THE DIVINE MADNESS OF ROMANTIC IDEALS

MERCER
UNIVERSITY PRESS

Endowed by

TOM WATSON BROWN

and

THE WATSON-BROWN FOUNDATION, INC.

THE DIVINE MADNESS OF ROMANTIC IDEALS

A Reader's Companion for Kierkegaard's

Stages on Life's Way

Kevin Hoffman

Mercer University Press MACON, GEORGIA
35 Years of Publishing Excellence

MUP/ P492

Published by Mercer University Press, Macon, Georgia 31207

9 8 7 6 5 4 3 2 1

Books published by Mercer University Press are printed on acid-free paper that meets the requirements of the American National Standard for Information Sciences—Permanence of Paper for Printed Library Materials.

Library of Congress Cataloging-in-Publication Data

Hoffman, Kevin, 1971-
The divine madness of romantic ideals : a reader's companion for Kierkegaard's Stages on life's way / Kevin Hoffman. -- 1st [edition].
pages cm
Includes bibliographical references and index.
ISBN 978-0-88146-499-3 (pbk. : alk. paper) -- ISBN 0-88146-499-6 (pbk. : alk. paper)
1. Kierkegaard, Søren, 1813-1855. Stadier paa livets vej. I. Title.
B4373.S833H64 2014
198'.9--dc23

2014034962

for c

my fellow maverick in the
art of leading an integrated life

Amare et sapere vix deo conceditur

—Publilius Syrus

Contents

Preface

The fictional publisher of *Stages on Life's Way,* Hilarious Bookbinder, prints "Lectori Benevolo!" in the place of a preface to the various pseudonymous manuscripts that make up the book as a whole, a common Latin phrase addressed to a sympathetic reader. According to the internal lore of the text one reason the Bookbinder gives for going to press was simply to get the collection off his desk in memory of a deceased wife who hated clutter. Initially, the sole merit Hilarius Bookbinder found in the set of manuscripts lay in teaching his son a rather splendid form of handwriting, only later to consider its content on the singular estimation of a nameless normal-school graduate and candidate in philosophy who abandoned pastoral training because he found himself a mere esthete and poet who could nevertheless deliver a good sermon, mainly due to possessing a particularly splendid pulpit voice.

However charming or ribald one may find such *ad hoc* rationale, as for my own motivation for going to press with a reader's companion I take a noble cue from the Latin, beginning with the fact that when I first read the book during a family vacation after my first year in college I understood very little of it, although my overall impression was that it seemed important and held me fast. By that point I had already switched majors from business administration to philosophy, a choice we may liberally blame on an encounter with Plato's *Republic* in Philosophy 101. Later, having repeatedly assigned *Stages* for class over a decade of teaching, I kept having to respond to student questions begging for answers. Gradually I came to realize a sympathetic reader is as tricky to find as a patient companion on life's way more generally, which applies to both books and actual people in turn. Fortunately I am happily indebted to a host of such people, including Merold Westphal, Edward Mooney, Dean Mel Piehl, Marc Jolley, my good, good friend Timothy Larsen, and many a fascinated student within Christ College of Valparaiso University for granting courage.

Introduction

Of his pseudonymous works, Kierkegaard's *Stages on Life's Way,* subtitled *Studies by Various Persons,* receives comparatively little detailed attention. When it does, the press is largely negative. As the most concrete and autobiographical characterization of the so-called three spheres of human life and their distinctively value-laden existential orientations, it is on the one hand both terribly personal and full of questionable personas. Each representative of the esthetic, ethical, and religious points of view come off smelling their worst, and readers are often anxiously sensitive to their outlandish, antisocial shortcomings. The otherwise cultured esthetes—the Young Man, Constantin Constantius, Victor Eremita, the Fashion Designer, and Johannes the Seducer—all appear reduced to intoxicated misogyny. As the representative of an ethical point of view, Judge William quips about domestic abuse by way of avoiding a serious question from his spouse about whether he might not have become something greater in the world apart from her. And the religiously driven diarist who breaks his engagement seems insufferably self-absorbed and patronizing toward his betrothed, itself an infamously veiled account of Kierkegaard's own experience of romantic joy and failure. More generally, many readers feel jilted by the ongoing Good Friday of the wan, inconclusive ending of the book as a whole, unbefitting a purported characterization of faith, hope, and especially love, whether human or divine.[1] Some of these crticisms

[1] Relevant preceding secondary materials include *Love Declared, Essays on the Myths of Love* by Denis de Rougemont (New York, NY: Pantheon Books, 1963), translated by Richard Howard; *The Nature of Love*, Volume 3, by Irving Singer (Chicago: The University of Chicago Press, 1987); *Feminist Interpretations of Søren Kierkegaaard* (State College, PA: Pennsylvania State University Press, 1997), edited by Céline Léon and Sylvia Walsh; *International Kierkegaard Commentary,* Volume 11, Stages on Life's Way (Macon GA: Mercer University Press, 2000), edited by Robert L. Perkins; *Kierkegaard and the Treachery of Love* by Amy Laura Hall (Cambridge: Cambridge University Press, 2002); *Wisdom in Love, Kierkegaard and the Ancient Quest for Emotional Integrity* by Rick Anthony Furtak (South Beach, IN: University of Notre Dame Press, 2005); *The Neither/Nor of the Second*

were already indicated in an offhand contemporary review by P. L. Møller in *Gæa* where the greater part of the book is characterized as a "Danaidean vessel of reflection" marked by "a pusillanimity at which our Lord and his angels must laugh," a review that later provoked a series of thinly veiled *ad hominem* cartoons of Kierkegaard's own dress and comportment in *The Corsair*.[2] As a respected translator and biographer even Walter Lowrie confesses he wished *Stages* had never been written.[3] Against these considerable interpretive odds, I offer a sustained close reading of the text in order to show the enduring significance of *Stages* as a complex, simultaneously poetic and philosophical exploration of the salient, tragicomic difficulty of leading a life suffused by romantic ideals, the ethical integration and kind of faith this life requires, and the sort of receptive agency that unfolds along the way.

In addition to the dizzying ensemble of main characters already metioned, most of whom appear in Kierkegaard's previous publications, the argument over romantic ideals and existential aspirations begins with William Afham posing a puzzling set of disjuncts between recollection and memory, solitude and fellowship, secrecy and disclosure, before relating five speeches about personal love delivered at a sumptuous banquet he did not attend, and which in fact never occurred, finally suggesting that he himself does not even exist. Apparently, it is all just a thought, a pleasant illusion, which may be true of ideals generally. The exploration of *Stages* as a whole ends with Frater Taciturnus composing and then commenting on what turns out to be a fictional diary recounting an unhappy love affair he claims to have found locked in a box with the key inside at the bottom of a pond. This additional character concludes his own commentary on the diary by turning to his fellow countrymen in contention that (a) Copenhagen

---

Sex, Kierkegaard on Women, Sexual Difference, and Sexual Relations by Céline Léon (Macon GA: Mercer University Press, 2008); and *Kierkegaard on Faith and Love* by Sharon Krishek (Cambridge: Cambridge University Press, 2009).

[2] Søren Kierkegaard, *The* Corsair *Affair, And Articles Related to the Writings* (Princeton: Princeton University Press, 1982) 101–22, edited and translated by Howard V. and Edna H. Hong.

[3] Kierkegaard, *Stages on Life's Way* (Oxford: Oxford University Press, 1940) 13, translated with introduction by Walter Lowrie.

lacks excitement, (b) the Danish language lacks complexity, and therefore, (c) to become a local author is a dubious achievement and poor way to make a living. Taciturnus then turns back to the reader to ask what his countrymen might say about *him* as such an author and claims they would probably warn a potential reader against him as a seducer, a qualified version of which Taciturnus readily admits. Having split himself into the third person and vanishing into the crowd of imaginary responses he cites, Taciturnus promptly leaves the reader entirely alone, who he suspects will be among very few by the end anyway given the length and content of his literary contribution. Between what Afham and Taciturnus offer appears a stolen, purportetdly anonymous essay attributed to Judge William in defense of a staid bourgeois marriage as the highest aim of human life that ends, rather abruptly, with the author being interrupted by his wife and invited to throw away his "wretched pen," which he is more than willing to do in honor of domestic bliss, but not before completing a really long, verbose sentence about it. It should come as no surprise that, after all this, most readers are left considerably perplexed about what has literarily happened to them, about what ideals and emotional reactions they are supposed to entertain. One might even conclude that Kierkegaard himself was artistically exhausted, or in Møller's words, that "he is completely finished (in both meanings of the word)."[4] However, these amusing, exhilirated, and paradoxical diversions suggest a delicate link between literary experience and romantic ideals and the mélange of the latter with actual, lived experience, falling in love and its pursuit being one of the most celebrated and vexing of those we undergo.

As this initial foray suggests, because *Stages* reads more like a novel than a philosophical treatise, my aim is to treat it as a self-contained, literary production and offer an interpretation of its significance as such. I do so apart from the tantalizing origins of the text that may be of interest to a biographer or source critic and do not offer speculations on settling the various whys and wherefores of Kierkegaard as the evident author of *Stages*. With this approach I hope to circumvent both historiographical and hierographical readings in order to directly focus on the delivered subject material. Furthermore, I avoid charging

[4] Kierkegaard, *The* Corsair *Affair*, 100.

Kierkegaard with specific points of view that can only responsibly be attributed to his characters.[5] Closely related, whatever external sources I employ along the way—including other texts penned by Kierkegaard himself as well as those he only might have or even could not have read—are all intended to serve and illuminate ideas standing on their own within the jacket of *Stages* itself. If there is anything like a Kierkegaardian point of view, it is more like what Dostoevsky presents in *The Brothers Karamozov*, where the interpretive task is to distill what a Karamozovian view of the *imago dei* really amounts to. In this latter case, we are simply subjected to a series of questions as an answer: are we supposed to fall in love, engage in duels, join a monastery, leave a monastery, defer to impetuously terrible fathers, perhaps club them to death, drink a lot of vodka, bend the evidence in a court case, break out of jail and flee to America, take upon us the guilt of others, even the whole world, or in a ruinous imitation of Christ slam our own finger in the door to patiently observe it blacken and bleed. It is not even clear that Alyosha is the sole or even primary hero even though the author explicitly announces him as such. In the case of *Stages*, one should expect to be similarly perplexed.

In an even more methodological vein, while *Stages on Life's Way* unfolds a latent, concretely universal existential mood, both its form and content imply it is the least of Kierkegaard's works to admit the kind of conceptual or systematic insight for which professional philosophers

---

[5] In part I take my cue from Naomi Lebowitz, who straightforwardly assumes the actual life of an author is often three parts literary anyway, one on the side of the subject, one on the side of the person telling the story secondhand, and another on the side of the reader, a perpetually vexing consideration for biographers. See Naomi Lebowitz, *Kierkegaard, A Life of Allegory* (Baton Rouge: Louisiana State University Press, 1985). The additional relevant scholarship includes: Walter Lowrie, *Kierkegaard* (Gloucester MA: Peter Smith, 1970); Henning Fenger, *Kierkegaard, The Myths and Their Origins* (New Haven: Yale University Press, 1980), translated by George C. Schoolfield; *Encounters with Kierkegaard, A Life Seen by His Contemporaries* (Princeton: Princeton University Press, 1996), collected, edited, and annotated by Bruce H. Kirmmse and translated by Bruce H. Kirmmse and Virginia R. Laursen; Alstair Hannay, *Kierkegaard, A Biography* (Cambridge: Cambridge University Press, 2001); and Joakim Garff, *Søren Kierkegaard, A Biography* (Princeton: Princeton University Press, 2007), translated by Bruce H. Kirmmse.

typically look. The literary trees are simply too thick and various to yeild such a consumate Hegelian *Begriff* (concept) beyond the purportedly one-sided *Gefühl* (feeling) and *Vorstellung* (representation) characteristic of imaginatively narrative worlds. Nor shall we uncover a pristine phenomenological disclosure apart from the stories and pre-ontological interpretations that populate both the surface and underground of *Stages,* distilled from which the language of Heidegger's fundamental ontology sounds like fury. Where Hegel stripmines various biblical and literary sources in order to elevate our minds above the persistant miasma of experiental conflict, and while even Heidegger cites the ancient fable of *Cura* crossing a river and sculpting an inanimate creature out of clay as a centerpiece in his analysis of *Sorge* as *Dasein*'s distinctive structural feature—a figure that Jupiter breathes into life, and after some dispute, Saturn (time) decides would indeed be named after the earth (*homo* from *humus*) though when it dies its spirit shall return to Jupiter, but that during its whole life it shall be possessed by Care—Kierkegaard more or less allows an anxious and evocative flow of literary blood to fill the veins of living ideals with relatively few neologistic abstractions to clot the arteries.[6]

In initial response to the specialized disciplinary doubts or biographical interest this tack might awaken, I would emphasize how the unusual authorship of *Stages* and the corresponding demands it places on readers is one major theme of the entire publication in question. Here and throughout I take this demand as an elaborate inside joke, but one worth exploring at length on the assumption that anything written according to an indecipherable genre is by design still supposedly readable and hopefully understandable. In doing so I unpack what is probably Kierkegaard's most spectacular attempt at indirect communication where that delivery is akin to sending an intimate package to an estranged lover accompanied only by a single,

[6] G.W.F. Hegel, *Lectures on the Philosophy of Religion, One-Volume Edition, The Lectures of 1827* (Berkeley, Los Angeles, London: University of California Press, 1988) 104–10, 432–70, translated by R. F. Brown, P. C. Hodgson, and J. M. Stewart, with the assistance of H. S. Harris, and edited by Peter C. Hodgson. Martin Heidegger, *Being and Time* (New York: Harper and Row Publishers, 1962) 242, translated by John Macquirrie and Edward Robinson.

cryptic word of explanation. In order to help the recipient decipher—and perhaps even appropriately laugh and cry along the way—I follow the primary text in a close, directly linear fashion, which in turn allows my own reader to follow alongside the original. In the process, I include extensive primary quotes and a few lengthier supplementary footnotes in a potentially penumbrous effort to relate universal and particular dimensions of the book as a whole.

Perhaps both *more* locally *and* universally the present reader's companion will further an understanding of formative romantic literature from the nineteenth century as a part of our collective tradition. This effort may be the husk of a seed Frater Taciturnus plants near the end of *Stages* about whether any generation can imaginatively move forward in the present without absorbing and appealing to a significantly shared but ambiguous past along with its cultural crises and innovations. Some ideas, feelings, and practices have an obvious shelf-life, just as outdated as they are disturbingly resurrected to bolster our own sense of progress. But others do not. Whether we are considering a religious tradition, civic identity, or personal history, the same distinction applies. *Stages on Life's Way* ranks among those compelling works of quirky universalism that locate us exactly where we are at, till death do us part. My approach will be reminiscent of Gadamer's invocation of a "classic" as both historical and timeless, a charitable but honestly evaluative encounter with which engulfs readers in a hermeneutical ciricle where they find themselves simultaneously judge, jury, and penitent, altogether caught between the various poles of embracing what is strange and critiquing what is familiar.[7] Both externally as a historical product and internally concerning its theme, one could say of *Stages* what C.S. Lewis said about the unprecedented late Medieval inscription of courtly love in general—namely, that our

[7] See Hans-Georg Gadamer, *Truth and Method* (New York: Crossroad Publishing Corporation, 1989) part II, section II, second revised edition, translated by Joel Weinsheimer and Donald G. Marshall. Such theory is best practiced on the ground, citing examples. For instance, what we want to know is whether Antigone understandably feels trapped between the exigencies of political prudence and the more personal, pious impulse to perform proper burial rites, or whether some bygone, kingly-aristocratic social protocol bars us from recognizing the conflict as such.

common humanity "does not pass through phases as a train passes through stations: being alive, it has the privilege of always moving yet never leaving anything behind," a tradition Denis de Rougemont also traces within our present cultural imagination as both irrepressibly inpiring and potentially destructive, hoping in the end that romantic ideals do not derail us in a tragically adulterous outcome with all parties hopelessly divided like Tristan and Iseult.[8]

Above all, I wish to model the kind of community it takes—both between readers and within ourselves—to reap the collective rewards of a careful, close reading of anything, be it a literary, philosophical, or historical document, and ultimately another person. Well before penning his own works, in an early journal entry Kierkegaard wrote that "[w]hen I read a book, what gratifies me is not so much what the book itself is as the infinite possibilities there must have been in every passage, the complicated history, rooted in the author's personality, studies, etc., which every phrase must have had and still must have for the author."[9] On the one hand this sentiment is a dramatic premonition of what has tempted so many readers to do with his own authorship, and especially *Stages on Life's Way,* given the lengthy devotion Kierkegaard offers in later entries to both his own experience of personal love and how he himself understood the development of this particular publication in its own right. On the other hand, the ensuing testimony of the journals also signals how the "infinite possibilities" and "complicated history" are just as rooted in "what the book itself is." The overall evidence suggests that Kierkegaard never supposed he or anyone else could resolve this dialectic since he so obviously lived in and through his own writing. My own interpetive gloss on these variously extended roots is correspondingly twofold: all we have left of Kierkegaard as a person is a book that can help us understand ourselves and shape our response to a

---

[8] C.S. Lewis, *The Allegory of Love* (Oxford: Oxford Univerity Press, 1936) 1. Denis de Rougemont, *Love in the Western World* (Princeton: Princeton University Press, 1983), translated by Montgomery Belgion as a revised and augmented edition with a new postscript.

[9] *Søren Kierkegaard's Journals and Papers,* Volume 5, *Autobiographical, 1829–1848* (Bloomington: Indiana University Press, 1978) 5297, translated by Howard V. and Edna H. Hong, assisted by Gregor Malanstschuk.

living neighbor, and that in this case it clearly begins with two or three gathered together reading something, whatever else they may end up doing along the way.

1

An Unprecedented Recollection

Before encountering the apocryphal speeches about love that form the first installment of *Stages* under the heading "In Vino Veritas," the literary and experiential links already introduced are frontloaded by William Afham's opening gambit on recollection, solitude, and secrecy. "The art of recollecting is not easy," he writes, "because in the moment of preparation it can become something different, whereas memory merely fluctuates between remembering correctly and remembering incorrectly. For example, what is homesickness? Homesickness is prompted simply by one's being absent. The art would be to feel homesickness even though one is at home. This takes proficiency in illusion."[1] This passage suggests a highly complicated relationship between actual experience and an ongoing affective construal of it as meaningful. Keeping with the example of homesickness, on the one hand we have a lived, historical experience prompted by actual absence. Something we cherish is not present, and so we miss it, perhaps noticing what we truly value for the first time. A sudden wave of feeling comes over us, marking out a salient pattern of what matters. On the other hand, this entirely passive, immediate feeling, stemming directly from experience, inevitably gives way to an ebb and flow of reflection upon it. Subsequently, and increasingly over time, we are not just subject to our experience but active participants in collecting and editing what we find so significant. Along the way, much that we continue to experience strikes us with an obstinate, prosaic ennui. The art of recollection, then, pits a poetic construal over against what is often brutally mundane. However, what makes it an art is that one must never make a complete

[1] Kierkegaard, *Stages on Life's Way* (Princeton: Princeton University Press, 1988) 13, edited and translated by Howard V. and Edna H. Hong. Further citations will appear in the main body of the text by page number in parentheses.

break with actuality. "To go on living in an illusion in which there is continual dawning, never daybreak, or to reflect oneself out of all illusion is not as difficult as to reflect oneself into an illusion, plus being able to let it work on oneself with the full force of illusion even though one is fully aware" (13). The kind of proficiency at issue here is an interpretive process in which one's feelings are derived not only from what actual experience delivers but also the active work of imagination. The delicate problem is how we might become given over to either self-deception or hardened realism. For his part, William Afham is an unapologetic creative writer.

> I know very well that I shall not soon forget that banquet in which I participated without being a participant; but just the same I cannot now decide to release it without having provided myself with a scrupulous written απομνημονευμα [memoir] of what for me was actually *memorabile* [worthy of memory].—Recollection's erotic understanding I have endeavored to encourage, whereas I have done nothing for memory. (15)

The trick, then, is to recollect what is most essential. Yet given actual life even the smallest things intrude, reveal, and are cherished, like tokens of a complex creation out of welter and waste. Our invariable lot and greatest responsibility is to act as editor in chief within a created order so overwhelming that every leaf, feather, and hair, every tender promise, angry failure, and insecure doubt count amidst the terrible beauty and seeming disorder. Truly humbling is it to consider how even the best of us stare blankly, inappropriately select, or change our minds. Truly wonderful is it to accept how every actual gift is the product of a sensitive and intelligent imagination. In either case we inevitably look for the essential and try to pick it out in our own lives whenever we tell a story. It is as if Afham has deliberately set out to illustrate Aristotle's dictum that "the poet's function is to describe, not the thing that has happened, but a kind of thing that might happen, i.e., what is possible as being probable or necessary"—that is, to describe what might have been said and perhaps necessarily had to be said given the topic.[2] The moral aim of fiction and our power of imagination within actual history is to

[2] Aristotle, *Poetics*, line 1451a 38.

consider the full range of what we could have done or said, or should have but did not. No doubt we shall be edited as we have been editors. Woe to the person who excludes important details, for they shall not inherit the earth, nor shall the kingdom of heaven be theirs. This is especially true when recounting a story of love or loss, whether personal or political.

Afham's proficiency in this regard thus comes at a peculiar cost. He seems aware that a ruminating imagination can betray and delude both us and those around us as much as it can provide fodder for tender acts of visible devotion. Its elastic delicacy will stretch, but can break at any moment, and therefore must fit properly according to contrasting standards of comfort, elegance, utility, and panache. Perhaps in light of these esthetic demands, Afham cuts himself off from others in preference for "out-of-the-way, hidden, and secret" places, just as lovers do (16). Having fled company he even goes so as far to assert "how rich is language in the service of desire in comparison with language when it describes actuality" (29–30). Nevertheless, the bond with reality is never finally severed, and its moral aim never finally submerged. Although he denies poetic recollection can admit a public fellowship, he is clearly communicating something to us, his readers, no matter how solitary he casts himself or how alone we may find ourselves. In fact, there is nothing left for us to do except enjoy his lavish description of the banquet and ruminate on the content of the tipsy orations. That is, we *could* put the book down and return to our unimagined lives. Or we could read on. But if we do continue to turn the page, we should expect a considerably indirect interpretive scenario that itself mirrors the inherently volatile but invariably seductive power of a romantic imagination. Afham finally signals all this by confessing that, as a writer, he might disturb his reader's inner life:

> Only someone who sought solitude unworthily can benefit from surprise, as if a pair of lovers did not even have the power to shape a situation. If this is the case, then one can serve Eros and the lovers by making an appearance, even if to the lovers one's service remains a mystery, just as the guilt does—they cling closer together out of irritation with the intruder, to whom they are nevertheless indebted for their so doing. But if they are two lovers who worthily seek solitude, how oppressive it is then to take them by surprise, how one

could curse oneself as every animal was cursed when it approached Sinai. (18)

In the end, the potential guilt is apparently worth the risk, though it bears a relation to something as terrifying, mysterious, and unpronounceable as YHWY. Judge William as well as the anonymous diarist will return to this thematic esthetic-religious hybrid. But for us, as readers and lovers, the drama gets underway with the "recollection" of a banquet.

The Drama Begins

From within the fiction Afham unfolds, the whole prospect of the banquet is first introduced and then summarily dismissed as a possibility by four of the five "actual" participants. The Young Man is declared "unsuited," the Fashion Designer lacks "the time," and Victor Eremita and Johannes the Seducer agree that such an event cannot even be planned, let alone executed, because the "good" must simply happen, immediately. This conclusion renders Johannes bored ahead of time and Eremita despondent that it could even occur at all. Along with Constantin Constantius, the proposal had indeed come up spontaneously as they all fortuitously found themselves together in a coffee shop. This preemptive speculation was fine by Eremita, who claims the mere talk of a banquet was satisfying enough, and thereupon "thrust his hand in his pocket, took out a cigar case, took out a cigar, and began to smoke" (23). So, what does happen? After protesting Eremita's "absolute power in thus transforming the projected banquet into an illusory fragment of life," Constantius takes them by surprise (23). But he does so with grave reservation. Having surreptitiously planned carriage rides for the others to a salon in a wooded area outside of town, Constantin worries that the mood of his fellows might derail in lavish anticipation, "for just as there is no force so proficient as the imagination in embellishing everything, so, too, there is no other force able to play havoc with everything when things go wrong for one in the moment of encounter with actuality" (26). His one consolation, what he counts on, is the effect of the natural environment on dampening any premature excitement that might kill the moment. "Driving on a summer evening," he ruminates,

> does not turn the imagination toward the sumptuous but does the very opposite. Even if one does not see and hear it, the imagination involuntarily creates an image of the evening's cozy, comfortable longing; thus one sees girls and farmhands on their way home from their field work, hears the hurried clattering of the harvest wagon, interprets even the bellowing far off in the meadow as a longing. In this way the summer evening lures forth the idyllic, refreshes even a craving mind with its tranquility, prompts even the fleeting fantasy to remain with autochthonic homesickness on the earth as the place of one's origin, teaches the insatiable mind to be satisfied with little, makes one content, for in the evening hours time stands still and eternity lingers. (26–27)

Before reaching the banquet, Afham here moves us another step toward the roles imagination and actual perception play in shaping what we think, feel, and value about our place in the world, roles that Constantin is clearly trying to manipulate in order to mitigate the disappointment he anticipates from having high esthetic expectations. But the particularly noteworthy aspect of this passage is how much imagination it really does take to think of a wooded area outside Copenhagen, prompting us to "remain with autochthonic homesickness on the earth as the place of one's origin," which is a downright evocatively romantic ideal, being suffused by which may or may not be under our control. Poetic souls can find themselves either crippled or enlivened, bored or excited, and usually with a mixture of both.

In any event, they each arrive at the prearranged site, carrying with them various states of inner life. The Fashion Designer, Afham tells us, "has charmed or bewitched himself, by the wizardry of his will has conjured himself into an almost silly character, but has not quite satisfied himself with it, which is why now and then reflection peeks out" (22). Eremita initially stood apart, and in response to hearing *Don Giovanni* in the background, shuddered, and said: "You secret, festive, seductive strains that tore me out of the cloistered solitude of a quiet youth and deceived me with a loss, as if it were a recollection, terrifying, as if Elvira had not even been seduced but had only craved to be!" (28). Johannes cries *viva la liberta*, to which the Young Man adds *et veritas*, followed by Constantin insisting that, in any case, and above all, it should be *in vino*. Needless to say, this latter requirement put them all in full swing, even though Johannes initially objected that he only becomes more sober the more he drinks while Eremita is characteristically of the opinion that, like every other good thing, it must happen spontaneously, for "to deliberately and experimentally to set out to become intoxicated would prevent one from doing so" (30). Nevertheless, and perhaps fortuitously, the members take their place at the table and "as if with a single bound, the little dinner party was out in the middle of a boundless sea of enjoyment" (28–29). "Before long" Afham reports, as if it were history,

> the conversation had so woven its beautiful wreath around the guests that they sat festooned in it; at times the conversation was enamored of the food, at times of the wine, at times of itself; at times it seemed as if it would mean something, then in turn at times it meant nothing at all. At times a flash of wit burst forth, that wonderful kind that blossoms but once, that delicate flower that closes immediately. Then came an exclamation from one of the diners: These truffles are superb; then a shout from the host: This Château Margaux! At times the dinner music was drowned in noise, and then it was audible again. At times, at the crucial moment when a new course was about to be served or a new wine offered and designated by name, the waiters stood quietly as if *in pausa*; then they were busy again. Silence intervened for a second, and then the exhilirating spirit of the music passed over the guests again. Now the one with an audacious thought took the lead in the conversation, and the others followed him, almost forgetting the food, and the music came trailing behind as it echoed the jubilation of the tumult; then at times only the clinking of the glasses and the sound of dinner plates were heard, and the task of eating proceeded in silence, supported only by the music, which festively took the lead and again called forth the conversation. (29)

Historical or not, only a completely unsensible person would balk at this description rather than earnestly want to participate. Even so, Afham wavers over the simultaneous poverty and power of language in describing what we *really* can, do, or should experience, "something that not even the theater can reproduce and for which language has but a few words!" (29). Cribbing from Plato, both language and love alike seem to be children born of poverty and plenty, always in need but ever resourceful.[3]

The speeches about romantic love that follow have been read as having little to recommend them. For starters, the Young Man is the only one who speaks about love *per se,* and even then nearly gets disqualified after admitting he has never actually had any experience in the matter. The others sidestep the topic altogether by making *ad hominem* comments about women, none of whom, happily, are present. Which seems to disqualify them. However, the debatable value and power of the kind of intense personal attachment we associate with romantic love is addressed at a level above the heads of the individual banqueteers. As with Plato's *Symposium,* on which "In Vino Veritas" is formally modeled, the aporetic delivery is precisely what we are meant to hear. But it begs for interpretation. And we should begin where Afham begins, with the Young Man, after by agreed requirement he is several sheets to the wind, "which was rather visible" (31).

The Speeches

The Young Man is a self-described thinker who will subject himself to nothing he does not understand, and love is chief among those things. He makes his point by describing a series of contradictions love implies or gets one entangled in and begins with what romantic lovers say about an unhappy affair. "They say that it is death, certain death, and the first time they believe it for two weeks" (31). Actually, he suggests it seems to take at least three times before literally dying of love, which is not unlike "the dentist's having to try three times before extracting the impacted molar" (31). Fortunately the Young Man has not contracted such a prolonged illness, and wishes to die only once, and from natural causes. What is the contradiction he is pointing out here? If love really is as salient and grave as people claim, then death should in fact accompany its loss. This does not happen, and therefore love must be an "imaginary construction in thought" (32). In that case, the Young Man concludes, love is a terrible illusion whose only real power lay in making one "gush about a bliss I did not perceive and a pain I did not feel" (32). In fact our

[3] Plato, *Symposium,* lines 203b–e.

passions are indeed mediated by a kind of fantastic conferral of value that does not arise from objective, inherent qualities in the beloved.[4] This has often been the basis for a fundamental critique of romantic love and its associated ideals. For example, more than one person has referred to the end of a honeymoon, not only in regard to personal attachments, but in regard to a new neighborhood, their work, even a political campaign, from which few of us even expect romance in the first place. We sagaciously know better, as it were. It was fun while it lasted, which it did not, and apparently does not. Indeed, the most generally accurate statement we can make is that there is something tragically comic about it. But the "contradiction" can be handled in better or worse ways. One can avoid it, embrace it, manipulatively engage it, reinvent it, let it slide—there are so many verbs. However, it does seem that very few are able to simply ignore it. Beneath the surface comedy that people do not ordinarily die of unhappy love—or if they do it takes three times—there lay the tragic fact that people do regularly suffer incomparable loss, and if it does take three times, it was evidentally the third love that was for the first time the most real. Numbers aside, for every delusional infatuation or marriage of conveneince, there are those who in fact die, either literally or in their hearts, from unreciprocated or fatefully averted passion. The truly blessed but locally tragic irony here is that if the infantile rationalist with no experience attributes even the latter to a mere "imaginary contruction in thought," then he is in fact lying to himself. No wonder then that the other banqueteers were reticent to let him speak at all.

The contradiction between romantic passion and actuality is further developed by the Young Man in his ironic perplexity over our not being able to give an account of what is finally loveable about those who suddenly stand before us in all their fully incarnate and arresting particularity as so bewilderingly irreplaceable.

> Aside from the utterly foolish explanations that end in a blind alley, that is, end by saying that it is the beloved's beautiful feet or the lover's much admired handlebar mustache that really is the object of

[4] See Irving Singer's opening chapter on "Appraisal and Bestowal" in *The Nature of Love,* Volume 1, *Plato to Luther* (Chicago: University of Chicago Press, 1984).

> erotic love, even when we hear a lover talking grandiloquently, he first of all mentions various particulars, but finally he says: her whole loveable nature; and when his speech has reached its high point, he says: that inexplicable quality of which I cannot give an account. (35)

At the high point of this part of his own iteration, the Young Man declares not just one contradiction, but two, partly because the explanation he has imagined "ends in the *inexplicable* and partly because it *ends* there, for anyone who wants to end with the inexplicable would really do best to begin with it and say nothing else in order not to become suspect" (35). Although he is fully cognizant that we cannot solve this puzzle by straightforwardly identifying the loveable with "the good"—which may as well apply to money or sports or even the truth, not to mention actual people, as Plato has Diotima via Socrates assert at a crucial point in the *Symposium,* and thereby completely overstep the concrete particularity of individuals—the Young Man nevertheless reverts to a residual, caricatured Platonism when he says "the person who listens to the talk of several lovers will learn that no two say the same thing, although they all speak about the same thing" (35).[5] What the Young Man is wrestling with here is that our love for another person in all their particularity constantly shuttles back and forth between their objectively good qualities that anyone could recognize and the purely subjective testimony of a lover, together which constantly throws only indirect lighting on a mysterious beloved.

Our apparent inability to account for the inexplicable draw of this kind of personal love is echoed in the manner in which it "seizes its prey" (36). In short, it is alarming that romantic passion appears involuntary, a feature of the experience that the Young Man finds additionally comic. He imagines someone who has seen hundreds of women; "he may be getting on in years, has felt nothing. Suddenly he sees her, her, the one and only—Catherine" (36). This hysterical introduction of a proper name, presumably out of nowhere, is an echo of the "freemasonry that is a continuation of that first inexplicable something" (39). A further manifestation of the paradoxical nature of love is the kiss following a pledge of devotion. What is baffling about

[5] Plato, *Symposium*, 206a.

such displays of affection is that two spiritual creatures who find themselves so charmed and wedded in their deepest personalities would then symbolically mark this fact by sharing a slippery exchange of saliva. "The psychical at its loftiest finds its expression in the extreme opposite, and the sensual wants to signify the psychical at its loftiest" (29). It is difficult, perhaps impossible, to explain how and why some form of physical communion in which we mingle our mere bodies attends relationships that are supposed to express our highest imaginative and spiritual aspirations. For the young thinker, this is all very contradictory, indeed tragic if it were not so thoroughly comic, and the mysterious incongruity of it frightens him. In actual fact, the way it goes is that one falls in love with another's lips, eyes, and hair, all the way down to their toes, *because* of the correponding thoughts and virtues of character within the heart and mind of the beloved. What should be obvious is that there are several ways for this to go wrong. On the best scenario, shrunken breasts and scarred features become even more attractive over time; in the worst-case scenario, shameful vices are increasingly hidden by a youthful appearance cloaked in bad ideas.

In spite of the Young Man's ironic detachment, but faithful to the topic, his lampoon of the lover's experience actually counts as indirect praise. Biographically, his declaration that he "shall not love anyone until I have exhausted the idea of erotic love" suggests he may indeed have fallen for someone, but somehow got burnt. He does after all accurately describe how we are inexplicably drawn to another and ascribe an involuntary, subjectively invested worth to a beloved and the ensuing relationship beyond any reasonable objective appraisal in a process Stendhal rather inelegantly refers to as "crystallization."[6] The Young Man also rightly points out how the seemingly selfish dimensions of romantic feelings walk hand-in-hand with a newfound sense of our own incompleteness, how we come to need an other, but need them to be their own selves, and so a third is born, during which we become ourselves as if for the first time by relinquishing that self to another. He makes this point literally by noting how seemingly odd it is that lovers suddenly become parents. Romantic ideals become merely nominal when "Catherine" prosaically turns into "mom." This underhanded

[6] Stendal, *Love* (New York/London: Penguin Books, 1975) chapter 2.

reference to both Aristophanes' and Diatomia's speech in the *Symposium* evokes the emotional equivalent of childbirth that romantics undergo in becoming a vulnerable *part* of a shared creative venture rather than remaining a separate self-satisfied whole.[7] It does seem contradictory that so apparently a selfish desire would be equally terrifying and invaluable, as if what the lover actually *wants* is to *relinquish* their self-containment. In conjunction with how Afham had initially described the Young Man as a "sleepwalker" who "had been neither awakened and inflamed nor disquieted and disturbed," it comes as no surprise that Constantin opens his own speech by astutely describing him as "a bewildered man who does not know whether he should laugh or cry or fall in love" (21, 47).

Perhaps prompted by the Young Man's contentious comment that, in the process of falling in love, a man and woman in fact only become merely one and a half, since presumably, unlike the woman, the man was already a whole self beforehand, Constantin makes the following two claims: "It is the man's function to be absolute, to act absolutely, to express the absolute; the woman consists in the relational. Between two such different entities no real interaction can take place" (48). This peculiar association of the relational with the feminine is followed by a set of other disparaging terms: frivolous, inflammable, whimsical, faithless, incomplete, and confusing, all of which threaten the purported husband with the prospect of cuckoldry. But happily, this fate may be avoided if one remains at a safely bemused distance in order to enjoy her whims without suffering from "jealousy as a tragic passion" (53). If the lover can manage to be "absolute" in this way the joy will be incalculable, just as others find amusement "in balancing a cane on his nose, in swinging a glass without spilling its contents, in dancing among eggs, and doing other similar routines just as entertaining as they are useful" (52).[8] On the other hand, if a lover gives himself over too

---

[7] Plato, *Symposium*, lines 189–93, 205–209.

[8] In a classic iteration of the Easter egg dance amidst which one ushers in new life by stepping among a series of fragile orbs placed on the floor, perhaps Constantin has in mind Goethe's riveting account of Mignon's blindfolded performance of the Christian appropriation of pagan festivity in *Wilhelm Meister's Apprenticeship* (New York: The Heritage Press, 1959) book 2, chapter 8.

completely to such a whimsical creature the outcome will likely be tragic. Whatever else we make of Constantin's perplexingly gendered rant and rather ridiculous advice on a literal level, most of what he says about women can be plausibly said of love itself. In addition to being inexplicable and involuntary, personal loves are also unstable, prone to "eruptions out of an inviolable romanticism" (52). And it is also true that there are better and worse ways to handle them, against which the Young Man has decidedly "backed away…terrified by the difficulty" (53).

The language of "absolute" and "relational" are paired in Constantin's mind with a contrast between esthetic and ethical values. This is our first introduction to two of the three "stages" on life's way, two of the value-laden existential manners of inhabiting life. The very end of his speech is worth quoting at length:

> [A]nd now let us empty a glass to erotic love and to woman. Beautiful is she and lovely when she is viewed esthetically no one can deny it. But as is said so often, so I, too, will say: One should not stop with that but should go further. Look at her ethically; just start doing that, and you have the jest. Even Plato and Aristotle assume that woman is an incomplete form, consequently an irrational quantity that perhaps in a better existence can be led back to the male form; here in life one must take her for what she is. What that is will soon be manifest, for she, too, is not satisfied with the esthetic. She goes further; she wants to be emancipated—she is man enough to say that. If that happens, the jest will exceed all bounds. (55–56)

This passage is especially evocative if one thinks of romantic ideals in close combat with ethical stability. Constantin suggests erotic love itself longs to be tamed or civilized, to become male, and by implication, free for the first time. But what shall we make of the final claim that if this paradoxical domestication occurs the humor of it will exceed all bounds? On the one hand, this seems to strike a despairing note, as when one might drunkenly laugh at a ridiculously tragic outcome. On the other hand, it may strike a hopeful, even ecstatic note, as one might laugh at an entirely unpredictable and wonderful outcome: star-crossed lovers fortuitously finding each other equally, excitedly, and ethically bound, together with an equally democratic vote, personally and politically. We cannot tell which it is, as is often the case in telling whether it would be good or bad to be liberated from the rude inconstancy of romantic love or the fickle pretentions of democratic rule. Perhaps "in a better existence" we could. But such an existence is evidently not our present lot, and so we are left to wonder, and interpret. It may already be right here that feminism reaches a third and fourth wave, with men wearing dresses and women applying fresh lipstick, or women with equal pay and men finally gaining an emotional thought by casting aside a lucrative status. On such a seashore wonders may never cease, even as they have been there from the beginning.

Victor Eremita, onetime editor of *Either/Or*, takes up the preceding references to Plato, and with him, thanks the gods he was not born a woman. In his own tipsy fashion, the primary reason he gives is that a woman's existence is thoroughly fantastic. "If the girl's name is Juliane, then her life is as follows: 'Formerly empress in the vast outskirts [*Overdrev*] of erotic love and titular queen of all exaggerations [*Overdrivelser*] of giddiness, now Mrs. Petersen on the corner of Badstustræde [Bathhouse Street]'" (57–58). But before arriving at this amusingly tilted, offensive conclusion about Juliane, Eremita claims more particularly, "the misfortune is that her life in the romantic consciousness has become meaningless" (56). The question is whether this misfortune belongs solely to her. After all, the "romantic consciousness" belongs to the man, since for her part, the deepest tragedy is that she "cannot come to know" the lack of significance behind her fate "because she is woman" (56). What we must attend to here is what explicitly lies latent beneath the disparaging surface. The meaninglessness is evidently shared between *both* the man and woman, although the analysis is cast in a brassy, gendered mold. In this regard Eremita's description of gallantry, which "befits the man," is particularly revealing (56). Gallantry, "quite simply, consists in conceiving in fantastic categories the person toward whom one is gallant" (56). This sounds like it has nothing to do with *her*, but is rather a self-deceptive trick the lover plays on his own consciousness. And yet Eremita claims that gallantry is a tribute to the fair sex, which she in turn instinctively though tragically accepts, since she does so without ever becoming aware that if "gallantry is to be genuine, it must be reciprocal and be the quoted rate for the specified difference between beauty and power, cunning and strength" (57). But again, she "cannot come to know" this. Know what exactly? That love is an illusion and only has significance as an illusion, or that our ideals have no reality? But if that is the case, then how is it better to be born a man?

Eremita is not unaware of this implicit question, since immediately upon his own treatment of gallantry he exclaims that while Juliane is in seventh heaven, and Mrs. Petersen is somehow un-self-consciously reconciled to her fate, "yet how much I have to renounce!" (58). It turns out the polite and amorous grace from a gallant social distance is a dubious tribute because the power the fair sex wields is merely her ability to poetically inspire. Many a man, we find out, has become a genius, a hero, a poet, or a saint because of a girl, but not "because of the girl he got," for through her he only became a cabinet official, a general, or a husband, and in the case of the saint, one literally can only become such without getting the girl (59). Her ability to inspire in this way in fact renders the man "a little inferior." Nevertheless, in contrast to an indefinite inspiration from a fantastic distance, Eremita would rather be "a concretion that means something than an abstraction that means everything" (59). What is especially provocative about all this troubled gendering is what "a concretion" that at least "means something" refers to in Eremita's speech. Does it refer to being a cabinet official, a general, husband, or father, or does it refer to being a genius, hero, poet, or saint? And for her part, does the "abstraction that means everything" refer to her former life as "empress in the vast outskirts [*Overdrev*] of erotic love and titular queen of all exaggerations [*Overdrivelser*] of giddiness" or her life as "Mrs. Petersen on the corner of Badstustræde [Bathhouse Street]" (57–58)? Eremita is not unaware of this question either. But he answers it rhetorically: "Indeed, who ever heard that anyone became a poet because of his wife?" (59). If we are paying attention, it must dawn on us that being a wife is after all "a concretion that means something" and that being a genius, hero, poet, or saint may very well be imaginary and entirely fantastic. Indeed, what can the unmarried Eremita say for himself in regard to having had his "ideality" awakened by love (59)? How has "woman" made him "productive" other than in a drunken, fleeting, and rather confusing speech about it (59)? No doubt his speech does not mean "everything," or presumably worse, it might mean just about anything, which is certainly no "concretion."

As with the other speakers, the argument once again seems to proceed just above Eremita's head. On the one hand he invokes the classic romantic notion that while love draws us out of ourselves toward the beloved in a way that exceeds their actual, objective value by conferring wonderful and mysterious qualities that de-center and inspire the lover, the very experience of which inspires creative ventures of all kinds, rendering the Polis warm and exciting by the tender means of Eros, such inspiration is predicated on actual love remaining in some significant sense unrealized. Thus Eremita himself does not know what to make of it. Is it pure illusion, or the best, most productive actual experience we might have? All he says about fully actualized love is that it "scarcely arouses ideality" (59). His explicit point is the internal equivalent of the shamelessly external, late-Medieval courtly assertion that true love is essentially adulterous put down by Andreas Capallanus.[9] Romantic ideals have a corresponding conflict internal to them: they are somehow inspiring only in virtue of the distance from reality they create and maintain and yet wish to dismantle. That conflict is what is so confusing, because it looks as if, for the lover, an excessive and purely internal conferral of value amounts to an actual discovery. In his own way Eremita externally poses this as a tragic either/or. He develops this view by asserting that love ultimately awakens the "consciousness of immortality," but does so only "negatively" by thriving on obstacles to a truly and fulfilling actualization (60). "If the idealizing element were positively present in woman, then the wife and only the wife might awaken the consciousness of immortality. Life expresses the very opposite. If she is really going to awaken ideality in her husband, she must die" (60–61). Eremita's particular version of this dramatically gothic side of the romantic tradition suggests the positive, full presence of the beloved can only engender a narrow, bourgeois-philistine experience of desire, a mere longing for "the time we were in Deer Park" and other "trifles of marital life" (61). This tension between

---

[9] Andreas Capallanus, *The Art of Courtly Love* (New York: Colombia University Press, 1960), with introduction, translation, and notes by John Jay Parry.

the poetic and prosaic within a personal love fueled by romantic ideals that Eremita casts as a gendered either/or goes back at least as far as Plato, beginning with Adam and Eve, presumably the first to become aware of death, and the first to produce an actual lineage through their love. But the immortality in question here is indeed Platonic in the lineage of Socrates' *Symposium* speech: artistic, intellectual, and spiritual. Eremita is preoccupied with the geniuses, poets, and saints. Literal paternity interests him about as much as it does Diotima. The Eros that interests her, and him, is that product of poverty and plenty that draws us beyond the beauty of actuality, beyond the finite and ephemeral glory of sharing morning tea our bachelors will shortly encounter between Judge William and his spouse. What naturally follows from this negative account of a truly inspiring form of love is that it would be best if love makes "her appearance at the right moment, when ideality is acquiring its vision. It is a brief moment, and then she does well to vanish again. For a positive relationship with woman makes man finite on the largest possible scale" (62). Adding to the misfortune of it, such a moment "is the courtesy of fate" and therefore out of our control. Thus, in a backwards agreement with Constantin, Eremita concludes that even if love is not inherently faithless, the greatest thing a lover or beloved can do is vanish as a stalwart matter of choice (63). On the part of the lover, leave the beloved in the lurch and she may very well make something of herself; on the part of the beloved, marry him and you will end up serving tea to a cabinet minister. And *vice versa*. That is the purported either/or, which is only incidentally about gender, and all about romantic ideals generally.

The end of Eremita's speech signals things to come from the anonymous Judge William concerning the heterogeneity of the marriage sacrament, itself a tragicomic display of contradictions already inherent in the involuntary and inexplicable qualities of love itself. As an institution Victor cannot figure out whether marriage is something pagan or Christian, something sacred or secular, or whether like turtle meat, it has a taste of all kinds.

> Is it the expression of the inexplicable eroticism, that *Wahlverwandtschaft* [elective affinity] between kindred souls, or is it a duty, or is it a partnership or an expediency in life or the custom in certain countries,

> or is it a little of everything? Is the town musician or the organist to furnish the music—or should we have a little of both; should the pastor or the police sergeant give the talk and inscribe their names in life's register—or in the municipal register; is it in comb-and-paper music that marriage can be heard or does it listen to that whisper that sounds like "the fairies' from the grottos on a summer night"? (63)

After this litany of dichotomies, the blessed unity of which he cannot even begin to fathom, Victor predictably returns to his original theme to conclude that if "a positive relationship to woman is thinkable, then it has to be so reflective that for this very reason it would not become a relationship with her" (64). What immediately follows is an even more consistently bizarre reflection: "To be an exceptional husband and yet secretly seduce every girl, to seem to be a seducer and yet hide all the ardor of romanticism within one would really be something—yet the concession to the first power is invariably destroyed in the second" (64–65). Mimicking Hegelian dialectic, he tempts us with how nevertheless "every man has his true ideality only in a reduplication. Every immediate existence must be annihilated and the annihilation constantly safeguarded by a false expression. Woman cannot grasp a reduplication such as that; it makes it impossible for her to state man's nature" (65). Thus we are left in a kind of limbo with the general implication that "since her nature so obviously is as it is, there is a disturbance of the erotic condition of man's nature, which continually has its life in the annihilation of that in which she has her life" (65). What is not quite so obvious, but should be, is that these are internal dynamics within human nature as such, whether one is a man or a woman. Underneath and on top of this dissimulation the reader is left argumentatively hanging in that Eremita resolutely refuses the ultimately logical conclusion of his namesake: the hermitage. "Away with the monastery. It, too, is only an immediate expression of spirit, and spirit cannot be expressed immediately" (65). We are then left to face not an either/or, but a particular neither/nor: neither the nunnery nor a prosaically unified trek to Deer Park, each as unpoetically inspiring as the other. What then?

At this point the Fashion Designer leaps to his feet, knocks over a bottle of wine, and proceeds to tell us that among his fellow "conspirators" it is only he who can articulate the weakest but nevertheless most compelling side of love. One way of reading "In Vino Veritas" as an overall argument about romantic ideals is to say that love is inexplicable and involuntary (the Young Man), entirely unreliable (Constantin), largely illusory (Eremita), and therefore spectacularly beside the point (Fashion Designer). Picking up the argument at this latter point, the Fashion Designer seems to say that what really makes the world turn is not love, but the ephemeral, arbitrary, often ridiculous, but nevertheless perpetual and even lucrative cycle of fashionable adornment. On this interpretation the laws of attraction and subsequent basis for poetic inspiration are entirely uncoupled from distinctively human values, and may very well end, the Designer threatens, with "a ring in the nose" (71). More broadly, one might also think the Designer's speech an opportunity to pause and reflect on the rise of consumer culture at large and how it threatens to override all human values, reducing even "the fear of God" to economic terms (71). This would certainly square with Afham's initial characterization of the Fashion Designer as one having "charmed and bewitched himself" who "by the wizardry of his will has conjured himself into an almost silly character, but has not quite satisfied himself with it, which is why now and then reflection peeks out" (22). The self-contradiction that Afham reports would then indicate a kind of Marxist diagnosis of bourgeois self-alienation. Indeed, our Designer neatly summarizes the insidious nature of middle-class pop-culture industry in the following confession:

> Whether I am serving the devil or the god, I do not know, but I am right and I am determined to be right. I will be right as long as I have a single farthing; I am determined to be right until the blood spurts from my fingers. The physiologist draws a woman's shape in order to show the terrible results of corsets; alongside he draws the normal shape. This is correct, but only the one has the validity of actuality; they all wear corsets. (70)

While the evidence for a critical, economic reading of a purely esthetic enterprise remains solidly in place, the Fashion Designer too has his own positive but problematic point to make about romantic ideals, in spite of himself. We know there is something more going on because, whether we believe him or not, he lays out: "I supply the finest and the most expensive things at the cheapest price—indeed, I sell below cost.

Hence I am not out to gain no—every year I lose huge sums" (66–67). For what, then, is the Designer willing to throw away his money, quite unlike a self-respecting entrepreneur? Our initial, rather baffling clue is that he frankly admits fashion "is not open sensuality, is not tolerated dissipation, but is a sneaky trafficking in impropriety that is authorized as propriety" (66). What, exactly, does this mysterious power of fashion that makes the world turn amount to? We do not find out until he describes in piquant detail the conditions under which he interacts with those who visit his boutique, the protocol they appear to follow, and the conflicted response this seems to elicit:

> Just as there are a special bathing costume and a riding costume, so there is also a special attire that is in vogue to wear for going to the boutique. This costume is not as casual as the negligee in which a lady likes to be surprised earlier in the forenoon. The whole point then is her femininity and coquetry in letting herself be surprised. Her boutique attire, on the other hand, is calculated to be casual, a bit frivolous without thereby causing embarrassment, because a fashion designer has a relation to her quite different from a cavalier's. The coquetry consists in appearing this way before a man, who, because of his position, does not dare claim the lady's feminine recognition but must be satisfied with the uncertain profits that richly pay off but without her thinking about it or without her dreaming of wanting to be the lady in relation to a fashion designer. Thus the whole point is that femininity is in a way left out and coquetry is invalidated in the exclusive superiority of the distinguished lady, who would smile if anyone were to allude to such a relationship. In her negligee on the occasion of a [surprise] call, she covers herself and thereby gives herself away; in the boutique she uncovers herself with utmost nonchalance, for it is only a fashion designer and she is a woman. Now the shawl slips down a bit and shows a little white skin if I do not know what that means and what she wants, then my reputation is lost. Now she puckers her lips apriorally, then gesticulates aposteriorally; now she wriggles her hips, then looks in the mirror and sees my admiring face; now she lisps, walks with a mincing gate, then hardly seems to touch the floor; now she trails her foot daringly, sinks weakly into an armchair, while I obsequiously hand her a scent-flacon and cool her with my adoration; now she roguishly hits at me with her hand, then drops her handkerchief and lets her hand remain

> in a loose, drooping position, while I bow low and pick it up, offer it to her, and receive a little patronizing nod. This is how a woman of fashion deports herself in a boutique. (67–68)

This quote is worth considering at length because, although sarcastic and despairing throughout, the triviality is so rich. What throws the Fashion Designer into such confusion, but for which he is willing to pay his last farthing, is the professional pretense of clandestinely interacting with so-called clients who have received a strangely anonymous social sanction to let their guard down. What both attracts and enervates the Designer is that he is more than willing to *pay* for *them* than to capitalize on this delicate and delightful, if otherwise disingenuous, interpersonal repartee.

But what is the capital gain in this scenario? Chiefly, the Designer conveys how our relationships are embodied in expressive forms that are a function of a culturally shaped imagination, within a play of possible moral worlds against one another, and the esthetic innovation that typically accompany them. Witness the specific manner in which listlessly dropping a handkerchief in order to elicit amorous recognition involves an intricate balance between hidden motivation and revealed intention, from a fig leaf to the broad cloth. Less concretely, love of any kind is not a reducible fact, like having five fingers in a world of four fingered gloves. It is an irreducible fact that offers itself as a gift to interpretively enact in one way or another. Our agency can be tragic, but we are not powerless, and our imaginations can be either morally sensitive or casually seductive. Ideally, the particular form a given affection takes should be as authentic as it is alluring, and remain as personally wonderful without ending socially ruinous. This possibility eludes the Designer because he does not think romantic ideals amount to anything, since what they materially unfold is simply a matter of arbitrary and self-deceived flirtation. But he nevertheless remains divided, as perhaps should we. Wrapping both aspects of this puzzling dilemma together, the Fashion Designer represents the most distilled, comically distracting version of the esthetes. Because his relations with his clients are the most abstract in their concrete embodiment, his irony is perhaps the most despairing, since love and its vicissitudes are fastidiously reduced to the ephemera of a contrived physical presence rather than a nakedly natural one.

Arguably, the Fashion Designer promotes the absolute low point of romantic ideals in order to set the stage for Johannes the Seducer, who is unprecedented among the bachelors for making something like actual contact with the tangible reality of others while nevertheless holding back. Before leaving the Designer's speech, however, we should be careful. While fashion plays a rather conspicuous role in the corrupt origins of inequality and itself becomes a later sign of degenerate moral sensibility, infecting both the bohemian and aristocrat alike, we should hesitate to knock the importance of a fitted red dress and patent leather boots, coat tails, or a properly feathered hat. One shall regret this and only appear a frump, as religiously dull as one would be esthetically insensitive. What we choose to wear plays a positive role in self-expression, and it is a genuine art to authentically cover and adorn the very bodies that are a divine gift to be passed on and revealed. As with any other gift of the sort, large or small, it can be squandered or debased, but it is the tailor's considerable job to uniquely fit both an occasion and us in a pleasing and appropriate way, whether that occasion is a wedding, a funeral, a day at the drawing board, or clearing a sewer. That we often attend to such things in the wrong way or at the behest of criminal industries is itself no argument against either their practical necessity or artistic appeal. The reason the Fashion Designer fully admits he does not know whether he serves the devil or the god in this matter is that it is very hard to tell the difference between well-turned outfits that render us legitimately more attractive or simply appear better than we are. The same would apply to wit or physical prowess.[10] In order to sort this ambiguity out we would have to get to know a *person*, a difficult enterprise in itself, all told. For example, taking his cue from Plutarch, Shakespeare reports that Antony and Cleopatra disguised themselves as servants in order to have private nights on the town, and exchanged their own queenly and soldiery outfits in the bedroom, which are not the

[10] For a classic treatment, see Rousseau's second essay on the origin of inequality, part II.

least significant details about them, including the considerable confusion it caused in the mind of the young and rigid Octavius Caesar.[11]

Johannes immediately picks up on the Fashion Designer's economic imagery and suggests he has never suffered a loss by having "paid too much for a kiss" (72). On the surface he claims to only enjoy the chase, the flower, the initial flush and swoon of love, and insists on turning his back on any enduring, concrete relationship that would render him "a prisoner of all the prolixities of finitude" (75). But the tale about Prometheus and Pandora he invokes points to something more complicated beneath the literary waters. According to Hesiod, separating the delight and wonder from the suffering Pandora brings with her charming box cannot be achieved in the way Johannes advises by avoiding the hook of marriage while consuming the bait. For one thing, having opened it, the one item retained in Pandora's box, even if one successfully avoids the "prolixities of finitude," is Hope.[12] The "devotee of erotic love," as the Seducer calls himself, is thereby nevertheless caught—hopelessly caught. Ironically, in relishing anticipation by breaking with actuality from a gallant distance—which amounts to an active refusal of hope—Johannes bears witness to the fact that his attempt to enjoy "the deception without being deceived" is spectacularly unsuccessful (79). The very strategy for which the Seducer is so infamous remains secondary to what he passionately believes about the power and value of romance, which actually requires quite a bit of work. Put otherwise, he inadvertently harbors the belief that the enchanting punishment for Promethean theft may in fact be our greatest blessing.

In spite of himself indeed, and despite his attempt to distinguish himself from his fellows, Johannes ends up praising the actuality of love by saying she was formed

> as delicate and ethereal as if of the mists of a summer night, and yet rounded as ripe fruit; light as a bird although she bears a world of desire within her, light because the play of forces is unified in the

---

[11] *Plutarch's Lives* (New York: Modern Library, 1975) 1120. Shakespeare, *Antony and Cleapatra*, Act I, scene IV and Act II, scene V.

[12] Hesiod, *Works and Days* (Loeb Classical Library, LCL 57. Cambridge MA/London: Harvard University Press, 2006) lines 42–105, edited and translated by Glenn W. Most.

> invisible center of a negative relationship in which she relates herself to herself; slim and firm, with clearly defined contours and yet to the eye surging with the undulations of beauty; complete and yet continually as if she were just now finished; cool, delicious, refreshing as the new-fallen snow, and yet blushing in tranquil transparency; happy as a pleasantry that lets one forget everything, soothing as the objective of the desiring, gratifying by being herself the incitement of desiring. And the gods planned the situation in such a way that man, upon seeing her, would be as amazed as one who sees himself and yet in turn as if he were familiar with the sight, as amazed as one who sees himself in the reflection of perfection, as amazed as one who sees what he never suspected and yet sees, so it seems, what must necessarily have occurred to him, sees what is necessary in life, and yet sees it as the riddle of life. (77)

Just above this hyperbolic tribute to svelte externals, which rightly deserves undiminished praise, our Seducer is confessing *he* is the one seduced, that romantic ideals concretely present us with a riddle as meaningful as they are necessary for seeing and understanding ourselves for the first time. Such as it is, Johannes's strategic response betrays not merely the moral depth to which he has apparently sunk, but from that depth, the very height of what love has the power to reveal, as within "a dream" that is nevertheless the "highest reality" (80). Otherwise, why would he bother trying to enjoy what he truly believed was an actual deception? It is from this simultaneous height and depth of such hopeless hope that we should read his initial entreaty: "Have enough fanaticism to idealize, enough appetite to join in the jolly conviviality of desire, enough understanding to break off in exactly the same way death breaks off, enough rage to want to enjoy all over again—then one is the favorite of the gods and the girls" (73).

But if Johannes has claimed that holding on to romantic ideals in this way makes him a favorite of both the gods and the girls, then what sense can we make of his final conclusion that with marriage the gods ultimately prevail in punishing both men and women in that "the once-upon-a-time seduced woman walks through life at her husband's side, occasionally looks back wistfully, reconciles herself to her fate, until she has reached the borderland of life" (79)? It appears Johannes draws a dichotomy between a distinctively romantic repartee and a fully embodied relationship such that both parties suffer in either scenario. By means of an instrumentally temporal breach, the lover "leads her and is led by her outside of time," while in marriage "she becomes temporal, and he through her," each ending both fragile and mortal in an apparently pejorative sense (80). Once again we face a neither/nor in which the concrete, experiential articulation of romantic ideals paradoxically becomes simultaneously a real impossibility and impossibly real. The one difference Johannes acknowledges is that, in light of his strategy, the Promethean punishment becomes a gift only in that, though love's glory is brief, "the pain is also quickly forgotten," while presumably the same cannot be said of marriage (80). The reader is left to wonder whether between such options lies a dreamy possibility in which the Seducer truly has "spied out the secret of life" in order to, in his own way, "serve something divine" and finally offer a toast of thanksgiving for it (78).

What each of the bachelor's speeches highlight are the arresting particulars that inexplicably draw us to one another, the unnerving role an active imagination plays in the process, and the degree to which we nevertheless remain agents in the process by how we choose to respond to and express that attraction. For the five in question the reactions range from intellectually throwing in the towel ahead of time, remaining coolly bemused, giving ourselves over to poetic inspiration at a distance, pandering to fashionable externals, or simply ending it after a dearly won kiss as they subtly negotiate a sense of reality amidst the purported illusion. Although largely negative and ironic, these reactions testify to how unaccountably struck we are by another's character and proclivities, allure and faults, manner and worldview, and how these simultaneously inspiring, wan, tearful, and exhilarating dimensions of the experience perennially overwhelm us with an attraction for which we are nevertheless responsible, whether flirting on a beach or standing before the altar, or both. As readers we should take no small delight in Johannes's ridiculously serious assertion that anyone "who, when he is twenty years old, does not understand that there is a categorical imperative—Enjoy—is a fool, and anyone who does not start doing it is a Christianfelder" (72). No small part of this delight would lay in imagining how baffling it would be for Kant to consider enjoyment such a primary element in the lawful requirement of morality and how much comfort we would have to offer the poor philosopher when he found out how entirely objectionable a spouse might consider it that a lover might stay by her side solely out of a sense of duty. Less personally heartbreaking and even more hysterical would be to witness the good Immanuel try and herd a whole flock of hummingbirds into a kingdom of ends while a singularly Vulcan feline sits in the corner yawning to death. But then again, perhaps our amusement should not exceed all bounds, but remain within those of reason alone.

A Significant Break in the Action

At this juncture Constantin calls a militant halt to the revelries, empties and then smashes his goblet against the back wall in an effort to break the depressing spell of the evening's theme and treatment it seems to have caused. The others follow suit with their glasses, at which point a prearranged demolition crew suddenly materializes to complete the task. Notable about all this dramatic interruption is Afham's commentary on it:

> One *breaks* off, and it takes strength to do it, even more strength than to cut a knot in two, for the obstacle of the knot provides the passion, but the passion it takes to break off, one must provide oneself. In a certain external sense the result may be the same, but artistically they are poles apart—whether something stops, comes to an end, or it is broken off by means of a free act, whether it is a happening or a passionate decision, whether it is over like the schoolmaster's ditty when there is no more or something caused by pleasure's Caesarean incision, whether it is a triviality everyone has experienced or that secret that escapes most people. (81)

Two hundred forty-eight pages later an anonymous, and it turns out fictional, suitor will break his engagement to his one and only beloved for reasons that are as much a matter of interpretation as *Stages on Life's Way* is as a whole, and even then it is recounted in a puzzling past tense fraught with an exhilarated sense of hope. But for now, Afham here signals the generally complex relationship and potential dichotomy between our passive experience of events and ideas as significant and the active manipulation of them in an effort to keep their interest, excitement, and meaning alive and in motion. In terms of romantic ideals, and in the case of personal love in particular, the issue is whether in pursuing and enacting them we are passively brought to our knees in becoming simple recipients of an involuntary and inexplicable wonder and so discover the truly sacred by relinquishing a ruinous preconception in the face of an unpredictably hospitable real world, or are responsible for imaginatively and faithfully crafting a meaningful reality of our own out of raw materials that threaten to pass on, each upon the other, as arbitrarily, tediously, and boringly as a schoolmaster's ditty. "Artistically," Afham tells us, the two "are poles apart." The question is where we stand in actual life. As elsewhere, the reader must interpret one way or another, which itself requires a receptive agency in the face of a surprisingly given wonder, therefore suggesting an implicit both/and. Where *do* we stand; where shall we look, how shall we act, in the face of such a baffling constellation of disjunctive conjunctions?

Once Constantin takes his leave and the others await the arrival of their separately arranged carriages such that each "could follow his own inclination, drive wherever he wanted, alone or if so desired in the company of whomever he wished," the remaining banqueters go for a stroll, and happen upon a country house with a hedged-in garden containing an arbor within which they discover Judge William and his wife having morning tea (81). In a telling reversal of both domestic and law-abiding intent, the arbor reveals the couple within even as the spies remain "as concealed and tense as police agents out to surprise someone," although "as far as that goes, their external appearance made a confusion possible—the police agents could be out looking for them" (82). Who is spying on whom, and *what* exactly is thereby revealed? Turning to this question, Afham cannot help but pause to signal the irony of the observational reversal that simply occurs, although he reports it as an author who was not actually there as a witness, and furthermore does not even exist. "They were surprised," he begins his next paragraph, and then summarily clarifies the subject of his sentence. Not the married couple—*they* were not surprised—*they* were "much too secure to think of themselves as the object of observation" (82). Upon the heels of this clarification, mid-paragraph, Afham simply declares it would have been obvious to any outside observer that it was a married couple in the arbor. The apparently obvious reason is because:

> Even if nothing, nothing in the wide, wide world, nothing undisguised and nothing disguised has any disguised or undisguised intention or desire to disturb the happiness of lovers when they are sitting close to each other, they are not secure in the same way. Blissful they are, and yet they cling so closely to each other as if there were some power that wanted to separate them; it is as if there were some enemy against whom they are protecting themselves and as if they could never feel sufficiently secure. It is not so with married people, and not so with that married couple in the arbor. (82–83)

So who are "they" who were in fact surprised, and what is the "power" that makes the mere lovers insecure, whether disguised or undisguised, intended or desired, to which married individuals are generally considered immune, including the particular couple in question? These are the interpretive questions that beg for answers, answers whose resolution is considerably indirect. For example, although it is apparently obvious that the two under scrutiny are married, how long they were married "could not...be stated definitely" (83). Neither do we find out what the wife's Christian name might be—Julianne for instance, or perhaps the incomparable Catherine. Given social convention, we might assume a common surname, except that it cannot be specified since William is presumably only the Judge's first name. Our perplexity about the exact status of this relationship mounts as the temporal activities surrounding the morning tea become increasingly ambiguous. Continuing in a concrete manner, Afham writes that the way the wife busied herself

> had a practiced sureness, but nevertheless there was so much almost childlike zeal about it as if she were just married, in that intermediate state where she still did not know for sure whether marriage is jest or earnestness, whether being a housewife is a task or a game, a pastime. Yet she may have been married for some time but did not usually function at the tea table; perhaps she did it only out here in the country, or perhaps she was doing it only this morning, which possibly had a special significance for them. Who can say for sure? Up to a point all conjecturing runs aground on every individuality with

an originality in his soul, because this prevents time from making its marks. (83)

The author, and reader, wonders whether what we witness here is a poetic moment or a prosaic habit, whether we find, or simply imagine, a delicious attraction only topped by "the wife's friendly inviting look" or a laughably dull bourgeois practice. Afham of course does not settle the matter for us, but simply concludes that if "anyone is not ordinarily a friend of tea, he should have been in the Judge's place" (83). But none of them, or any of us, is actually in the Judge's place. In terms of romantic ideals, here as elsewhere one is invited to entertain fabrication of importance when nothing is there versus a hard-won passion no third party is actually in a position to either deride or celebrate.

This unsettled and unsettling ambiguity is forcefully sharpened by what happens next. After solicitously suggesting that "the least" thing she can do is encourage William to drink his tea while still hot, followed by a laconic response about it being perhaps "the most, or the only thing," his wife returns to an interrupted conversation from the previous day about whether he might have become something greater in the world had he not married, adding "and you know very well on account of whom" (84). Before answering the Judge took up his tea, lit a cigar, "put his arm around her waist while she leaned against his shoulder, turned his head to blow away the smoke, then rested his eyes on her with all the devotion a look can communicate, yet smiling, although this smile of joy was tinged with sad irony" (84). Not only do we never discover "on account of whom" this question arises, Afham does not actually report the specific content of what greatness she has in mind, although she "went into detail with feminine eloquence" during which Judge William drummed his fingers on the table while humming a ballad (84). Was it the unrealized talent of a poetic soul she spoke about? Perhaps she speculates he could have become a lauded writer, a political magnet, or someone responsible for raising an entire generation's vision of religious passion. Is he happy being merely *Assessor Vilhelm*? We do not find out. All we hear is William's indirect response to this underreported explication: "very likely you are not aware that Danish law permits a husband to beat his wife; the only trouble is that the law does not state in which situation it is allowed" (85). Vaguely amused at this "threat," she insists on an honest and serious answer. Turning down this persistent request, he responds with: "I must either laugh at you or make you forget it, as before, or beat you, or you must stop talking about it, or in some other way I must make you be silent. You see it is a jest, and that is why there are so many ways out" (85). Upon this final reply he stands, kisses her on the forehead, and they leave arm in arm "down a thickly wooded path leading away from the arbor" (85). Laughing or crying, or perhaps outraged, but certainly piqued with interest, we are left in the lurch with evocative, but scant, and finally ambiguous evidence about what to conclude.

To say the least, the actual witnesses are left ungratified by this outcome, and except for Victor Eremita "the others were content with making a malicious remark" (85). Given the content of his speech Eremita would have taken particular interest in William's serious and honest answer, which may explain why the others found him stealing a manuscript by the Judge spotted through an open window facing the road. His justification for this theft is that he was responsible for publishing other work by William. More intriguingly Eremita may very well be the character "on account of whom" the Judge's wife pursues her question. Equally notable, just as Victor is getting away with the document, Afham slips it from beneath his arm, which is a curious antic for someone who was not there and furthermore only exists as a mere thought. But much more significant for *Stages* as a whole, in pitting himself as Victor's "nemesis" and publishing Judge William's manuscript on his own (although we know the task in question was actually performed by Hilarious Bookbinder), the reader is led to conclude that the stark contrasts between esthetic values and ethical commitment, romantic ideals and the actual world, love and death, hope and despair, vulnerability and detachment, the temporal and eternal, and all the real or imagined attendant feelings and choices these dichotomies pose are only going to become more complicated, and perhaps unravel altogether at our very fingertips.

As readers ourselves spying on the silhouetted "refugees" of the banquet observing the couple in the arbor at the break of day, we are left with a conflict of interpretation. Do we witness a romantically cloistered affection that truly would "transform and embellish all life," or are we simply privy to a longstanding resignation thinly cloaked in apparent tenderness, laughably bolstered by some kind of creepy internal compromise (36)? Afham does not resolve this for us, but rather carefully includes opposing hints within his snapshot in order to elicit introspection about our own esthetic longings and moral imaginations. That is, one can *look* at it in two ways, which brings us half circle to Afham's epigraph: "Such works are mirrors: when an ape looks in, no apostle can look out" (8). As Judge William and his wife are opaquely revealed within the literary bushes, our response to the text of their lives may very well expose us as either monkeys or saints, depending. Part of what this gaze depends on is that we have more text to deal with, while at this point the "enemy occupation troops," including Eremita, as we shall see, are forced to retreat without any tangible plunder (85).

2

A Purportedly Anonymous Rhetorical Flourish

The discordant hermeneutical suspension circumscribed by the reportable events in the arbor is immediately transposed in that the high-jacked manuscript ascribed to Judge William entitled "Some Reflections on Marriage in Answer to Objections" remains on the page as anonymously authored by "A Married Man" (87). For whom was it written, and from what quarters have the objections arisen: from one of the bachelors, his wife, those of the author and husband himself? The very first paragraph declares that "marriage is and remains the most important voyage a human being undertakes," for only the married person "has properly immersed himself in life" (89). No poet of course, the author continues, will be able to say of such a person what was said of "the wily Ulysses." But "the question is whether he would have learned just as much and things just as gratifying if he had stayed at home with Penelope" (89). The sentence immediately following this set of claims reads: "If no one else is of this opinion, my wife is, and if I am not very much in error, every wife agrees" (89). But which opinion, and in whose mind exactly? Does the author refer to the opinion about "the most important voyage" concerning whether marriage can provide adventurous material for a poet, or simply about what "the question is"? Given what we have witnessed in the arbor, the most literal candidate, in *her* case, would be agreement on *the question,* which "the married man" had refused to answer. We simply do not have enough information about whether at least she would agree to potential poetic material, since the content of her "melodramatic discourse" in response to what her husband could have become if he had not married remains unreported. But clearly Judge William seems to mean the first claim about marriage being the most important voyage when he concludes that since presumably every wife agrees, this is "a bit more than a simple majority, all the more so since he who has the wives on his side no doubt has the men, too" (89).

Coming from a "Judge" marshalling a defense against objections, it turns out we the readers are the ones who must judge, and our main task is to decide just how defensible or defensive that account turns out. And we are not decisively helped by the deeply conflicted tone of the unofficial court transcript. But that is precisely what is meant to help us, since it is we who must form an opinion on our own. To initiate us into this cross-referential ambiguity, as far as his wife is concerned, William claims her as a co-author and asserts "a literary firm such as that does not seem unlovely to me if one intends to write only about marriage" (96). She not only sanctions, but also forgives him—he is quite sure—for "using the opportunity to say one thing and another about her that I otherwise cannot manage to say except in solitude, because I cannot say directly to her how much she means to me, lest my eulogizing become oppressive and perhaps almost disturb our good understanding" (96). Then, after waxing lyrically about how that understanding is a "venture in natural magic," how "everything revolves around the little things that the divine element in marriage nevertheless transforms by a miracle into something significant for the believer," and that to believe it takes "absolute faith," the Judge ends by concluding that this must all be written anonymously in order to avoid his domestic life becoming "an object of anyone's curiosity" (90–91, 96). One wonders what exactly he might be protecting, since he assures us that he is "invulnerable to laughter" just after admitting that he also has "a presentiment of the terror that can overwhelm a man along this way" (92). Although he claims "if I could mean something more to more people by being an author, I far prefer to mean as much as possible to my wife," the laughter to which he is apparently immune as a husband he may not be as invulnerable to as an author. Just after describing how the main ideals contained within marriage are like root consonants, and that "while these remain fixed and unchanging, one can have the joy of adding new vowels and then rereading it," he ends by insisting that he is not thereby—"as a malicious mocker has said"—making "erotic love and marriage have the same consonants and the vowels constitute the difference" (97). The reference here is to a Hebrew spelling in which, by changing a vowel, to kiss means to bite, as if the synthetic eloquence Judge William lauds could be either genuinely romantic or spell a bourgeois lack of passion. Apparently, we must be prepared to read between the lines, and this may disturb *our* "good understanding."

The Formal Predicates of Marriage

The anonymous Judge begins his formal reflections on marriage by announcing that erotic love "does indeed have its own god" and has poetry on its side, along with all that is comfortable, fragrant, and inexplicably arresting (99). In contrast, when two lovers find themselves in the presence of "the God of spirit," who presides over the bond of marriage, all this "disappears," as if the King himself had just arrived at the party. In the presence of YHWH Cupid must suddenly behave himself. As for the lovers themselves, this will likely "disturb" them. One would think the party in question would be the occasion of a wedding, but William's chosen example is that of a baptism. Having just announced the potentially volatile rivalry between our romantic and ethical ideals, this detail suggests he is eager to move on and is not entirely content to start at the beginning when he claims that marriage is "a higher expression for erotic love" (100). At this point a "malicious mocker" would likely retort that, apparently, the truly sacramental moment that unites a couple literally emerges from a fallopian tube, presumably nine months later. But above this provincial perspective, and significant for *Stages* as a whole, the tension between romantic and ethical ideals does indeed split into three, not two, leaving open whether the pregnancy in question refers to that of an actual infant or a platonic brainchild.

With such a multivalent christening in the background, and because "the difficulty is to be able to preserve the qualifications inherent in the erotic so that the spiritual does not burn them up and consume them, but burns in them without consuming them," the marriageable partner must steer clear of a specific Skylla and Charybdis:

> [I]f the individual has not in faith placed himself in the relationship with God as spirit, paganism haunts his brain as a fantastic reminiscence and he cannot enter into any marriage; and on the other hand neither can he do it if he has become totally spiritual; even if one

> of the latter type and one of the former type were married, such falling in love or such a match is no marriage. (100–101)

Against the backdrop of these two specters Judge William describes the third way of marriage as "the highest *telos* [goal] of individual life" (101). Why, the reader might ask, would the Judge claim that marriage is a higher expression of erotic love, and indeed the highest aim of human life generally, and then feel it necessary to clarify by writing that "it is the highest *telos* in such a way that anyone who evades it crosses out the whole of earthly life in one single stroke and retains only eternity and spiritual interests, which admittedly at first glance are not slight, but in the *longitude of time* are very strenuous and also in one way or another an expression for an unhappy life" (101)? How did we get from the preoccupation with whether a staid bourgeois marriage counts as a romantic institution to the acetic threat of purely spiritual interests? At this point we do not have enough text to tell. All we know is that, as the highest *telos*, marriage "includes the particular qualifications, in which it is exhausted as in its predicates, thus under itself, so that they have their meaning precisely as immanent and, on the other hand, are meaningless as soon as they attempt to go on their own, for a detached thought that wants to be all on its own is comical and thoughtless" (101). Marriage, then, is a semantic construction that fully conveys all the relevant romantic meaning of a human life without other, and presumably meaningless, connotations. The careful reader will no doubt be unable to resist asking: in what sense shall we take this? Apparently, the interchangeable vowels in the lead-up have here not yet become stable predicates. Correspondingly, the relationship between the content of our actual life and the form of literary imagination reappears on another register, but not without inducing considerable anxiety. Unlike the esthetes, Judge William does not seem to ethically suffer from ironic detachment—at least not in what he chooses to write about. But the problematic relationship between our romantic ideals and ethical aspirations remains with him, dramatized in the deeply ambivalent though emphatic nature of his discursive treatment of them. For instance, in steering between the purely esthetic and religious exceptions that threaten the marriage bond, we find that romantic and ethical ideals must themselves form a partnership of true minds:

> The difficulty is this: erotic love or falling in love is altogether immediate; marriage is a resolution; yet falling in love must be taken up into marriage or into the resolution: to will to marry—that is, the most immediate of all immediacies must also be the freest resolution, that which is so inexplicable in its immediacy that it must be attributed to a deity must also come about by virtue of deliberation, and such exhaustive deliberation that from it resolution results. Furthermore, the one must not follow the other; the resolution must not come slinking along behind but must occur simultaneously; both parts must be present in the moment of decision. If deliberation has not exhausted thought, then I make no resolution; I act either on inspiration or on the basis of a whim. (102)

What Judge William articulates in this decisive paragraph is how the impulse of erotic love is necessary but not sufficient to carry us forward in an ethically authentic and enriching way. Since the form of personal love in question presumably has all the features the tipsy bachelors variously lampooned and celebrated, it is not surprising that he would think something within the human personality must compensate for it and thereby tame, stabilize, and finally guarantee its life, perhaps by having an actual child. What remains curious is how impotent and self-deceived he thinks erotic love turns out to be, taken on its own terms between two alone, and about which he seems quite sure ahead of time.

That he *is sure* that either "nothing more is needed at all than the prompting of erotic love, which like a magnet steadily points without deviation toward the same point, or the resolution must be present from the beginning" leads the anonymous Judge to declare a very specific uncertainty: "When it is a matter of immediate falling in love, it is utterly impossible to determine whether it is a knight or a seducer who is speaking, for the next moment decides that" (102–103). In contrast, the simultaneous "safeguard" of ethical resolve relieves us of anything potentially treacherous about romantic love, along with any attendant "anxiety of immediacy over its own happiness" (103). The problem with starching and ironing out the difference between the seducer and saint is whether this will leave the world bereft of knights. The courtly tensions that seem inherent within a personal passion worthy of the name enfold the apostle and playboy and give birth to those spiritual bastards we come to somehow, at our best, involuntarily cherish as our very own. Of course, we could always simply ignore such tensions and turn our backs on the children they produce. At the same time Judge William seems aware of this corresponding anxiety. Just after criticizing Aladdin for pleading with a jinni to guarantee his "exorbitant" love rather than drawing on his own free resolve, he admits that "in every generation there perhaps are not ten young men who have this blind courage, this vigor in the unlimited" (104). Setting these few romantics aside, most others would not even wish as Aladdin wished, let alone face the prospect of their wish being granted without "growing pale" (104). Nevertheless, although Aladdin is great, William diagnoses him as a seducer because "it is never sufficiently clear and emphatic" whether he is "a justified individuality" (104). Over against a poetic "faith in immediacy and its power" to fill the sail of falling in love, the marriageable person "has permitted himself a doubt, an innocent, a well-meaning, a noble, a lovely doubt, for he really is far from wanting to offend erotic love or wanting to do without it" (104–105). Ironically, although these claims are certainly emphatic, the final clause remains enervatingly opaque.

When it comes to faith, doubt, and romance, Judge William continually reverses tack to avoid a prosaic dead calm in his own account of the emotional epistemology of love. Nevertheless, it is clear the Judge earnestly wishes to embrace the poetry of knighthood within the ideal of marriage, which "must not be a fragmentary something that comes along with time and opportunity, something that happens to the lovers after they have lived together for a while" (105). The way it seems to work is that all the creative tensions within romantic love get built into the foundation of ethical resolve by acknowledging and then stalwartly turning away from the difficulty by means of an act of will that consolidates our feelings and aspirations into a concrete and satisfying whole. How one pours this foundation as an unhesitant result of exhaustive deliberation raises a question about whether Judge William thinks any marriage actually accomplishes this or is simply *meant* to. The drama in the rhetoric here is that we could read him as saying that ideally it actually does so, or that this is the ideal to which one must commit, whether achievable or not. Significantly, as he spells it out, his own agency and the power of the ideal fold in on one another. After insisting there must be no haggling and compromising between husbands about marriage ideals and how things actually go, he writes: "No, an open fight—marriage's idea is bound to win. Humble before God, submissive to the divine majesty of love, I proudly hold my head high above all witticisms and do not bow my head to any objection" (106). We must keep in mind the existential role Judge William has cast for himself in this fight, the simultaneous humility and pride of having and holding to an ideal he claims is itself bound to win and the corresponding place in which this puts his reader.

This particular battle over romantic ideals begins with a treatment of "negative" resolve with which one might "fritter life away looking for the ideal" or "prudishly" reject any possibility of meeting it (107). He apparently has in mind unmarried idealists standing around at a ball, illegitimately stalling and ridiculously looking around for a thunderbolt on a clear day. Virtually in the same breath he is at pains to avoid the impression that he would prefer a resolve "speedily arrived at in line with others and resolved on the basis that the next-door neighbor and the neighbor across the street have so resolved,…for whether there is poetry at second hand I do not know, but a resolution at third hand is no resolution" (108). Although we may agree that neither an infatuated romanticism nor the sham aping of others is authentic, of what concrete help is the positive description of ideal resolve other than to restate an abstract, unrealistic, and potentially heartless "synthesis of falling in love and resolution" (109)? As the reader turns the page, it gets worse. When it comes to genuine ethical resolve we must avoid two category mistakes. The first is to think in terms of "*probability*—a spineless fellow, a dabbler, and Jewish peddler, with whom no freeborn soul becomes involved" (110). The second is to ruminate about "the *outcome*" (110). Conjoining these mistakes, William writes that if "a person in the moment of resolution is not so glowingly surrounded by the brightness of the divine that all phantasms created by the fogs of drowsiness vanish, his resolution is but a greater or minor forgery—let him find consolation in the outcome" (110). In contrast to both, the apparent task is to suddenly grow confident ahead of time, without the consolation of any decisive knowledge concerning either the qualities of a potential beloved or the likely prospect of a happy result. How this comes about remains shrouded in an arbor of entangled duty and desire, not unlike that from which the Judge and his wife recede from the view of the skeptical bachelors. In the end all we get is: "Cheer up, then, venture boldly. Have the courage to will the difficult; then the difficulty will be of assistance, for the difficulty is not an old grump, is not a chicaner, but an omnipotence that wills to do it so very well" (111). Among the difficulties we are encouraged to face are the limitations of our powers of attraction and the available options of those with the power to attract. It is quite possible, even probable, that we have to make it up as we go, humbly speculating on what might be a good fit and thereby bring about something worthy of being called happiness in the end.

As readers, the difficulty we are encouraged to face *is* the very difficulty we face with our highest ethical ideals generally. The "ideality of genuine resolution," William writes, is "just as temporal as eternal," "just as sympathetic as it is autopathetic," "just as concrete as it is abstract," "just as dialectical with regard to freedom as to the divine dispensation" (112–15). The example of marriage simply distills the problem of romantic ideals from a singular scenario. As an example, what seems to render it the highest *telos* is the greater prospect it offers for ethical obligations to actually coincide with our warmer emotional aspirations.

> Let a poor wretch who does not have an understanding with the temporal in the resolution of marriage nurse the sick, feed the poor, clothe the naked; let him visit the prisoner, let him comfort the dying—I commend him, he will not miss his reward, but neither is he in divine madness an unprofitable servant. His sympathy is continually seeking its deepest expression but does not find it, seeks it far and wide as his solicitude goes from house to house, whereas a married man finds opportunity in his house, in his home, where to him it is bliss to will to do everything, and an even greater bliss, a divine *poscimur* [we are called upon], that he is and remains without meritoriousness. (113–14)

The synthetic ideal of marriage as a romantic institution thus weds personal desire to a sacred duty, and in doing so most fully articulates the meaning of a human life. But it does so in a curiously wordless fashion:

> The highest expression of falling in love is that the lover feels like nothing before the beloved, and vice versa, because to feel oneself to be something conflicts with falling in love. The resolution has no words, because words themselves are almost too concrete. The vow is silent or that immortal 'yes'—and this abstraction is expressed in such a way that if all the writers of shorthand joined together they would be unable to describe what takes place in a week of marriage. (115)

The very wordlessness of the marriageable synthesis then issues in an even more curious dialectic. In coordinating the sheer helplessness of falling in love with ethical resolve, one

> ventures out of infatuation's hiding place with the beloved one, with the beloved ones—what can happen there? He does not know; if he would devote himself to this thought, his hair would certainly turn gray in a single night. He does not know what would happen—he can lose everything; and this he does know—he cannot evade a single thing, for the resolution holds him firmly there where his love imprisons him but also holds him undaunted there where falling in love laments. (116)

In all this our anonymous author is saying and not saying several things at once. On the one hand, Eros is happily received as a freely bestowed gift, however scary as a shot to the heart. On the other hand, the considerable risk involved in joining our desire to duty presents us with a sadness no less irresistible and threatening. There is so much in our emotional lives that eludes our control and that we must vulnerably and wonderfully receive, without falling prey to the contingency of what we cannot know, and perhaps do not even feel. We can only construct and revise it as we go, in the dual sense of taking moral responsibility and literarily crafting the script. In a single sentence Judge William evokes the simultaneous glory and ennui involved: "A married man risks every day, and every day the sword of duty hangs over his head, and the journal is kept up as long as the marriage keeps on, and the ledger of responsibility is never closed, and the responsibility is even more inspiring than the most glorious epic poet who must testify for the hero" (117). In its own way this high sentiment ominously anticipates the extended diary about a broken engagement that follows William's own defense of marriage to objections.

Near the heart of this impending prosaic equivocation lies the ancient and perplexing relationship between Eros and the Polis. "What interest can anyone who refuses to let marriage have its reality [*Realitet*] have in the ideal of the state, what love can he have for his fatherland, what civic patriotism can he have for everything that pertains to the woes and welfare of society! The more abstract the ideality, the more imperfect it is!" (114). All of us are placed in a larger social world that demands our care and investment. We variably play vocational roles in political life, education, medicine, as members of a parish, a string quartet, in national theaters, neighborhood associations, or charitable organizations. As we navigate any of these waters along with their native but contested values, we invariably encounter the institutional obstacles of conflict and disgrace, boredom and apathy. No one person can change things for the better, which is precisely what makes intense involvement with them so unrewarding. Any community seems to rely on its members to form close, personal, and often erotically charged friendships as a comfort and release from inhabiting such otherwise chilly and corrupt environments. The problem is that these personal attachments can lead us away from larger and longer social and religious aims into a perilous and equally empty world entirely set apart. A Polis without Eros lacks warmth, and Eros without a Polis lacks depth, each of which taken separately lay waste. One way to read Judge William is to say the bourgeois family structure ideally resolves this dilemma. We witness him working out on the page the sense in which he actually believes this over against the fragile and often tragic romance of love-struck youth, along with the god who inspires it and the austere resignation of eternally minded souls who know all earthly ideals are bound to disappoint and the God who inspires them. But the well-trimmed arbor of domestic life between them remains fraught. In fact, if the Polis is a macrocosm of the individual soul, the tensions within each are only further dramatized between just two, although it may be singularly worth our time, and not only in the bedroom.

A third of the way through his "reflections" in defense of marriage all this dissonance comes to a particular head as the author pauses, as if wrapping up a eulogy. At the center of this pause we find that marriage "is the fullness of time," an image of a divine incarnation annunciated and presumably christened in a stream of opposing modifiers. Marriage is "divine," "the wonder," "earthly," "nature's most profound myth," "sacred," "civic," "poetic," "light, like dancing in the meadow," "happy like a child, and yet solemn," "solemn and yet mitigated in jest," "humble and yet courageous," "satisfied and yet full of expectancy," "plain and everyday" even as "the recollection of eternity listens and forgets nothing" (117–18). Amidst all this fluid vocabulary we read that marriage is "secure, at peace, enfranchised in life; no danger is a real danger, but only a spiritual conflict" (118). Only? Meaning a mere and insignificant danger? No wonder seven pages earlier he felt compelled to write: "Cheer up, then, venture boldly." In the story of our lives it somehow seems as if between Christmas and Easter comes the ambiguous wonderland of Marriage. But how much of Good Friday might that inevitably include? If we go with the Gospel of John, strength, warmth, and comfort abound, while the arrest and crucifixion remain momentarily alarming but finally voluntary and ultimately harmless. If we go with the Gospel of Mark, the disciples are all as forsaken as is Christ himself, while of all people a Roman centurion is compelled to announce that divinity is finally revealed in helpless agony.[1] That Judge William would weld marriage ideals as a romantic institution to the Gospel narrative is a pivotal Archimedean point for *Stages* as a whole. The evocative thought that our ordinary lives of love and loss mirror the actual Passion of the very incarnate God who began his life in a manger is both wonderfully edifying and profoundly disturbing. And the particular turning point is revealing: "All I wanted to do is jack up the price a bit" (119).[2] On either side of this statement we have what comes

[1] John 18:6 and 19:28–30. Mark 14:46–51 and 15:33–39.

[2] In the overall internal tragectory of Kierkegaard's authorship, the echo here is clearly that of Johannes de Silentio's treatment of Abraham in *Fear and Trembling*. In that work de Silentio jacks up the price of faith as a humble courage in facing the certain threat of losing the beloved Isaac while remaining gloriously open to recieving him back. Here and throughout a fully implied double-movement of faith occurs just above Judge William's head in regard to what it takes to long for, receive, renounce, and then receive again in the case of a spouse. See Søren Kierkegaard, *Fear and Trembling/Repetition* (Princeton: Princeton University Press, 1983) 15–53, edited and translated by Howard V. Hong and Edna H. Hong with introduction and notes.

off as a genuine confession about his own imperfection as a husband and a renewed defensiveness aimed at "chicaners," "freebooters," "spies," and "vagabonds" (119). Thus an injured admission ends with an insulting pretense, like listening to an insufferably sophomoric disciple. Peter, for example. Or Judas, whose kiss was indeed a bite.

Another Beginning

Having provisionally completed his reflections, the Judge proceeds to more specifically address "the objections," as if they were not right there from the beginning (119). In doing so our anonymous author finds himself forced to return to what ironically amused the Young Man about the involuntary and inexplicable peculiarities of our personal affections, only to epigraphically announce that "the deceived is wiser than the one not deceived" (88, 119). But given the fact that he claims that to "elaborate the objections as such is only a waste of time," and given that the epigraph originates from an ancient Greek insight about the salutary effects of a tragic spectacle, it is difficult to identify where exactly the "defense" and the "objections" stand or rest. Between these two we find that the objections will arise either from one who "has gone astray in desire and thereupon become callous" or from one who "is infatuated with the understanding" (119). He then concludes that it is "indeed true that it takes a quite different kind of wisdom to remain in the blessed deception of ardor and of mystery and of erotic love and of illusion and of the wonder than to run away from house and home split naked, half-sappy from sheer sapience" (119). In all this we find a confluence of the epistemological, volitional, and imaginative dimensions of our emotional lives, each containing a corresponding ambiguity. The trick, apparently, is to be sufficiently informed and simultaneously naïve. Or to put it the other way around, we must be neither hopelessly naïve nor worldly-wise. In attempting to spell out where exactly to locate the objections in order to defend marriage against them our author finds, or places himself, in a very tight corner, beginning with dismissing the "degenerate who ends a perhaps dissolute life by wanting to ridicule everything that always knew how to elude his profane touch" and turns rather to the "more acceptable form of objection" from a young man "pure in regard to the erotic" but who, "like a prematurely wise child, has skipped a stage in the development of the soul and has begun his life with reflection" (120). The reason the corner is so tight is because the particular "stage" in question is the momentous immediacy of falling in love, which William rightly wonders whether the degenerate has ever really experienced, and therefore feels genuinely sorry for the overly reflective and emotionally inexperienced virgin who has carefully stepped around it.

At issue is exactly how choice, imagination, and tangible experience figure in the moral life in regard to personal love and what role our understanding of the matter can or should play. Our author's own position is that we must "choose" that which is involuntarily granted and simply accept the wonder of being romantically struck in such a way that we avoid the danger of "wanting to set someone up as the beloved" and thereby become "a laughing-stock by starting a silly, critical lecture on the beloved, that I love her for this reason and for that reason and finally for this reason—because I love her" (121). Along the way, precisely "when the understanding stands still, it behooves one to have the courage and heart to believe the wondrous and, continually strengthened by this vision, to return to actuality and not just sit still and want to fathom it" (122). In contrast, the "rueful knight of reflection" wants to "fathom the synthesis at the basis of erotic love" and thereby loses "the immediacy that carries a person through life" (121–22). This preempted response to the naively burnt-out reaction of someone like the Young Man belies a full half of the Judge's point. Nonetheless, William seems aware of the complicated battle in the process, a battle in which the involuntary, wonderstruck urgency of a fully incarnate attraction must "find its equivalent in an immediacy reached through reflection" (123). It is amusing to think of our dear Judge offering the intangible counsel that we must indeed exhaustively think through things, but do so immediately without interruption lest the phenomenon in question spoil before our very eyes. On the other hand, maybe that is the way love actually goes, if it goes anywhere.

At this juncture, William decorously tips his hat at those verbosely experienced in the art of love, from whom "the objections take another direction" (124). These objections also remain entirely implicit, since such "amorous, seductive worship of the sex ends with insults," presumably because their assumption is that "the brief period of falling in love is supposed to be a woman's culmination, and therefore the point is to leave off again" (124). Surely we should have the speech of Johannes the Seducer in mind at this point, which all amounts to a bunch of nonsense according to the Judge, ironic enough given he has just enjoined an innocent reader to simply accept the wondrous as a gift of the gods (124). Then we hear an account of William's own love story, worth repeating at length given its brevity:

> As a critic of marriage, I am a *tiro* [novice]; I have no shallow introductory studies from a man-about-town period, which at times is more poisonous than one thinks. My love story is in a certain sense short. I have minded my own business and tended to my studies; I have not inspected the girls at parties and on the promenades, at theaters and concerts. I have not entered into it recklessly, nor have I done it with the idiotic seriousness in which a marriageable male is pleased to think that a girl must be extraordinary to be good enough for him. Thus without any experience I became acquainted with her who is now mine. I have never been in love before, and my prayer is that I may not fall in love later on, but if for a moment I were to think what for me is indeed unthinkable—that death took her from me, that my life underwent a change such that I would be dedicated to being a husband a second time, I am convinced that my marriage has not spoiled me or made me more competent to criticize, select, and inspect. No wonder one hears so much silly talk about love, since to hear so much talk is already an indication that reflection is universally forcing its way in to disturb the quiet, more modest life where love prefers to reside because in its modesty it is so close to piety. (124–25)

In turning to the more experienced sensualists, and telling his own story, Judge William suddenly takes the side of the Young Man at the banquet, aware that he might be declared incompetent to discuss either the glory or danger of love because not only does he lack a sufficient amount of experience but also because that experience does not seem sufficiently complicated and tangible enough since, "despite being married for eight years I still do not definitely know in a critical sense what my wife looks like" (125). In his own way, he perfectly agrees with the Young Man that such personal and particular affections cannot be explained, but he also defensively refuses to try because "just as it must be nauseating for someone entering the temple in an exalted frame of mind to hear the jingling of coins, so it is nauseating to me to hear the noise of words such as 'slim,' 'shapely,' 'svelte,' etc.," concluding that "all this slimness and svelteness and the eyebrows and flashing eyes do not constitute falling in love, still less a marriage" (126). As a concluding judgment, this one is fair enough. But can we really trust a Judge who finds the word "svelte" positively nauseating rather than imperfectly delightful? What exactly has barred him from wanting to definitely acquaint himself with the architecture of his own wife's neckline? Does he not find her particularly attractive, and then convinced himself that such attraction is no different than the jingle of coins in the narthex?

It is clear the Judge would not have been a very welcome participant at the banquet, much worse than even having ladies present. Nevertheless, he cannot help but take part by speaking in praise of love in such a way that both squares with and detracts from everything previously stated, all the way from the Young Man to Johannes the Seducer. But because he has carved for himself such a restricted space for positively describing marriage as a higher expression of romantic ideals, what he must now do is defend himself against being insensitive and ultimately humorless. In gearing up for this part of his defense he mentions a book he once read that purportedly demonstrates the superiority of the Female Sex, which he found amusing, although he shares with us none of its content except that he appreciated the concluding "poem…that refuses to have anything to do with any turgid [*vaniloquax*] praise of man" (126). He then explains more precisely what he is getting at by mentioning a speech delivered at the "Twenty-eighth of May Society," which he found not amusing but actually absurd, since the content seems to have been about how new discoveries in natural science brought us closer to God, a paragraph which, as an illustration, is anything but precise (126–27). After this he returns to his memory of the formerly amusing "little book" to say that, "while I never speak to my wife about her being slender, etc., which would certainly displease her and be a failure for me, yet sometimes, if I do say so myself, I am very good at the kind of arguments and observations that please her, probably because they demonstrate nothing at all and therefore simply demonstrate that our marriage needs no prolix critique but that we are happy" (127). Somehow all of this dissembling is connected with the previously declared conviction against the "loafers and bachelors" that "woman is certainly just as good as man—period" (124).

In the paragraph immediately following, the announcement that he is adept at making "arguments and observations that please" his wife without volatilizing her begins with how "it has often amazed me that no poet really portrays a married couple conversing" (127). He adds that if they ever are portrayed, "they are only minor characters" and "much older" than the real lovers in question, and that furthermore poetic love must be threatened with external obstacles while married love must have its dangers within, all of which he regards "as a sad indirect demonstration that marriage is far from enjoying the recognition is deserves, for it indeed seems as if a married couple were not just as poetic as a couple of lovers" (128). Having geared up in this way he is now finally ready for his own defense and illustration, with which he begs "the reader to have enough sense of humor not to regard as demonstrating anything" (128). Here is the example he offers: While on a summer excursion with his wife William noticed an advertisement in five consecutive country inns posting a paternal gratitude for the expert hand of a doctor who relieved his family of some bad corns, including a daughter, who "like an Antigone...was not exempted from this family evil either" (128). The Assessor thought it tactless of the father to reveal such an infirmity, and wondered out loud to his spouse whether a potential suitor might not be offended, since "this nasty corn, even after it was removed, has a most disturbing effect on an esthetic romantic view of the beautiful," and furthermore, whether un-removed corns or even the memory thereof may not be sufficient grounds for divorce (129). Apparently his wife found this light banter amusing enough, as should the reader, but what remains unclear is the "anything" about which we are supposed to have enough humor not to suppose it demonstrates. Since it would be definitely perplexing if the chosen illustration by the humorless Judge demonstrated nothing at all, he immediately clarifies that what he means to show is how it is "precisely marriage's sense of security that sustains the humorous," even though "based upon experience, it does not have the restlessness of erotic love's first bliss, even if marriage's bliss is far from minor" (129). One might conclude from all this that the Judge has narrowed the "esthetic romantic view of the beautiful" as well as the entire field of particularly wonderful and vexing personal loves to their most superficial dimensions in order to then humorously dismiss them. Then the question becomes whether we are supposed to find *that* funny. Debatably, such an outcome might provoke laugher, in a tragic sort of way. For one thing, apart from the topic of conversation, we hear no more about her side in the exchange than we did when they were having morning tea in the arbor. For all we know, she might suffer from a corn or two, as painful as they are unbecoming, which she has kept carefully hidden from her husband. Furthermore, after recounting his bemused reaction to the repeated public announcement concerning a family relieved of an esthetic epidemic a married individual is secure enough to humorously handle, Judge William cuts himself off with "enough of this" as if immediately sick of his own joke in the retelling of it. The way he really wants to talk is the way "every husband wants to talk," not as a critic "who admires or sees the lack of some earthly beauty," not as infatuated, but as someone "deeply moved" (129–30). More specifically, what he really wants to discuss is his conviction that "within my wife's breast beats a heart, quietly and humbly, but steadily and smoothly," how it "beats for me and my welfare and for what is mutually ours," and his belief that "through her I absorb peace and contentment into my life and many times am rescued from the death of despondency and evil torment of vexation of spirit" (130). None of this, he intently points out, has the passion of an "emotional blaze of the moment" (130). What the reader may find difficult to tell, however, is whether this latter statement is a description or confession, given or assuming how the way "every husband talks" is "better, provided he is a better husband, better, provided he is talented" (130). The amount of defensiveness, finger-wagging, and sheer protest within the prose at this point is downright feverish.

The implicit suspicion that William has narrowed the field of particularly inspiring and vexing personal investments, and has in his own way fled from them, is perhaps what leads the author, after eight years of marriage, to suggest "in what direction I seek woman's beauty," though incidentally *not* in terms of his wife in particular. Dramatically showing something less than a poker face, just as he starts trotting out the thesis that feminine beauty unfolds and increases with age, he interrupts himself in a long footnote to effusively adore the actress Mme. Nielsen for being able to traverse all stages of life with a range of understated nuance that entirely transcends the momentary demands of theatrical spectacle. In itself this is telling, although he admits it is "dubious" and "misleading" given his stated point of view (131). What is significant about the footnote is that it indirectly evokes the problematic intersection of romantic ideals, artistic representation, and actual life, and is amusing in that it comes from the pen of a husband who claims he is not a critic, or at least does not want to think of himself that way. On a deeper level, the fact that he can so eloquently appreciate a theatrical display of what is "essentially feminine," given the abbreviated character of its performance, once again renders the main body of his text ambiguous. For example, that body continues with

> [i]ndeed, who, unless he is desperately in love, has not looked at a young girl without sensing a certain sadness because the fragility of mortal life shows itself here in its most extreme contrasts: vanity as swift as a dream, beauty as fair as a dream. But however fair that first beauty is, it is still not the truth; it is an envelope, a garment, from which only with the years does the true beauty extricate itself before the husband's grateful eyes. (132–33)

With Mme. Nielsen in mind the final paragraph of the footnote begins with "[a]lthough at the theater one ordinarily tends to think about the vanity of life and youth, beauty and charm, one is safe in admiring her, because one knows that this does not perish" and ends with:

> For this reason she may not have her admirers among the critics who register the pulse of the moment, or among the devotees of the theater who are obliged to have seen this one and that one, or among the messengers who want something to gossip about, or among the triumph-bearers who like other carriers seek day labor bearing someone away, or among young men who, failing otherwise to situate an adolescent love, cast it upon an actress, or among the dissipated who sustain themselves by a momentary excitation, but instead has her admirers among those who, themselves happy and contented in life, do not miss the theater, do not hanker after it, whose

> right hand does not promptly run to the left in applause on the spot, whose pen is not busy on paper that same evening in connection with some detail, but who are slow to speak and perhaps rejoice all the more discriminatingly [*skiønsomt*] in seeing the *beautiful* [*skjønne*] when *in truth* it *is.* (132)

The contrast between the sadness one often feels in actual life in the presence of a young beloved given the fragility of life and the enjoyment of feminine essence one may witness at the theater is linked to the corresponding contrast between the true beauty that must "extricate itself as if from an envelope, a garment" in real time and Mme. Nielsen's understated presentation which, surprisingly, *is in truth beautiful.* To round out these complications, the temporal and visual contrasts are strikingly premised upon a crucial qualification: "unless he is desperately in love." This qualification appears in the main body of the text where the garment covering true beauty is likened to an envelope, which ordinarily contains a letter, not a body. This confluence of moralism and a subdued attempt at esthetic rumination raises further questions about the character of Judge William's own love. When did the sadness of young love that drives him into a footnote on an actress overwhelm him, and was this prior or subsequent to his actually having fallen in love, and how desperate was that love? It is as if we really are confronted with a sealed envelope from a lover whose words have yet to emerge, which in a way they do.[3]

[3] Under the psuedonym *Inter et Inter,* Kierkegaard will three years later write an essay in honor of the actress Luise Heiberg in which he presents another side of the coin when evaluating an aging actress. In that essay, the author highlights a different tragectory in which an older woman enacts the tension-filled youthfulness of Juliet given her wisdom of years in a way that the "damned pretty and devilishly pert wench of eighteen years" may not be qualified to muster. From a truly esthetic point of view, the beauty here emerges from the character. But unlike what Judge William emphasizes, the erotic charge is lauded throughout. Outside the theater, the moral implication is that we become starstruck exactly when it counts. An actual person might be eighteen and older than the rest, or forty and younger than than the others, and vice versa. This pivotal essay in Kierkegaard's authorship as whole is significant because it coordinates an extatic bit of theatrical criticism with an en route commentary on the spiritually laxidasical admiration we may have for God, who presumably does not change with the seasons or fall out of vogue by turning forty, but who,

Just after the footnote and passing comment about "a certain sadness" one might feel upon considering a youth in bloom, we are forthwith asked to gaze upon an actual woman of years and enjoined to be careful, for "it is not the fleeting kind that hurries away like a dream" (133). This beauty, this love, now that the envelope has been scrupulously unsealed, is "reconciled with life, and if you once again feel the urge for a reconciling word, if you should feel the urge to forget the dissonances of life, then go to her, sit worthily with this worthy one" (133). Unlike the "froth of the moment" with which the critic, reviewer, and connoisseur in foaming despair rush along "shouting: Let us love today, for tomorrow it is all over," a mature woman arrives at and provides "life's solution" (133–34). In contrast, men do not provide such a solution, since "ordinarily his accounts are more complicated," while a housewife "has only elementary events, the everyday distresses and the everyday joys, but also this happiness, for if a young girl is happy, then the woman of years is even happier" (134). It is plausible, but rather difficult to think Judge William believes all this, since he then immediately leaves "the woman of years, whose company I am not, however, really avoiding" (134). Why would we suspect he was avoiding anything as one whose accounts are apparently more "complicated"? One reason might be that he has narrowed, truncated, and simultaneously reconciled himself to an imaginary solution he resolutely wants to be real. And that would be complicated given how truly romantic he otherwise claims to be. As for *her*—"the woman full of years who accomplishes a work of God, who provides the solution to the worried person and for the cheerful person is the best eulogy on existence"—there is evidently nothing to avoid (134). As William develops this part of his thesis, his rhetorical strategy is to work

---

alas, cannot "even by dying ever make them feel what they lost. Oh human admiration, what sheer vanity you are, and not least when you think you are being constant!" Søren Kierkegaard, *Christian Discourses/The Crisis and a Crisis in the Life of an Actress* (Princeton: Princeton University Press, 1997) 305, 318, edited and translated by Howard V. and Edna H. Hong with introduction and notes. This coordination may very well be the best clue we have on the relationship between the so-called esthetic and religious writings. See Søren Kierkegaard, *The Point of View* (Princeton: Princeton University Press, 1998) 29, edited and translated by Howard V. and Edna H. Hong with introduction and notes.

backwards in time in order to properly locate the significance and salience of personal love, turning to the topic of motherhood and agreeing with Victor Eremita that a maiden's life is but a phantasm. As a mother, however, she finally belongs to actuality, no longer "nimble, light, flirtatious" but "caught, imprisoned" (134–35). In order to immediately mollify how pejorative this might sound, he hastens to add that "I certainly do not imprison her...No, no, she has trapped herself and sits imprisoned beside the cradle; imprisoned, and yet she has complete freedom, a boundless freedom in which she binds herself to the child; I am sure that she is willing to die in her nest" (135). No doubt much could be said here about internalized gender roles foisted from without along with the entourage of presumptuous aspirations attending them. But if we again think of the author's reflections as a qualifying speech at the banquet, the claim that only within a family does love become fully tangible and concrete and therefore real for the first time raises a more global issue.

What confirms that the Judge has more on his mind other than the beauty of motherhood is that William once again interrupts himself, now in the main body of the text, with a parenthetical thought about jealousy. Although the pretext for it is "the mother's partiality for the child" which "good Lord" will "certainly be surmounted," he seems to be thinking of Constantin's witty and detached stratagem for avoiding cuckoldry (135). But now that he has suddenly mentioned the dark passion of jealousy we are informed that, as with anger, in a "noble love there is also a righteous indignation that really is both troubled and resentful and is an altogether normal psychical condition if the terrible thing has happened," a condition he considers to be "love's ethical sorrow over someone who has died" (135). Somewhere near the jealous heart is a laudable attachment that insists love is stronger than death and our passionate investment is not in vain. In making this point he is fully aware that in contrast to the sort of troublesome weeds that arise from the fragile soil in which love grows, he is also aware of a "not very commendable fearlessness that, plagued by an evil spirit, wants to be pure spirit, and also wants to have the power to become what is just as reprehensible as raging in jealousy—the power to become cold, thoroughly chilled in the icy passion of wittiness. For there is a hell whose heat blights all life; but there is also a hell whose cold kills all life" (135). Cool detachment and heated possessiveness equally choke the life of the garden, planted as it typically is somewhere east of Eden.

How did we arrive at this foreboding juncture that interrupts a thought about the truly esthetic glow of motherhood that actually begins with his speaking "as inoffensively as possible" about a mother's partiality, and the "terrible thing" that could prompt feelings of jealousy and resentment, and why does the Judge feel compelled to defend a salutary version of those feelings and mention an even darker and more troubling state of disaffection? The nagging irony behind all this paradoxical reflection is that in defending marriage as a romantic institution, a cloister of two apart from the world, it suddenly becomes a small Polis that potentially includes diffused affections and divided loyalties within its own borders. And even though William notes that poets typically portray erotic love as having threats only from without, in his own eulogy on the increasingly wonderful stages of love he suddenly must address how the solution of a respectable marriage appears to inherit such obstacles and now must absorb them, which may or may not involve children. It might include higher longings and larger neighborly obligations, or perhaps most threateningly, an adjacent personal affection. In fairness to the dear Assessor and the obvious affection he is so intent on expressing for his spouse, we must say that just above his head he is admitting a world in which loyalty and disaffection do haunt us and call for a larger perspective and comportment in which an amorous gaze is not outstripped by our inability to finally possess another person and the kind of detached investment this requires.

To be sure, William does not seem entirely aware of all the implications of such a larger romantic perspective. Rather, he enjoins us not to dwell on it but get back to the beauty of motherhood, "an actuality so infinitely rich in variety" that "love has enough to do day after day to discover something new," a rich variety that a husband does not consume "even though he feeds on it, for it is like the food in Valhalla; and even though he does not live upon it, it is nonetheless certain that he does not live on bread alone but also the approving admiration that accompanies the mother's achievements" (135–36). Apparently, cherishing the beauty of motherhood is like partaking in a rich and intoxicating soldier's fare, although it does not nourish. But then again, we do not live by bread alone. There are two readings of this: either the domestic scenario provides a spiritual food unlike any other, or the Breadwinner remains famished. In a severely ironic twist, the text implies the opposite of each, since in his home Judge William fortuitously finds both "*panis et circenses* [bread and circuses]" (136). This inversion of an unwelcome neither/nor into a fortuitous both/and forms a *non sequitur* in the light of which we must embrace what does not follow as a matter of course.

What does textually follow are four paragraphs lauding the unexpected beauty of motherly love that is visible to the Judge from a rather dubious distance. He recounts two instances. One day, while "walking steadily at my businesslike pace from one end of the city to the courthouse to render a verdict," he witnesses a presumptively upper class woman on the street attending to a charming and curious boy who, in "a breach of agreement," suddenly demanded to be carried. "Several people turned around," but in her face the Judge detected no "trace of embarrassment or of any repressed anger or of any growing impatience," a face he felt qualified to read since he has had occasion to sit as an examiner on a "commission of inquiry" (136–37). The second manifestation of motherly charm occurs in church with a mother accommodating her fidgety offspring while maintaining a devotional mood with equanimity, although the scene made the Judge "what I ordinarily am not—an inattentive and distracted listener to a sermon" (138–39). What he finds remarkable in the first instance is a singularly tolerant affection amidst a breach of socially enfranchised protocol. In the second case he is distractedly absorbed with the woman's ability "to divide in this way, to have joy in the child even when he is disturbing, or at least seems to be about to disturb, or is being somewhat of a nuisance," and to do so in such a way "that she also was concentrated on her devotions with undivided soul" (140). What these examples have in common are those features of personal love that threaten to unravel us, divide our social or religious attentions, and that we must learn to handle and enjoy in a particular way. But the Judge can only appreciate this from a distance, and only in sentimentally excusable cases that involve a "little underworldling" (139). Far less beautiful to him, one might imagine, would be two adolescents who cannot manage to keep their hands off one another, particularly in church. The sequence of this section begins with the wonderful and tender resolution of motherhood but ends with what "multiplicity of collisions mother love is exposed," concluding with a return to jealousy and other similarly dark passions, which surely are not the only phenomenon equipped to keep a man "clear-sighted" and "alert" (136, 140). The repeated references to Othello are telling. It appears Judge William can only imagine that what lies between a misinformed jealous rage and chilly indifference is a staid fondness. What he does not quite admit, as far as solutions go, is that this one remains problematic.

More Dissembling

Less beautiful than either the woman of years or the young mother, the bride is more beautiful than the maiden, whose charm is more extensive but also more abstract and less intense. We know this is Judge William's thesis. But the initial literary analogy reveals the real complexity of the issue: "Is an author less rich in ideas because ordinary observation finds nothing, while the reader who has made him his sole study nevertheless discovers an ever-greater wealth?" (141). While on the surface this appears to be a rhetorical question, which could be asked of any stage of esthetic or moral development and ultimately of love itself, the answer to it is anything but obvious since it is followed by two other questions: "Is it a perfection in human works of art that they look best as a distance? Is it an imperfection in the meadow flower, as in all the works of God, that under microscopic scrutiny it becomes lovelier and lovelier, more and more exquisite, more and more delicate?" (141). As a set of questions bleeding from the anonymous pen of a married Judge who thinks of himself as an a-vocational author, we are bound to wonder about the answers. The perfection visible at a distance in human artwork suggests there is something deficient about it up close. The presumptive imperfection in the given, created order right at hand suggests its natural beauty unfolds as we get closer.

Amidst these rhetorical suggestions the author has caught himself, as well as the reader, between a rock and a hard place on the road to genuine esthetic evaluation. Natural beauty appears mundane at a distance, and artistic renditions seem better from far away. If we transpose these claims back into the topical key, personal loves and romantic ideals more generally are both natural and constructed, both entirely given and poetically created out of and in response to a kind of welter and waste. They are divinely dispensed and humanly penned, which means that to recognize and authorize them for what they really are, we must have one eye in a telescope and the other on a microscope.[4] These sound like empty platitudes until we consider the way in which we actually live in both stories we read and ones we tell, the most salient of which are often about relationships old and new, broken and healed, reinvented, and broken again. We all wish our greatest affections were reciprocally met, our most peculiar feelings concretely shared, and our highest values fully embodied. For all this to occur, however, we must strike a delicate artistic balance between fact and fiction, in both word and deed. And failures along the way can be devastating. No wonder, then, that in the midst of articulating the superior esthetic validity of the mother and wife, Judge William finds himself on the subject of death. "There is indeed no one who welcomes the arrival of a baby as joyfully as a mother, but neither is there anyone who is able to grieve in this way when death comes and takes it. But a grief that is precisely just as ideal as it is actual is the most poetic grief" (141). Here the death of a child is compared to the death of a young husband and in comparison to which the latter loss of a mere beloved lacks "the dedication and epic presuppositions" to amount to anything other than a relatively abstract requiem (141). At this point the Judge no longer pulls any punches. There can be no question that the thought of mortality undoubtedly puts our most cherished attachments in dramatic and final relief. But whether it can clarify our values ahead of time still remains very much in play. *Is* a maiden's loss so obviously less, and why so? Seemingly it is because

---

[4] In a journal entry Kierkegaard writes that "I would like to write a novel in which the main character would be a man who had gotten a pair of glasses, one lens of which reduced images as powerfully as an oxyhydorgen microscope and the other magnified on the same scale, so that he perceived everything very relatively." *Søren Kierkegaard's Journals and Papers,* Volume 5, *Autobiographical, 1829–1848,* 5281.

the relative timelessness of her investment was so short. And yet it may have been more imaginative, and therefore more significant in its own way. It may have brought out her inner self more truly and deeply than any given marriage might. Who is in a position to creatively enjoy, authentically relinquish, or eloquently say? Speaking on behalf of his wife, all the Judge can muster in answer is that his wife's memorial at his death will be his greatest honor, about which, of course, he can only imagine. Darker than death, and in halting circumspection, William writes "let the wife be tried and tested in the worst of fates: let her be unhappily married" (142). In comparison the brief pain of a jilted lover is but a momentary wound. What is this supposed to demonstrate exactly? That bearing the torment of an esthetically dry commitment is more beautiful and ennobling than the emotional weight of a single summer of love lost? It seems like it would depend on who is telling the story. The Judge can only abstractly imagine the "angelic patience" of the former which, if it were described, "would fill more books than the largest library contains, even if it were nothing" and which "indeed, almost stimulates the hunger of passion" (142). What immediately precedes this claim is a web of renewed references to *Othello*. Desdemona pacifyingly confesses to a nameless guilt in forbearance of her husband's inexplicable rage, itself combustibly fueled by love. The light and heat William draws from this is that true romance and its associated glory is on the side of forbearance rather than jealousy. But how *could* we judge between forbearance and jealousy? The difference may be as wide as an ocean or slight as a hair, and both of equally terrifying measure. We are left to literally experience, and decide, outside the parameters of an essay, or stricter still, a court-case document.

The specter of an unhappy love borne with either patience or jealousy brings the Judge to consider woman as the weaker sex, addressing a theme raised by Constantin and Eremita, and like their treatment, does not seem to be about women *per se*. For example, the calm and submissive devotion he associates with a wife and mother is first contrasted not with the needs or demands of a husband, but with how odd and even comic a young girl might appear "when things get out of control, when she is thrown into the extreme dismay of a decision, into a state of confusion in which a man could hardly stand and keep from being blown away" (143).

What are these "things" that may become uncontrollable, make her appear weak, and require the firm stance of a man? Our clue is that after dismissing the "perpetually gallant and rude, titillating and insulting talk" about maidenly bloom, he turns to compare a wife's weakness to the strength is must take to act the part of Don Giovanni simultaneously holding the hand of the Commendatore while appearing to wrench himself free. This allusion suggests it is actually the husband who is the weaker actor when it comes to dealing with upheavals within our most delicate and unpredictable passions, since he just has to stand there while the woman must both hold on and pretend to writhe in pain. In the world of the opera, and on the analogy of God's omnipotent care for even an insignificant blade of grass, the weakness one associates with our limitlessly seductive passions rather oddly becomes, in actual life, the domestic support and balm of "less significant tasks" that continually equip a man with a merely "conspicuous strength." In turn, this leads our author to believe his wife "can do wonders; and I more readily understand the greatest feat I read about than the dainty embroidery with which she clothes my earthly life" (144). Apparently, dainty tasks are more significant, though less understandable, while great feats are more understandable, though less believable. The vigor of his own feelings remain correspondingly and suspiciously suspended. Furthermore, the allusion to acting the part of the Commendatore additionally suggests that, in *his* actual life, the firm arm of a husband is but a pretense. This uncomfortable series of ambiguities gives way to an insistence upon the basic equality of the sexes against those who would ascribe to a wife merely "the strength of the scream" and ridiculously reserve ethical categories for bachelors, who can only remain faithful in rejecting something as presumably faithless as love itself (145). This feverish defense of feminine strength then breaks with the admission that a good-natured characterization of the unhappy fate of a woman's life can have a "certain comic and tragic effect," the ironic and amusing aspect of which "carries the stamp of fiction to such an extent that it cannot insult even the weakest" (145–46). The reason is because if what is most attractive, inspiring, and salient about love must be sacrificed on the shore of marriage, then everybody loses either way. The beloved maiden, preserved as such, then "signifies nothing positive" and merely becomes "the occasion of the unhappy lover's ideality" (146).

When considered at the level of *Stages* as a whole, this takes on much more than "a touch of deep irony" since it is not clear what Judge William thinks he can legitimately assert about marriage as a romantic institution by pointing out how those who renounce it remain unhappy in their own fashion. At the meta-textual level, the theatrical tragicomedy of romantic ideals keeps emerging and retreating amidst the ecstatic prose of a multilayered book out of which we are asked to interpret our own lives and loves, and in the light and darkness of which we must nurture and develop certain feelings and make particular choices. For his own part, Judge William—intentionally anonymous by design to keep out spies—obliquely confesses he cannot quite coordinate exactly what he believes, understands, or feels about all this embroidery, which brings him momentarily back to the subject of falling in love in the first place.

An In-Flight Holding Pattern

After reiterating how the glory and wonder of immediate attraction must be bolstered by resolution, William offers an illuminating analogy. The native talent of a "genius," presumably a corresponding gift of the gods, must be enacted in order to express itself for the first time. For example, one cannot really be a writer without doing what it takes to write something. Similarly one cannot really be in love without the "convoy of marriage," since it is only on that voyage that "love is already a subsequent immediacy, a heat lightning that commences at a time when the will may be sufficiently developed to comprehend a resolution just as crucial as falling in love, taken in its immediacy, is crucial" (147–48). Whether writing or loving, each will take time and commitment, sweat and probably tears, although the latter two and the parallel more generally are not what the Judge chooses to mention. Instead he provides an extended commentary on a particular lover *and* genius: Goethe, as he presents himself in *Aus meinem Leben*.

Apart from the poet's writing skills, it is with considerable irony that Judge William begins his treatment of Goethe by saying his "personal life is extraneous; I refrain from any judgment," and then proceeds to cite him as a chivalrous but nevertheless deeply corrupt subterfuge in matters of personal love (149). According to the autobiographical record, as the Judge reads it, Goethe is not a malicious seducer. But perhaps more ruinous than this, he politely and amicably backs out of the various romantic affairs he finds himself in. He falls in love easily, and just as easily terminates it. A poetic existence such as this can appear benign, but its very esthetic detachment is disingenuous. One might not notice that such a life is only attractive on the page rather than in actuality, and even then what is engaging is invariably forlorn, "the strangest romance of sad events," as Goethe himself writes.[5] As a judge, William feels he is diagnosing a case that contains neither the galvanizing power of Eros nor the authentic gravity of resolution and concludes that, far from tragic, the whole existential portrait amounts to a satirical pantomime of actual love, sorrow over which must be feigned. Nevertheless, the Judge's pronouncement is divided. Full-blown seducers he can understand ethically as corrupt but consistent. They at least provide clear cases. However, a romantically distended life such as Goethe's is far more opaque and therefore requires a more harsh reprimand:

> He sorrows a little over the poor girl, it is not pretense, he really sorrows—no, really! This, however, is carrying politeness rather far; it is, after all, a sympathy and condolence that will only increase the pain. The break itself or, to put it more precisely and accurately, this polite and amicable agreement about a departure is precisely what is most insulting; this final forgery, that any girl, when it is established that a man has a contractual obligation, should not be a preemptory creditor, is really the most shocking thing of all, and yet it is with this politeness that he bought the world's forgiveness. ...He is sorrowing not over his instability, over this flare-up of ardor, over this shift in the world of the spirit, not over his sins. (151)

Even so, the ongoing diagnosis remains unclear:

> This kind of existence, which essentially is scarcely a paradigm, can nevertheless figuratively assume a paradigmatic character or be

[5] Johann Wolfgang von Goethe, *The Autobiography of Goethe* (Boston: Dana Esthes & Company) 178, translated by John Oxenford, Esq.

> paradigmatic by the accident of being an irregular declension, according to which several lives are indeed formed. One dare not say that they form their lives according to it, for they are too innocent [*uskyldig*] for that, and this is precisely their excuse [*Undskyldning*]: it happens to them; they themselves do not know how it happens. Indeed, at times such people are even visionaries who are pursuing the ideal. They do not learn any more from their love affairs than what a lottery player learns from losing. (151)

In the very next sentence the Judge signals that this does *not* apply to Goethe's portrait. Then who or what is the Judge writing about? Apparently there are irregular declensions that are paradigmatic, at least "figuratively," although William is extremely reticent to admit them to the realm of actuality, since such individuals only become representative by means of an innocent, passive, and visionary idealism from which they apparently learn nothing of real value. As an aspiring writer himself, and without quite saying it, one gets the impression Judge William is casting doubt on Goethe's status as a *genius*, in light of which his "personal life" appears anything but "extraneous." The entire paragraph ends in confusion. Purportedly of Goethe, William writes that he

> is too great not to learn, too superior not to harvest advantage, and if he had been just as ethically inspired as he is gloriously endowed, he, more than anyone else, would have discovered and solved the problem: whether there is an intellectual existence so eminent that in the profoundest sense it cannot become commensurable with the erotic, for the response that one loves many times, that one parcels out one's superiority, is merely a disorientation that neither esthetically nor ethically satisfies what could be termed a decent man's more serious demand upon life. (151–52)

In comparison to the other irregular, but nevertheless paradigmatic declensions, Goethe stands apart only in being less passive about it, without having identified or indeed solved the real problem. But what kind of solution is it to discover and admit one's life or proclivities were somehow incommensurable with romance fully realized?

In answering this question we must first note that a good deal of what William is haltingly objecting to is the longstanding experience of summer loves that bloom only until early fall and the peculiar staying power they nevertheless have over our imagination. Literature is full of such instances, as it is also full of staid, middle-aged offense at the timeless spectacle of desire in some cottage down by the lake, surrounded by gentle trees and warm winds, gloriously set apart from everyday life, bursting with leisurely picnics, skinny dips, campfires, sandcastles, suntanned shoulders, and stolen glances freely given, all retrospectively preserved in a present tense of sad unreality.[6] However, once felt, the memory never entirely leaves one alone, and poetry is its muse in reverse. Although the Judge denies the legitimacy of all this, we must grant that he at least reads, and takes seriously, the life and work of Germany's great poet. But we must add to this the literary architecture of *Stages* itself, where what follows the Judge's reflections on marriage in answer to objections is the extended tale not only of a correspondingly anonymous diarist who both seems and himself feels irregular, but also the testimony of the fictional author who conjures such a figure and claims him as somehow paradigmatic. It is as if we are in the middle of a detective novel where the true culprit remains unclear. That culprit may turn out to be ourselves, negotiating as we do between the kite and string of high-flung resolve and terrifying weakness while the wind blows wherever it wills.

At this point William returns to his original thesis and final conclusion, namely, that falling in love must be immediately married to resolution, although the aisle down which the reader has been walking here is apparently thick with mud and brambles, and ends not at an altar but a gravesite. In this regard the Judge mentions Goethe's "strict religious upbringing," which seems to have issued in a dark intellectualism that blocks the daylight of authentic human contact (152–53). The poetic pathos written on the autobiographical page thus serves as an idol for the reader, a false impression forged in the smithy of a depressed and ruined soul. What Goethe's portrait represents is a romance of distance in which actual women and his relations with them are perpetually transposed into one-sided masterpieces of well-drawn characters, lovely to behold, but essentially unreal. Even so, while the Judge, "who is so rash to talk about him" while admitting he himself is a

[6] Witness, for example, Kate Chopin's *The Awakening*.

"bourgeois-philistine," also claims Goethe is a hero of sorts, although in the same breath cannot finally confer legitimacy on such a temperament (154). What William is wrestling with is the degree to which our imaginations can or should play a creative role in shaping our perceptions of and feelings for a beloved. He admits Goethe's portrayals are superb in regard to individuals and that "it is not so much they who are dishonored." And yet, ambiguously, "it is womanhood that is dishonored in their persons, because in relation to them the condescending sensibleness that knows how to enjoy, relish, but also how to distance them and itself when the pleasure is over, almost seems to be justified or at least excusable" (154). The Judge seems partially aware of how his own act of writing may be a form of idealization at a distance, and therefore may also seem "justified or at least excusable." At their dogmatic height, ethical requirements, which must intervene in order for the truly poetic to emerge, turn out to be "so incorruptible that if our Lord himself had been obliged to allow himself a little irregularity in creating the world, ethics would not let itself be disturbed, although heaven and earth and everything found therein is nevertheless quite a fine masterpiece" (155). But it is not clear what kind of irregularity the Judge has in mind; nor is it evident how the global qualification of the third clause relates to the second boldly transparent claim that an ethical view of life would remain undisturbed. Slipped into the middle of all this William inadvertently concludes: "Thus the natural tendency to poeticize an actual human relationship is both rather common and dubious" (155). Whether this claim applies to Goethe, himself, Kierkegaard behind the scenes, or indeed the rest of us looms as an unsettling backdrop, while he, Judge William, front and center stage at this point, confidently returns to how resolution must be added to falling in love. With notable but unbeknownst ambivalence, the Judge takes this up after having ten pages earlier initially addressed the topic of falling in love itself, only to interrupt himself for those ten pages to occupy us with a simultaneously inspired, depressed, romantic connoisseur and subterfuge salted with sober religiosity. On the face of things it is almost as if he is competing with Goethe as both a lover and a writer, which is frankly amusing. It is as if in the interim he himself neither believed that falling in love could be either presupposed or quite real, nor whether resolution could truly resolve the matter, since we find out the latter itself presupposes "reflection," and this turns out to be "immediacy's angel of death" (157). He is then quick to distinguish between two different directions reflection can take upon holding a beloved in mind.[7]

Disparagingly, we are informed the first sort of reflection is a nascent form of criticism masked as adoration. Under this heading the lover inspects whether the beloved meets "the ideal abstract conception of an ideal" (158). Such reflection is an occupational hazard of the poetic soul. What is perplexing, enervating, and even disturbing about such inspection is the degree to which it includes the particular details that one might otherwise naturally list in a description of a beloved: the inimitably embodied manner and look from eyelash to calf, the range of cavalier to gripping humor, the sense of fashion to vocational outlook, all including not only the way the beloved holds an opinion, wry or earnest, but holds their head, slightly cocked and alluring. We might suppose that any one of these could just as well become an object of distaste as well as celebration. And none of them taken alone either finally inspire or amount to love. But it is not clear how we can pass them over in order to modestly reach "the loveable substance of her nature" and so avoid becoming an "insipid babbler of words" or a "birthday poet" (159). Surely an authentically modest approach does more than recognize the beauty of a person that discloses itself "as gently as when the grave opens" (160). A particular embodied individual is presumably neither a corpse nor a ghost, however gently or arrestingly revealed. Therefore, "reflection" must take another direction, even though we have been invited on this other path along the way.

In contrast, the proper direction reflection takes involves absolutely no detour, no indirect path, no pause, no critical assessment or taking stock. All these would be an affront to the wonderstruck immediacy of love. But what happens, then, when the lover does not twist and turn, does not measure the quality and weight of his experience and consider particulars and imagine alternatives or even simply wait for signs of reciprocal feeling? According to William's train of thought it turns out

---

[7] Thomas Mann explores the ambiguous significance of Goethe's romantic genius in *Lotte in Weimar: The Beloved Returns*, where the initial inspiration for *The Sorrows of Young Werther* shows her actual face, now an aged widow.

that, neatly apart from the usual forms of reflection that rest on a comparative treatment of the beloved in light of an "abstract ideal," in a

> perfectly ideal reflection the resolution has ideally emptied actuality, and the conclusion of this ideal reflection, which is something more than the *summa summarum* [sum total] and *enfin* [finally], is precisely the resolution: the resolution is the ideality brought about through a perfectly ideal reflection, which is the action's acquired working capital. (160)

It seems the Judge trades one ideal for another, and cannot extricate himself from a peculiar logic of exchange that circumvents the prospect of any risk or possible disappointment, let alone outright loss. In holding on so tightly to both romantic and unquestionable ethical ideals, he inadvertently erects a vision of love so purified of taciturn thoughts that we are not allowed to so much as look at the beloved before committing. What he does not notice, or does not admit, is that in securing love against attendant vicissitudes the certainty of conviction symbiotically feeds on what is strictly forbidden: "For the lover, the most certain of all things is that he is in love, and no meddlesome thoughts, no stockbrokers run back and forth between falling in love and a so-called ideal—this is a forbidden road" (160). Along the way he hastens to add, *en medias res*, that a "resolution is still always an ideality: I have the resolution before I begin to act in virtue of this resolution," but then questions "how I come to the resolution" (160). Before getting around to a "perfectly ideal reflection" he provisionally concludes that a "resolution is always reflective; if this is disregarded, then language is confused and resolution is identified with an immediate impulse, and any statement about resolution is no more an advancement than a journey in which one drives all night but takes the wrong road and in the morning arrives back at the same place from which one departed" (160). If we are paying attention, a corresponding conclusion is that we might as well go ahead and eat the apple, and find ourselves naked, since wisdom at a lower cost just seems cheap.

Having painted conscious reflection into such a tight corner, it comes as no surprise that it must be "discharged into faith" (162). The infatuated immediacy of love which can only serve to carry the lovers away to a remote region of illusory and anti-social bliss must be just as immediately tempered by a religious view of life, in which the fragility of human indecision and esthetic ennui is fortuitously swallowed by a particular form of passion which can "pave the way, so to speak, for falling in love" and "secure it against any external and internal danger" (162). Saying so William is clearly of two minds, a divided soul in spite of himself. Nevertheless, we are again summarily reassured that an ethical resolution "is not so difficult, especially if one has the impetus of the passion of falling in love" (163). This way of characterizing the existential task might seem to beg the question, as if romantic passion is both ethically indispensable and unable to preserve itself. But the Judge thinks the sheer fragility of our truest affections contain elements of their own transubstantiation.

> Precisely because the reflection that precedes the resolution is altogether ideal, a single imagined danger will be enough to bring the one making the resolution to resolve religiously. Let him think what he will, even if the danger is only that he cannot take the future in advance by thinking. In using his powers of thought and his concerned love to think this, he *eo ipso* [precisely thereby] thinks it [the danger] to be so terrible that he cannot surmount it by himself. He has run aground; he must either let go of love—or believe in God. In this way the wonder of falling in love is taken up into the wonder of faith; the wonder of falling in love is taken up into a purely religious wonder; the absurdity of falling in love is taken up into a divine understanding with the absurdity of religiousness. (163)

Imagining the dangers that threaten the irreplaceable singularity of a personal beloved, so transformed by a blessing of religious consecration, is a particular comfort to the lover in that "he is just like other human beings and in this common humanity is in relationship with God by faith and by the resolution" (164). Thus our most pedestrian romantic longings and divine self-understanding are seamlessly wed like unquestionably true lovers. To say the least, whether this conclusion is the height of folly or astonishingly convincing will depend on the status of how we have poetically put ourselves together, the exact dangers we have imagined, and what we have made of the evident conflict of values in play.

Our anonymous Judge once again interrupts himself to briefly mention certain "anomalies" a lover might encounter along the way that may interrupt the seamless sequence that normally follows a genuinely ideal reflection. Specifically, he writes how one might not trust how one's passion neatly fits into universal expectations of ethical resolve, having presumably christened them in the font of religious presuppositions. Reflecting on so great a promise of desire may take a wrong turn of some kind within the temperament or worldview of any given knight or heroine. Far from the comfortable assertion that the bold adventure of love is common, and not so difficult, William hints that if the lover "encounters repentance, then it may last a long time, and if he is really in love, as is indeed assumed, then he can regard himself as someone selected to be examined by life, for when he is questioned by love up one side and by repentance down the other side about the same thing, his examination can become much too rigorous" (164). The scenario he has in mind entails that the outlandish hope and tremendous investment love involves might appear utterly daunting, issuing in a paradoxical conjunction of passion and existential anhedonia. Without further comment, William simply says that such difficulties "have no place in a general consideration" (164). The additional diary and commentary that make up *Stages* is a sword in this particular side of the overall argument. Whether it bleeds water, legs unbroken, head merely bowed before resurrection, remains for any of us to estimate.

Cruciform anticipations aside, the hesitation and inner conflict such "anomalies" might engender do not entirely evaporate when on the next page William pictures two lovers on their wedding day. Insisting that one truly in love and resolved to remain so is simultaneously young and old, naïve and mature, his own "reflections on marriage" suddenly issue in a series of rhetorical questions about his own inner status as a husband. These questions only raise furher puzzles about whether his thoughts are a protest or celebration, within themselves containing all the defensive ambiguity of an apologetic. This series is couched between a set of other rhetorical questions whose subjects are variously and tellingly modified by certain definite and indefinite articles. The paragraph begins: "That a young lover is a pleasing sight need not be said, but it may be necessary to say that a husband is an even more refreshing sight, unless the altar is unto offense, because it is wrong, of course, to be only a young lover when one steps up there" (165). The indefinite articles here fit modestly, though uneasily, between that which is obvious and what it may be necessary to say. Then the article shifts: "But the husband is the young lover, totally so. His love is unchanged, except that it has something the youth does not have, the holy beauty of the resolution. Is he not just as rich and happy as the young man?" (165). Then the subject becomes personal, interestingly ending with an exclamation rather than a question mark: "Is *my* wealth less because I possess it in the only adequately secure way; is my claim upon life less because I have it on stamped paper; is my happiness less because God in heaven guarantees it, and not in jest, as Eros would do it, but in earnestness and truth, as truly as the resolution holds him fast!" (165, italics added). At this point the definite article makes a comeback: "Or is the language the young lover knows how to use supposed to be more divine than the married man can understand?" (165). But then the following sentence begins with a definite article, and then after returning with an indefinite one, ends by including anyone: "Is not the wedding ceremony itself such an obscure discourse that it takes more than a poet to understand it; is it not such a boldly ventured promise that anyone who understands but half is bound to lose his senses?" (165). How is it that the wedding ceremony itself becomes a subjective agent in all this, leaving some given poet speechless and the rest of us senseless with only half an understanding?

There are two things to notice about all this grammatical altercation. First, it should come as no surprise that this extravagant defense of the husband against a young lover and his attendant poetic sensibility comes just after William raised the specter of singular anomalies against the backdrop of our common moral lot. Ideally the Judge would have any possible tension between the particular and universal resolved. But it is not without considerable irony that the "anyone" who "understands but half" of this is "bound to lose his senses." The reason behind this possible nonsense is that it remains profoundly unclear, between youth and old age, naïveté and maturity, how we are supposed to understand the relations between experience and imagination, poetry and obligation, happiness and security. Who *is* in a position to recognize and feel the nature and quality of true romance? And what exactly is it that God earnestly guarantees that Eros would only promise in jest? Judge William simply reiterates the two halves, punctuated by his characteristic exclamations:

> To talk about duty to a pair of lovers—and to understand it and still be in love, bound to the beloved with the strongest bond of immediacy! To talk about the curse that rests upon the human race, about the difficulties of marriage, about woman's pain and man's sour sweat—and still be in love and in the immediacy of being in love be convinced that nothing but happiness awaits them! To hear this, to envision the resolution, to keep one's mind fixed upon it, and also to envision the myrtle wreath upon the beloved's head—truly, a married man, a genuine husband, is himself a wonder! To be able to hear his beloved's voice while the organ plays! To be able to hold on to the delight of erotic love while life concentrates the full force of earnestness upon him and his beloved! (165–66)

As a veritable cornucopia of colorful contrasts, this does sound miraculous. But as readers, we are left to distinguish for ourselves whether what we hear is the tongue of an angel or a noisy gong, in the event we still have at least half our senses to complement a partial understanding. It does not seem extreme to ask at this point, echoing Genesis 3:9, "Where are you?"

Two Apart at the Altar

Having initiated us into the mysteries of a religiously exalted ethical immediacy upon approaching the altar of marriage, and after noting that only a person with an exceptionally odd personality would find themselves overthinking the matter, we find out that a proper sort of reflection only applies to a man in the first place. As for *her*, the transition from esthetic immediacy to religiously ethical resolve occurs as "swiftly as a bird" (166). Each of them begins by falling in love. That is their common ground. But for her, the integrated temporal development love requires involves no reflection at all:

> That is, when an intimation of the thought, the content of which the man's reflection ideally exhausts, passes through her consciousness, she faints, while her husband hurries off and, equally moved but also

> through reflection, is not overwhelmed; he stands firm, the beloved leaning on him until she opens her eyes again. In this swooning, she is transferred from the immediacy of erotic love into that of the religious, and here they meet again. Now she is ready for the wedding, for without resolution there is no marriage. (167)

As with elements of the bachelor's speeches we could chalk this up to an antiquated, misogynist twist of imagination. But *her* side of the matter is also the truly fitting, albeit silent half of the Judge's entire discourse, the very half that may well make us lose our senses. For one thing, "she" stands in for an ideal synthetic development the Judge lauds but does not recognize in himself, or men generally, or anyone for that matter. According to his description, "she" manages to achieve a seamless whole amidst the persistent beckoning of romantic ideals, having become spiritually awakened without thereby having had her innocence volatilized by her own existential doubt or imaginative exploration, each of which under ordinary conditions perplex us and invariably provoke extended and often tortured meditation. That she would simply swoon in unreflective acceptance is hard to believe, entirely apart from her being a woman. We know this because William himself claims that while "[f]eminine romanticism is in the next moment the religious," it could just as well only be "sensual ardor and the demonic inspiration of sensuality; the holy purity of modesty…transformed into a darkness that tempts and incites" (167). Moreover, the fact that fainting in this manner would require someone else to hold on suggests that the difficulty of preserving all the best within our esthetic, ethical, and religious ideals gets compounded when the drama is not simply internal to one, but shared between two, especially if they are assumed equal, standing on common ground. What "she" represents is the whole "he" cannot quite picture.

The ensuing commentary on a lithograph of Romeo and Juliet's farewell kiss during the final scene of act III confirms this interpretation. Apparently, the image portrays Juliet sinking in submissive adoration, esthetically arrested and transfixed, having succumbed in a way that requires Romeo to meet her total abandon with a firm assurance so they would not completely fall apart. Somehow Romeo manages to be the stronger one such that what might otherwise amount to an un-reciprocal, volatile fragility will not work against them. As the Judge sees it, the beauty in this lies in its momentary synthesis of opposites, and hence its "eternity." So represented, the scene immediately points beyond itself to a subsequent moment.

> She is, then, not kneeling adoringly, for the difference that is fixed in the immediacy of erotic love, the man's strength that gives him the advantage, is sensed to be raised into a higher unity, into the divine equality of the religious. She is only sinking down; she wants to kneel in the admiration of love, but his strong arm holds her upright. She is drooping, yet not before the visible but before the invisible, before the excessiveness of the impression; then she grasps him, who is already holding her supportively. He himself is moved as he grasps her, and if the kiss were not their mutual support, they both might falter. This is no picture, there is no repose in the artistic situation, for as one looks at her almost sinking in adoration, one sees beyond this interrupted posture the necessity of a new one, that she stands upright at his side. One has intimations of a new prototype, the authentic prototype of marriage, because married people are contiguous angles on the same base. What is it that produces that incompleteness in the first picture, what is being sought in this faltering—it is the equality of the resolution; it is the higher immediacy of the religious. (168–69)

What the kiss represents is a perfect union of the esthetic and religious, without the troublesome bother of the ethical distention that typically shapes an actual life together. Its eternity is therefore illusory, and so we inevitably imagine a second, third, or perhaps fourth moment. This implicit projection is already captured in the fact that the image is of a farewell kiss, and as such, is burdened within by the weight of an unmet future. Thus it is as sad as it is inspirational.[8]

What the Judge draws from this imagery is oddly circumspect. He does not actually object to the pictorial representation or its literary inspiration so much as he anticipates a cynical response to it that shuts out all genuine imagination based upon it. Under this heading he

---

[8] On the extant nature of this image see Lasse Horne Kjaeldgaard's "'The Peak on which Abraham Stands': The Pregnant Moment of Soren Kierkegaard's *Fear and Trembling*," *Journal of the History of Ideas* 63/2 (April 2002): 309–11.

includes "all objections, which merely exclude themselves" (169). The response he has in mind is from those who might gaze upon such an image of pure, fragile abandon between two lovers destined to part, in one way or another, and mockingly retort "*Habeat vivat cum illa* [Let him have her, live with her]" (169). In other words, he imagines responses from those who know the story, and how it goes. Equally star-struck, but also equally and tragically at cross-purposes, the lovers may be roundly dismissed. In turn, all William can think of writing is "indeed, I will have her, which is precisely what I want" (169). Somewhere amidst the initial "I want her" and "you can have her" and "but that's it, I do want her," all manner of failures of nerve and belief, along with their corresponding self-deception take place. But for those with eyes to see, the sweet sorrow of the frozen visual representation is prosaically overcome at the tip of Judge William's pen. Or so he would indicate, and have us believe. Notably, the impasse here is ironic and itself indicates a higher point of view. Putting the formerly produced imagery together with that of the lithograph, as Romeo upholds Juliet she apparently plays the part of Don Giovanni holding the hand of the Commendatore while simultaneously appearing to wrench herself free. Somewhere amidst this cacophony of gender and type lies the weak strength of a true lover's disoriented devotion, which brings William to a particular brink of inadvertent confession.

A Decentralizing Caveat

At the Judge's behest, but against his own will, the fortuitous synthetic account of erotic magnetism and ethical resolve that culminates with his vivid reflection on a fictitious portrait of Romeo and Juliet suddenly appears even more radically penultimate. The image of the lovers, side by side, equally conscious and resolved yet variously holding on, now takes a new direction: "I do not say, then, that marriage is the highest life; I know a life that is higher, but woe to the person who gratuitously wants to leap over it" (169). It is as if the very attraction that is driven to ethically preserve itself through religious presuppositions outstrips its own desire and thereby threatens to render it entirely spiritual. Speaking from within a bourgeois post-Reformation world, we find out from William that a monastic trajectory may very well make a comeback, "not on dogmatic or hypermoral grounds," but due to a "recklessness of spirit" (170). Such recklessness not only "does not want to recognize the corruptible body in which it lives, this temporality in which it has its home, its transient residence, this piecemealness out of which it must collect itself," but also "desires to belong to God alone," intolerant of any duplicity within one's focus and desire (170, 173). Religiously outstripped in this fashion, an entirely abstract and thoroughly inhumane idolatry inversely appears in the form of "not wanting to have any concrete idea of what for most people is the reality of their lives," the very concreteness of which "is and remains a condition just for his being able to have the appearance of being in the right" (174). The peculiar pathos this abstraction entails is therefore inherently conflicted in a way that Judge William wants to admit as a possibility but cannot accept as an actuality. He makes this clear in rhetorically negotiating the conflict by pitting the virtue of humility against the vice of pride in such a way that, caught between spiritual interests and ordinary human longing, the subject becomes exhausted on the shore of both moral and religious confusion. "Inhumanity toward human beings is also importunity toward God" (174). We can sympathize with someone whose love has taken a spiritual direction only insofar as the "impertinent camaraderie" with God is rebuffed due to a corresponding inappropriate superiority at a human level.

> He can even be truly humble, but in the very same way, humanly speaking, a subordinate can have the most loyal enthusiasm for his king and be far superior to those who are neither hot nor cold but are *numerus* [numbers] and *pecus* [cattle], but yet when he seeks an audience with the king he can wish to be permitted to enter through a door different from the one assigned to all subjects. (174–75)

That is, we can sympathetically accompany such a soul to the degree that the king turns the reckless subject away to get in line with other regular souls:

> For the person who has actually had sufficient inwardness to comprehend that the religious is the highest love, how heartbreaking, how annihilating it must be to discover that he has allowed himself too much, that he has been too free, has grieved the spirit, has offended his love [*Forelskelse*]—alas, all the more grievously if he

actually was intending to give his relationship the highest expression. (175)

We can even further sympathize with this possible exception in that during such tepid, officially Lutheranized Danish times, it is "obvious the religious has been laying fallow long enough; when it begins to move with ideal energy, it is not to be wondered at if it makes a mistake again. To find the true concretion for the religious is not easy, for the religious continually has the infinite abstraction as its presupposition and is no simple immediacy" (172). In this vein, "people may talk very beautifully and truthfully about the religious, and at times, perhaps with a single word, retract everything without being aware of it themselves, since it appears they are speaking of the purely immediate" (172). Admitting the ardor and potential draw of such lofty magnanimous humility, the Judge nevertheless invites us to locate the green valley of marriage between the two heights of pure romanticism and spiritual asceticism, between the fertile land "the Middle Ages despaired" of reaching and toward which "the last few centuries" have advanced in a way far more secular than sacred. But confusingly, he himself regards the search for "the true concretion" "*a pium desiderium* [pious wish]," although salutary enough to ponder and write about, especially if married and aspiring "to be something of an author" (172). Just below the surface our judge seems dimly aware that a thoroughly bourgeois Christendom may be just as unromantic as it is irreligious. While William tries to appreciate the complexity of a monastic "exception" to the times, the main problem is that an unhappy personal love religiously outstripped in this way remains wholly abstract. The renunciation involved is not tied securely enough to the reality of what is supposedly given up. The break must have occurred ahead of time and is therefore premature and uniformed. Thinking of oneself as superior to a human beloved and then sublimating this by intellectually attaching all one holds dear to a higher divine ideal will likely end in a paradoxically arresting form of depression. He may have the story of Abelard and Heloise in mind, which Frater Taciturnus explicitly cites 235 pages later.

As we have come to expect from the good Judge, he cannot help but interrupt himself in his very judgment on this score: "But he is unhappy, unfit for this joy, for this security in existence; he is depressed, a burden to himself, and feels he must be that to others. Do not be quick to judge—the weaker person also has his rights; and depression is something real that one does not delete with the stroke of the pen" (175). Delete it with his pen he nevertheless does, since such depression ends fraudulent and not without "an admixture of fantasy" (176). Consequently, William can only acknowledge such a higher form of life by tightly circumscribing it within extraordinary existential preconditions and requirements. He already stipulated that the case in question does not involve the "futile contradiction" of skipping over married life in order to "relate directly and immediately to the state," presumably because simply trading in one's personal attachments for mere citizenship is not worthy of being called sympathetically human in any considerable sense (171). Barring this, if renouncing married life is to be legitimate, one must actually be in love (176). Minimally, any sacrifice of significance assumes that we truly cherish what is relinquished. Stronger still, insofar as marriage represents the warm, temporal attachment to a particular individual and the various concrete projects and activities this ordinarily entails, to renounce it one must be experientially invested in its reality, potentially including a role as "captain of the popinjay shooting club" (170). Therefore, as a second requirement, one must actually be married (177). These are two initial conditions for counting as a legitimate exception, "provided there is such a one" (177–78). But William provides further, ongoing criteria that ensure the moral gravity of this hypothetically considered, legitimate break with the teleological norm. After the break, one must not become inimical to life, but continue to love it all the more, for "in this enthusiasm he must find each beautiful thing even more lovely and delightful than does the person who rejoices in happiness, because the one who wills to reject something universal has to be better informed about it than the person who is peacefully living in it" (178). Attending this enthusiasm the exceptional individual must feel the break itself "as a fatality and a horror," must understand that "in making this step he has ventured out into the trackless infinite space where the sword of Damocles hangs over his head if he looks up toward heaven, where the snare of unknown temptations clutches at his feet if he looks toward the ground," and must know that "no one can understand him and must have the composure to reconcile himself to the fact that human language has only curses for him...and must feel the torturing of misunderstanding just as the ascetic constantly felt the prick of the hair shirt..." (179–80). In all this he still "must not harden his own heart against it, for at the same time he does he is unjustified" (180). At this point one might wonder whether being captain of the popinjay-shooting club is trial enough—an earnest example of incarnate feeling, thought and activity—or simply a joke.

The moral psychology implied by all these requirements is reminiscent of Johannes de Silentio's characterization of Abraham in *Fear and Trembling*. The only way we can understand Abraham's decision to bind Isaac is to think about what it would mean to be thoroughly prepared to relinquish a beloved by holding the very knife in our own hand, simultaneously believing the best, and therefore paradoxically knowing and not knowing the outcome. Having to love and act in the face of such excruciating, relative uncertainty has a parallel here in that Judge William suggests the truly legitimate person who, for whatever reason, cannot rest happily in the ordinary conditions of temporal life and its deeply personal and specific attachments also cannot know whether they are justified in doing so, and in fact "never finds out in this life whether he is" (183). Presumably this last qualification forms a contrast to Abraham's scenario, since we know how that story ends. But even de Silentio emphatically points out that everything of existential significance occurs before the angel appears and delivers the counter-order. Abraham was fully prepared to give up Isaac and fully invested in receiving him back ahead of time, no holds barred either way. And that is what renders him heroic. The difference in William's account and in *Stages* as a whole is that we are not afforded the luxury of an actual outcome. The present story and narrative requirements end just as penultimately as William's re-imagination of Romeo and Juliet's farewell kiss:

> To repeat the most essential points, he must not feel himself above the universal, but lower; he must *à tout prix* [at all costs] want to remain within it, for he is actually in love and, what is more, is a married man; he must want to remain within it for his own sake and must want it for the sake of them for whom he is willing to sacrifice his life,

> whereas instead he now sees their misery as if he were someone whose hands and feet have been cut off and whose tongue has been torn from his mouth—that is, without a single means of communication. He must feel himself to be the most wretched of men, the scum of humanity, must feel it doubly precisely because he knows, not *in abstracto* but *in concreto,* what the beautiful is. Then he sinks down, desperate in all his wretchedness, when that single word, that final, that ultimate word, so ultimate that it is not within human language, is not forthcoming, when the testimony is not with him, when he cannot tear open the sealed dispatch that is only to be opened out there and that contains the orders from God. (181)

What many readers will find distracting is the requirement of actual marriage *in order to be* considered a legitimate exception, as if the sacred bond is supposed to play second fiddle to a more elegantly strung separation. How is it exactly that one is simultaneously committed in good faith and then abruptly divorced, or simultaneously separated and yet hopeful? It just seems like not only a moral, but practical anomaly. But as with Abraham, in whose case we must be distracted neither by the outcome nor the raising of the knife, and where the point is to catch a glimpse of his inner life *while* traveling to Mt. Moriah, so here the issue lies beyond the literal externals and within the very real and sacred chamber of an imagined exception. The social conventions and trappings surrounding how our personal affections are embodied and enacted are not thereby irrelevant. These are the outer forms that provide the dramatic moral setting for a complex internal struggle. The larger hermeneutical question behind the hypothetical scenario William imagines is whether it spells the height of romance or the depth of delusion. It is inconceivable to the Judge that one could forge or glean from such suffering any larger significance. All he concludes is what faith it must take "to believe that God could intervene [*gribe ind*] in life this way" (181). For his part, the tormenting possibility he conjures only seals his own knowledge of "the happiness of marriage," shrewdness and mockery aside (183). In true character, he qualifies this self-assurance in the very same sentence with: "or, more correctly, my conviction of the happiness of marriage" (183).

At this point his quiet wife patiently passes by his study, "lest she disturb," and the Judge scratches down his final eulogy, perhaps while dinner is getting overdone:

> Just one minute, my beloved, just one moment—my soul is so rich, I am so eloquent at this moment that I want to write it down on paper, a eulogy on you, my lovely better half, and thus convince the whole world of the validity of marriage. And yet in due time, tomorrow, the day after tomorrow, in a week, I shall throw you away, you wretched pen—my choice is made, and I follow the beckoning and the invitation. Let a wretched author sit trembling when a thought presents itself in a lucky moment, shivering lest someone disturb him—I am afraid of nothing, but I also know what is better than the most felicitous expression on paper of the most felicitous idea and what is infinitely more precious than any secret a poor author can have with his pen. (183–84)

We have seen from the beginning the interpersonal and vocational ambivalence Judge William manifests in regard to being an author and husband. From his jovial but dismissive response to his wife's question about his greatness in the world, to his final verbose sentence about throwing away his wretched pen—"in due time, tomorrow, the day after tomorrow, in a week"—the life of the writer and that of a husband may very well be foils for one another. They both involve existential choices, choices that place in dramatic relief the possible weaknesses of one another. Could the life of the artist and that of the lover both be romantic in their own fashion, and yet mutually exclusive? All we know at this point is the elastic fancy of the poet and the faithful engagement of a courtly knight fold in on one another in a reflection on bourgeois marriage that itself somehow gives birth to the dire possibility of a religious exception to the entire project of wedding our esthetic and moral values. Both involve a salutary use of the imagination, but each can go awry in adjacent directions. This may mean that art and actual love remain in tension but cannot be neatly separated, which would not be a surprising outcome given how dramatically Judge William attempts, in his own writing, to both distinguish and then neatly relate them. All this culminates in a purely hypothetical introduction to how difficult it would be to maintain a distinctively religious existential point of view in actual existence, to which the rest of *Stages* is devoted. To anticipate, the following hallelujah shall be a broken one.

3

The Major Interruption in a Minor Key

In his introduction, "Notice: Owner Sought," Frater Taciturnus claims to have found an anonymous diary locked in a box with the key inside at the bottom of Søborg Lake while accompanying a naturalist friend out inspecting marine plants. It turns out the diary is a fictional product of his own psychological imagination, but the report of this odd fortune is not simply a playful literary dissimulation. First, the fact that he is out in a boat with a naturalist fills out a spectrum already evoked by Judge William's afterthought concerning his own imaginary experiment about a possible higher form of life than a marriage like his own: "besides," Taciturnus adds, "everything else has been treated, even astronomy" (172). The thematic task performed by this bears comparison to *The Phaedrus*, where Plato begins his classic treatment of love as a form of divine madness and subsequent pharmaceutical account of writing with Socrates' central Delphic preoccupation: "Am I a beast more complicated and savage than Typhon, or am I a tamer, simpler animal with a share in a divine and gentle nature?"[1] We problematically find ourselves somewhere between angel and beast, beneath the stars but above the marshland. What we can expect from the diarist, then, is a thoroughly human subject appropriately pursued not on behalf of science, but "for the sake of friendship and curiosity" (189).

This complex spectrum of subject material is mirrored by the fate of Søborg Lake itself. Before inadvertently resurrecting the diary using a tool provided by his companion, Taciturnus informs us the lake has been steadily getting smaller, giving way to fertile land only too gladly claimed by peasants on the one side and a local parish minister on the other. The contrast and comparison between the stars and marshland is thus transposed into a "boundary dispute" within the distinctly human

[1] Plato, *Phaedrus*, line 230a.

domain of culture and value. We also find out the lake is singular in all of Denmark, so enclosed and thickly overgrown is the quagmire surrounding it. A naturalist would of course be informed about such places. What Taciturnus notices, however, is the forlorn cry of a bittern and the attendant anxiety one often feels in a spot "so infinitely far from people" (188). He even asks of the strange bird: "why do you wail and lament this way—after all, you indeed wish only to remain in solitude," which he fully admits is not a very scientific question (188). These parallels between the natural world and the diary itself suggest that the universal and particular within the human breast fluctuate between something winged and fishy, between a healthy transparency and wounded deviance, between the "flustered clamoring" of disclosure and a melancholy reserve, the sigh of which rises with the bubbles out of the depths (188–89). And so while we should expect from the diarist a spectacle of inner life, it will be one that belies a neatly universal anthropology. Two minutes earlier Taciturnus would not have dared pull up such a thing. The anxiety he feels once again echoes that of Socrates, for whom natural landscapes have nothing to teach us outside the walls and social order of the Polis. Nevertheless, the stream where Boreas carried Orithuia away on the banks of which myth and reality vie for equal attention lures him outside the city gates along with the attractive young Phaedrus carrying a speech about the benefits of *not* having a lover tucked beneath his cloak.[2]

When Taciturnus gets around to locating the year covered by the diary's calendar dates, the anthropological oscillation between the universal and particular becomes further transposed into the ancient and familiar contrast between history and fiction. Since the historicity of the diary remains uncertain, one might assume of its authorship

> that a poor wretch of a psychologist who dares to count on but little sympathy for imaginary psychological constructions [*Experimenter*] and unreal fabrications has made an attempt to invite sympathy by giving it the aspect of a novel. A psychologically accurate sketch that does not ask whether such a person ever lived is perhaps not very interesting in our day, when even poetry has snatched at the expedient of wanting to have the effect of actuality. People certainly

---

[2] Plato, *Phaedrus*, lines 228d–229c.

> want to have a little psychology, a little observation of so-called actual people, but when this science or art goes its own way, when it ignores the many inadequate manifestations of the psychical states that actuality offers, when it slips away by itself to create an individuality out of its own knowledge and to make this individuality the object of its observations, then many people get weary. That is, in actual life the case is that passions, psychical states, etc. are found only to a certain degree. This, too, delights the psychology, but it also has another kind of delight in seeing passion carried to its extreme limit. (191)

Without deliberately claiming, following Aristotle, that poetry is more philosophical than history, Taciturnus is alerting us to the distinctive self-revelation literature offers by presenting characters that compel us in the dual sense of being idealized and yet made up of all the accidental foibles and obsessions found within actual human drama. But for Taciturnus this serves as a warning. Compelling fictional personalities can be fantastic or mundane, strange or prototypical, wholly themselves or somehow like all of us. What Taciturnus in fact suggests is that the diarist manifests a singularity of passion that could just as well repel as attract us, transforming all such disjunctions into uncomfortable additions.

The inner tale of the diary is in some respects deceptively simple: a highly intellectual and passionate man falls in love with a charming young prospect and, to his considerable delight and relief, finds his feelings reciprocated; they get engaged. He then breaks it off. She resists as he retreats, but they continue to see and think of one another. As socially awkward as it may be, such things do happen, as it were. But these are only the external facts. Internally, the story is about how we find ourselves irresistibly drawn to a single beloved who renders everything else paltry in comparison and in light of which we cast about for a larger narrative context and ethical content. This is often terrifying because the investment proportionally exceeds any prosaic rendering that might provide a place of rest, and so the cost and possible loss of meaning feels far too high. It could be an illusion, the product of an overly romantic imagination. But this too seems faithless, itself a product of an overly sagacious realism. So the sheer inwardness, inspiration, and intensely focused desire strikes one as paradoxically worth it, or not.

Overwrought in this way, we are thus here torn by a conflict of interpretations as well. The possibility of self-deception and the actuality of self-transcendence vie for equal attention, which drives the outward demand for decision inward through a paralytic frenzy. For the reader a central question becomes how this fairly common experience of love may be related to the peculiar set of stethoscopic frames the diarist puts around his own story.

Unfolding the Diary

The diary extends in time from 3 January to 7 July, which subdivides into morning entries recalling events a year past and midnight passages ruminating in the present a year later. Along the way we are informed that after 7 July *midnight* the author's period of withdrawal and hibernation begins. The time of "unrest" shall begin again on 3 January, "the half year of that actuality that comes back again and again until I become free" (396). As far as the narrated present goes, by the end of the diary, he feels glad the whole ordeal does not have the temporal structure of a church calendar, for then the period of mourning would be unremitting, as if "the moment I was through with the old one, I had to begin a new one" (396). What occurs during the second half of the year—the time of rest—remains unexpressed, like the future itself, and perhaps not unlike our experience of time generally if one is neither trapped in the past nor frozen in a present. In the end, the possibility to which hope clings still awaits the diarist. What happened, in a crucial sense, is still happening. The "story of suffering" is unfinished, its outcome suspended, resolved in neither a comic nor tragic fashion, which is why the second, unwritten half of the year strikes us as a silently pregnant, watery depth, giving way to the fertile ground of imagination for cultivation, whether by a peasant or priest, or some other curious farmer or shepherd who may lie between. In this way, the sacramental cycle that regularly interrupts and extends ordinary time on any given Sabbath, but which overwhelmingly occupies a single Holy Week, bleeds its way into the singular pattern of a wholly individual life along with the passion that life longs to preserve. Predictably, then, the diary begins *in medias res*:

> So it is a year ago today since I saw her for the first time, that is, for the first time with a resolute soul. I was no fantasizer, was not in the habit of becoming intoxicated on fine words and brief dreams; therefore my resolution certainly did not mean that I would die if she did not become mine. Neither did I think that my soul would be scattered and my life become completely empty for me if she did not become mine—I had too many religious presuppositions for that. For me my resolution meant: Marry her or do not marry at all. That is what was at stake. (195)

Already here there is enough to unpack, as the stark declaration of his position is just as immediately offset by self-interpretation. First, he is not a one-dimensional romantic in the throes of a single-minded figment of affection that has swallowed his existence whole. For one thing, something has presumably led up to the qualification "that is, for the first time with a resolute soul." Although we are not privy to what precedes this part of the narrative, an educated guess leads us to suppose he has seen her before, knows a few things about her, and is drawn in such a way that holds him fast by a power outside himself. What else could explain why he would cryptically confess, down the page, that he was as much in love as anyone "even though not many would understand that I, if my deliberation had not allowed me this step, would have kept my falling in love to myself" (195)? Not only were the feelings real enough to act on but a measure of their substance also implies that knowledge of them belonged to someone else. Any great love begins in the twilight of an uncalculated and reckless preoccupation that involuntarily risks a reciprocal response. Such emotional honesty includes taking responsibility for a dramatic disclosure that renders the beloved equally and correspondingly responsible. What few would "understand" about this is how our most salient personal loves simply erupt in this fashion, so long as we allow them, invariably beginning with initially admitting them. One might say we need not admit anything so tenuous, however large it seems. But this would be to accept an equal and opposing risk, the solitary investment of a buried talent. The diarist is too self-respecting, too emotionally intelligent, too romantic, to take this sagacious route. It is truly all or nothing. He is not comparatively looking around for someone more suitable, or worse, someone "worthy." At our best, we do not alternately fight and go slack or generally become arrested in such a sagacious manner. "I marry her or I do not marry at all," he repeats (195).

The interpersonal dynamics of falling in love pose difficulties enough, so much so that we cannot altogether trust him when the diarist writes he would not die without her or that his soul would not become scattered and his life empty if she did not reciprocate his feelings and investment. What he claims is that he is protected from such a fate by a battalion of "religious presuppositions" unfolding a larger worldview in which our more fragile desires and incarnate aspirations can breathe beyond the pale of earthly tragedy. The problem is that his religious preoccupation does not serve as an intellectual balm of perspective above the fray but is existentially interwoven into the entire structure of his personality in ways that give rise to "so many anomalies" that place him at odds with himself. The only language he has for this is "a primordial depression" against which he must stand guard even during times of truce (195). In the arsenal of slings and arrows romantic longing typically throws our way, the particular angel he wrestles with is whether a person so spiritually stationed should get intimately involved in the first place. The fact that he takes the risk anyway simply raises the ordinary stakes.

Our first clue that we are dealing with an especially complicated case of a general dynamic is that his "defense" in this battle lies in an ability to hide his depression behind a foil of "good common sense, dispassionate reflection, and above all a candid face and an openhearted nature" (196). Quite apart from whether such a talent only wins a one-dimensional audience, and even then only at a distance, the deception is threatened by exposure when he thinks of her. "Am I perhaps being somewhat sophistical toward myself? I am in love—is it the delight of falling in love that fooled me into thinking that I was capable of this?" (196–97). Along the way he notes his own father managed well enough, "and he was the most depressed person I have known" (197). While it may not fit the scale of everyday passions, he is conscious that a makeup such as his cannot be categorized as a straightforward aberration. His intelligence, wit, sadness, elation, and sheer creativity do stand in mortal combat, but they also work with and upon each other to form a complete and irreducible manner of engaging the world: "From the bitterness of depression there is distilled a joy of life, a sympathy, an inwardness, that certainly cannot embitter life for anyone" (197). Still, the impulse to safeguard her interiority drives him to trim the tumultuous wick of his own longing. "My joy, such as sometimes overflows in my heart, belongs entirely to her; for everyday use I work honestly to earn a livelihood of joy for her; only the occasional dark moments do I have for myself—she must not come to suffer under them" (197). The romantic secret thus heroically borne and then reduced to the "scantiest rations possible" is the very awareness that "my joy, my bliss, my first and my only wish is to belong to her whom I would purchase at any price with my life and blood, but whom I still refuse to weaken and destroy by initiating her into my sufferings" (197). To say the least, pulling this off and forging an open and generous union without eclipsing her with his peculiar and troubling inner strife could indeed "become the most difficult task, a matter of concern, even though it is my supreme wish" (197).

Switching to the present, a year later, the diarist echoes the warning from Judge William against taking a monastic shortcut through life and insists one does well to consider "whether there is something in the circumstances of his life that for the time being binds him and makes it his first duty to work at getting another person afloat if that other one can be rescued" (197–98). As the story of the past unfolds into this earliest of the present tense, we learn of the diarist's impetuous proposal of marriage, her acceptance, and his subsequent break with their engagement. The details follow later. What we learn here is that somewhere along the way she insinuates he is a murderer. Multiple sides of this charge throw him into alarmed confusion. He initially wonders whether she meant it seriously or whether for her, and those around her, it was simply "an exaggeration, a momentary mood" (198). But *he* obviously takes it seriously, and what is tormenting about it is waiting around to find out whether he is in fact guilty, which would be true if *she* meant it seriously. However, if she does not fall apart, then he is off the hook. But that possibility implies her love was somehow relatively easy to give up while his is evidently not, as the rest of the diary will make perfectly and painstakingly clear. This puts him in an extremely peculiar emotional spot. On the one hand he desperately wants her to survive, but on the other hand, if she moves on just fine then their love was never really shared, never a truly common passion and thorough-going joy, which would make his whole manner of taking responsibility for it unnervingly laughable. Such deflated laughter seems to be the demon he fears most. Here, a year later, he actually confesses to his earlier denial about exactly how much she means to him, as his whole life would become scattered and empty if the enormity of his affection turned out to have been unreciprocated in the first place. As a result he is in two places at once, literarily and morally. On the one hand, he refuses

> to forget any of it, not any; only to the faithfulness of an alarmed imagination that returns to me what has been confided more terrible than it was, only to the memory of a troubled conscience that sets a high interest rate on guilt, only to an honesty such as that will I and dare I entrust myself! —She is dying. How loathsome that I could believe for a moment the craftiness of the understanding or almost heed the demon of laughter—abominable! (199)

Even so, and on the other hand, he must remain calm and collected, virtually indifferent. Melding these involuntary responsibilities together, he writes: "Strangely enough, when I was courting her I was anxious lest I be too intriguing; now I am compelled to be that" (199).

What follows is the first of six narrative interpolations that appear on the fifth of each month from January to June. "Quiet Despair" begins with a reference to Jonathan Swift, an unmarried satirist and troubled cleric with an infamously uncharitable record of personal loves who funded an asylum to which he himself was later committed. This is significant enough, but the main topic is that of Swift looking in a mirror. The rest of the passage is devoted to the shared, but split image of a father and son who echo each other in a particularly oblique fashion, full of indirect communicative sympathy breeding a terribly uncertain intimacy. Swift simply looks at *himself,* and says: "Poor old man." In contrast, the father in this story says to the son: "Poor child, you are in quiet despair." Just prior to this declaration the son notes how their daily round contained "the cheerfulness of high-spirited, lively conversation" (199). But what follows this prescient statement is how nothing more was said about the previous comment or how it should be understood. All we get is how "the father believed that he was responsible for his son's depression, and the son believed that it was he who caused the father sorrow—but never a word was exchanged about this" (200). Then the whole passage ends, after the father's death, with: "For the father was the only one who had understood him; and the father was the only intimate he had had, but the intimacy was of such a nature that it remained the same whether the father was alive or dead" (200). What all this suggests is how our intimate bonds are constantly in the process of eclipsing our own identity and self-understanding, an eclipse we long for and simultaneously dread. This general dynamic gravitates around the thirst for a common language that would ideally alleviate our spiritual loneliness, the very wound for which we seek healing in the presence of some salient other self. A separation by death is the ultimate earthly threat to this dialogical exchange of heart and mind. But this ultimate breach is also simply the specter of what haunts our lives during a long day's dying. So it is no surprise that Swift's apocryphal self-relation is paired with a dying father, a son growing old, and then: "just as love devises, so longing and loss taught him—not, of course, to wrest any communication from the silence of eternity—but it taught him to imitate his father's voice until the likeness satisfied him" (200). Whenever we love, we long to see ourselves named, confirmed, understood, and justly celebrated. We simultaneously seek but cannot find this solely in ourselves, and so we do so with another, in tactile form, orally in both senses of the term. Whether we are speaking or kissing makes little difference. Both are articulate, and each grow and perish in the same earth and under the same sunlight, with the same roots. The fundamental desire both to be a self and to be overcome by another is precisely what joins the cognitive and bodily halves of our selves, but is also what divides the spiritual from the sexual. And this mad pursuit of agreeable union is exactly what makes the romantic individual universally human, a child of God, but potentially broken and melancholy, left alone gazing into a mirror rather than the eyes of another.

Marriageable Youth Lost and Found

The following four entries are all *morning* passages recounting the past. 8 January tells us "today I saw her at her uncle's, where I was together with her" (200). The same entry announces that "[f]or about a whole year now, ever since I realized I was in love with her (for prior to that time I had, of course, seen her), I have secretly and clandestinely been absorbed in this love" (202). 11 January recalls the impetuous and no doubt perplexing declaration of his love, and the ensuing letter to her father asking for her hand. The next day she and her father agree to the proposal, to which he responds, to himself, in print, sunk at the bottom of a pond, a year later: "The testing period is over—if only it has not been too short, if only no one hurried her into making a resolution, if only they made the whole matter difficult enough for her" (210).

The first thing to acknowledge about these passages is how detached, self-enclosed, and even creepy many readers find them. On the face of it, we have an older, depressed, possibly sick intellectual infatuated with a younger, healthier, presumably more cheerful beloved whom he observes at a distance from a half-rate coffee shop on her way to singing lessons. He even embarrassingly reveals that escorting her home a year prior to their meeting on 8 January, he

> walked happily along at her side. And yet it seemed to me that I was almost happier in my hiding place; to come so close to actuality, yet without actually being closer, results in distancing, whereas the distance of concealment draws the object to oneself. What if the whole thing were an illusion? Impossible. Why, then do I feel happier in the distance of possibility? For the very reason I myself have given; anything else is dark imagining. She is indeed the only one I love and have loved, and I will never love anyone else. But neither will I stoop to learn, as they say, to know her by testing and investigating her nature. She is my beloved, and the secret task of love is to imagine everything lovable about her until I almost perish from impatience. (205–206)

All this smacks of an overly reflective dissembling, more obsession than love, and fed more by illusion than reality.

There is no doubt the diarist is a peculiar lover, approaching his beloved from such a distance, and arriving with such a screeching halt. But it is also clear that he cannot help himself. He is in love. And she, for equally mysterious reasons, responds positively. As third parties, our task is to understand the universal dimensions of the affair, and this requires assembling a number of elements any genuine romance places in dramatic relief. This hermeneutical demand does not mean all of us will finally relate to it, but that too is part of the very drama of having another's happiness depend on the inner quality of our own proclivity and desire, each of us invariably mixed and pure only in our complexity. For instance, more central to the diarist's story than the seemingly prudish distaste for "the more free association with the opposite sex that our milieu permits, as they say, to make passes" or his alarm that any future spouse might have been the "object of a philanderer's attention," is his cryptic habit of indirectly brooding over love "from an earlier time and even more from the time of preparation for this *tentamen rigorosum* [rigorous examination]" (200–201). We can only guess what experiences had fostered such brooding, to which he has now grown accustomed, but he clearly indicates the kind of test for which he has been prepared in the present scenario. Ordinarily, a fully realized romantic longing has a pre-history of false starts and thwarted understanding, which Judge William would find utterly distasteful. In any case, behind his scrupulous reservation is the following:

> I do not know if cunning can ever be united with the erotic, but this I do know, that when one is struggling with God and with oneself whether *to dare* to follow the beckoning of love, whether to dare to reach for the desire that is the eye's delight and the heart's craving, then one is protected against this kind of going astray. But this is the reason I am so cautious, cautious to the very last moment—ah, what if there came to my interior being a counterorder that I should not have presumptuously intervened disturbingly there, and I should not only have the pain of an unhappy love affair but would also have to make the retreat of repentance. (201–202)

In the same vein, having been secretly and clandestinely occupied with her during the previous year—at parties, in her home, on her way—he reports, "I imagined many a terror and drilled myself in it while the pleasure of love hummed along with the task" (203).

There are at least four aspects to these coy passages we need to be aware of, each of which assume and only make sense in light of having actually fallen in love. The first concerns the nature of resolve, next the role of imagination, third the nature of the task, and all of these, so intimately related, issue in a question about the appropriate form of expression love should take. Upon falling in love, we find ourselves immediately faced with an unknown future we must somehow recon with ahead of time, and do so with a terrifying lack of assurance. Large portions of this have nothing to do with us, and are entirely out of our control. The rest *is* up to us, but we are typically full of unfitted dimensions in terms of what we have the power to feel, imagine, do, and finally say. For example, the terror that he drilled himself in while the pleasure of love hummed along occurs largely in his imagination, by virtue of reflection. But what it requires in actuality is that we realize how much one "does spontaneously in order to know what it means not to do the slightest thing without calculation" (203). More concretely, one needs to know "the difference between coming to a lively gathering and being promptly happy and, on the other hand, coming out of the deepest darkness of depression and yet arriving precisely at the time stipulated in the invitation and with the kind of blithe spirit that the company and surroundings demand. If one is not in love, one becomes weary on the way" (203). The difference here concerns not only the starting place before arriving, but also the authenticity of a hard-won, blithe spirit versus a prompt and presumably facile, happy demeanor. We may very well ask whether that difference is a matter of immeasurable scale, or existential and emotional depth about which it is very difficult to judge. We all must manage ourselves socially, and this may come easier for some personalities than others, but that is itself doubtful. In any case, authenticity and genuine reciprocity are what a romantic longs for, as opposed to a crudely struck interpersonal compromise. Casting about for his own balance along the way the diarist is intensely aware that the whole matter of his love may be an illusion, which he promptly declares impossible. What seems to make this impossible is how fantasy and imaginative construal are an essential part of any warm, morally engaged relationship of significance. It is the part we play in resisting and reconfiguring the prosaic world of brute facts. Poetic personalities do not always handle this very well. There is a constant danger of self-deception about how the texture of our inner lives and commitments do or ought to feel. But the risk on the other side of artistic gloss is the equally self-deceived, uncreative, and finally passive acceptance of what we nevertheless pragmatically interpret as a delivery of fate. This approach too is a form of immunity, as banal as it is calm. The difference is striking, but cannot be easily weighed. More generally, the whole existential state that a particular personal love throws into relief is how much of our moral passion is first mobilized and finally centers upon something or someone quite specific.

Although the diarist is loath to "stoop to learn, as they say, to know her by testing and investigating her nature" and only wants "to imagine everything loveable about her" to the point of virtually dying of impatience, he has nevertheless learned enough of her "life situation" to guess whether they might be suitable (206–207). Principally this situation includes the death of her mother, which has "helped the children to draw closer together more earnestly and to center their thoughts on their home, where the father, not without sadness but all the more solicitously, protects his children and not ungraciously lets himself be rejuvenated by the legitimate demands of the young people upon life" (207). What is particularly revealing about this information is that the diarist doubts whether *he* has the gumption to strike a similarly and authentically mollified sadness appropriately balanced with a friendly stance toward life, uninfected by "the prolix company of every Tom, Dick, and Harry" (207). In fact he worries whether he would simply make her unhappy. Having "adorned" his inner life "with the magic of love" he wonders whether the whole affair may not be just a dream, a spectacular failure of nerve (204). And yet the marks of its reality are everywhere evident.

Along the way the diarist nostalgically ruminates on a lesson delivered by a certain Latin teacher in his youth. The content of the lesson from Terence was that of Phaedria falling in love with a cither player, reduced to following her to and from school, during which his waiting took place in a grammatically subjunctive mood. Pedagogically speaking the initial point was a correspondingly grammatical one. The teacher explained, "that we were not to regard the subjunctive mood in an external way as if it were the particle as such that took the subjunctive. It was the internal and the psychical that determined the mood, and in the case at hand it was the optative passion, the impatient longing, the soul's emotion of expectancy." Thereupon, in a voice "completely changed" his teacher went on to say the

> person sitting and waiting there in that barber shop as if it were a café or a public place such as that is not an indifferent man but a man in love waiting for his beloved. In fact, if he had been a porter, a chair carrier, a messenger, or a cabdriver who was waiting there, then the waiting could be thought of as occupying the time while the girl was at her music and singing lesson, which is not to be considered subjunctive but indicative, unless it was the case that these gentlemen were waiting to be paid, which is a very mediocre passion. Language really ought not be allowed to express that kind of expectation in the subjunctive mood. But it is Phaedria who is waiting, and she is waiting in a mood of: If only she, if she would only, would that she might only soon, soon come back; all this is appropriately the subjunctive mood. (205)

Although the point of the lesson was grammatical, the diarist plausibly concludes the instructor "could have taken on other subjects as well as Latin" (205). Although none of these nostalgic ruminations seems particularly linear as a revealing thought progression, amidst the same passage we find the diarist manages to declare his love, though he cannot recall exactly how he put it. He is clear he conveyed "the interior truth of [his] passion," but as a diarist, as a writer, he has forgotten (209). The disjunction between memory and recollection upends him, both then and in the present, and no doubt in a subjective mood. As a fragile lover what he is committed to and fully aware of are all the interpersonal elements that could misfire, lose their point, and miss the meaningful mark. He is immensely nervous about giving an over-calculated, underhanded, or overwhelming impression. He hates the fact that he might be too weak, she might be too shocked, and the whole thing might end in misunderstanding, offense, and despair, all as a result of an "unexpected and passionate outburst" (209). And then—then—the proposal is settled, the period of testing is over, the sickness is healed; they kiss for the first time, and all stands interpretively, blissfully still.

At this point in time, however, he has occasion to jot down in scrupulous penmanship:

> If yesterday I became ten years older, today I became ten years younger—no, younger than I have ever been. Is this a crisis? Is this the wavering of decision? *Estne adhuc sub judice lis* [Is the case perhaps still before the court]? Have I really become ten years older, I who was almost an old man—the poor girl, who has to nurse one who is dead; or have I become young as I never was young—what an enviable fate to be able to be so much to a person. (211)

This is a *morning* passage that recalls the past. The theme of premature age conjoined with a returning sense of youth echoes throughout *Stages* as a whole. The existential connotation suggests a mixture of hope, uncertainty, fulfillment, and resignation. What we unreasonably long for and practically expect vie for allegiance within the breast of all those who feel themselves so problematically inspired. For his part, the diarist is caught between a noble risk and real doubt. He cannot make up his mind whether he has stepped where no angel would fear to tread or solidly affirmed what lesser gods have every right to claim. The breath of personal love does indeed require oxygen, as necessary and exhilarating as it is potentially explosive. But for now the subjunctive mood is met with satisfaction.

Switching to the *midnight* date of his engagement day, a year later, the diarist continues wondering whether he has a murder on his conscience, and having seen her crossing the street tries to glean information about her interior state. Naturally, this is a hapless venture in interpretation. He can only guess, chide himself, and hold his own conflicted feelings at bay. However, the most revealing rhetorical flourishes include a question without a mark and a bald declaration: "Was it chance that brought us so close, or what power is pursuing me with her, from whom I am fleeing and yet do not wish to escape" (211). And: "Only by enduring and suffering, by deferring to every argument against my shattered soul do I maintain any meaning in my existence" (212). What must be made clear is how his pursuit of her, brought happily to a resolution, turns on him and becomes a power pursuing him. The attraction and resistance so near the heart of any romantic affair and ideal are quadrupled in such a way that the inherent tensions take on a thaumaturgical significance. On the one hand this echoes the classic courtly tradition of desire thriving on obstacles already invoked by the banqueters, but the diarist has something more cosmic in mind. Prematurely old and perpetually young, he is transfixed by a future beyond his grasp and the interiority of a beloved he cannot pin down. Holding out, but nevertheless holding on, he can only compare himself to an elder tightrope dancer walking beneath a child precariously training on a wire far above. In the following *morning* entry he transposes the anxiety of the tightrope trainer into that of a jeweler witnessing a child obliviously playing with various precious and ordinary stones, in a "happy mood" and with no thought of distinguishing between them (215). If his beloved is supposed to be the child in either case, the diarist is obviously torn by a helpless adoration of her so-called youth. Innocence and immediacy are a wonder to behold and a fragility to fear. His reserve and her silence only accentuate the dramatic tension internal to any highly invested passion. Rather ominously, he locates this drama *between* them:

> Yet how strange it must be to be a young girl, to enter into life so briskly. I believed I would be released, that I would be changed, that I would have seen myself in love and by looking in love at her I would see myself saved—then I would have become like her, a bird on a branch, a song of joy in youth. I believed that we would have grown up together, that our life would be happy for us in our union and in its happiness understandable to others, like a happy person's greeting as he hurries by and throws us a kiss. (215)

Having distinguished the so-called refined and precious from the naïve and ordinary, he admits the dramatic tension is an active development within himself, since just prior to this passage he once again asks himself: "have I become ten years older or have I become ten years younger?" (215).

While on the surface some of these passages can seem insipidly off-putting, what she presents to his imagination is a person for whom "there is no absolute distinction between the idea that bursts into thought and language, as does the precious stone in its radiance, and the idea in which this is lacking" (216). In his engagement he longs for the ability to hold two such ideas together, and perhaps play with them accordingly, and thereby enter the kingdom of heaven as a child. Emotionally, religiously, and romantically, he would embrace his aged reflective nature together with an immediate feeling, and have the faith, the courage, to relax into a rich present union. In part, whether *she* is capable of this or not is both directly relevant and beside the point because the tale is an interior one for each of us to take stock of and settle on our own. Still, his unmitigated conclusion is: "Lovers ought to have no differences [*Mellemværende*] between them" (216). Even so, he finishes this thought with: "Alas, alas we have been united too briefly to have any differences. We have nothing between us, and yet we have a world between us, exactly a world" (216). The world that is between them contains all the geography that would simultaneously fascinate and frighten any given traveler on a voyage Judge William claimed is more rewarding than anything Ulysses ventured. But this view is itself romantic, and exactly what the diarist both comprehends and despairs over. The following entry is confirmation enough: "This much I certainly do realize—that it is not with her, it is not with Eros that I must struggle. It is religious crises that are gathering over me. My life-view has become ambiguous—how, I cannot as yet say. And my life belongs to her, but she suspects nothing" (216).

Past and Future Tense in Full Swing

It is at *midnight* on 17 January when we find out the order and timing of the entries and read the dreaded phrase "the current year" (216). There are at least five interrelated topics here: taking legitimate heed of another's interior life, presenting your own self with appropriate calm and distance, the use and abuse of third parties in doing so, acknowledging your own passion, and despairing over the unnerving confluence of the first four, in either person or writing. These all converge in a series of disjunctions between feeling and expression, agency and impotence, knowledge and imagination, all summed up in having a "soul full of reckless courage and the mind of plans and the words available—and then to have a pen that cannot write or with great toil write one letter of the alphabet every other hour" (218–19). On either side of this bravado he compares his passion to that of a gambler and fisherman, two active preoccupations that rely so heavily on the outside forces of chance and timing. A year later, he is still clearly invested in nurturing his love, in recognizing within that love some salient part of himself, and in having that feeling reciprocated. And yet he cannot reasonably expect her to follow along in what is evidently an agonizing ordeal for him. This agony of thought causes him to wish she *had* immediately died so that he could take full responsibility for initiating her into his own tragic difficulties, concluding that at least then "there would have been meaning in the whole affair" (220). But not knowing the character and level of her grief, the seriousness of her own words and feelings, he remains suspended. What particularly concerns him in such midnight passages is exactly where she is at with the relationship, whether she is a rare goddess "whose deification did not begin with death but with grief" or in some sort of fanciful manner has simply become "commonsensical" (214). More cryptically he writes "the slightest intimation of how she preoccupies me would be the absolutely most dangerous thing; it might lead her in false hope out into the indeterminable and let her be saved—that is, perish, be lost in half measures" (217). On one level this makes him appear like he is trying to act cavalier and removed while simultaneously stringing her along when he could simply cut her loose out of straightforward compassion. On another level he brazenly declares he has no desire to let her go, to kill his love in either sense, and is trying to discern whether her own passion is an equal match to his own or a culturally constructed emotion, as shallow as it would be prosaic. What is crucial about the electrically charged interpersonal static in this scenario is how the battle to maintain his own love, while carefully concealing the inner conflict, is a mirror image of what he hopes is happening within her own feeling and resolve. But this he cannot risk, for the very sake of love, without seductively enervating her by revealing his own. In all of this the fearsome either/or shared between them and potentially borne within the guts of each somehow links death with meaning and false hope with salvation, incredulously mediated by halves, and all mysteriously put together in something rather obviously "indeterminable."

Unsurprisingly the following *morning* entry opens with the inability to preserve his soul in the otherwise arresting immediacy of love. There are several incommensurable aspects contained within this ambiguous "cannot" (221). First, his unaccountable attraction to her, and second, not wanting to throw "the passion of my soul in that direction" (221). This disjunction gives rise to an odd third sentiment concerning how he is "most unhappy when she is most beautiful" (221). But fourth, because beauty is both entirely arresting and incidentally ephemeral, "it seems to me that she has such an indescribable claim upon life" (221). This speculative observation is followed by a most revealing confession: "I cannot comprehend that every human being has a claim upon life—I alone do not" (221). Here he absurdly wishes she were unattractive. How shall the reader put all these thoughts together? One way is to say that any incarnate magnetic draw between lovers alternates between the erotic in the highest and lowest senses, between sheer physical delight and elevated companionship, along with the depressing aftermath that often accompanies each of them. What he wonders, and apparently does not know, is whether she is on the same page, at the same stage. And so he cannot help but contrast and imaginatively resolve her physical beauty with existential unhappiness. In his own mind, they might come together, since "like loves only like" (222). In a rather circuitous reciprocal motion he thus juxtaposes her "childlike happiness," her "buoyancy in the world," with his own courage, his own "buoyancy in dancing over abysses of which she has no idea whatsoever and with which she can sympathize only unessentially, as with a dreadful story one reads and whose actuality one cannot conceive..." (222). The tension here points in both personal and political directions, with whomever we share bedclothes and with whatever social causes awaken us as if from a dream. He is clearly trying to put them together within and for himself, as must we all.[3]

[3] A fruitful comparative test-case to help illumate these tensions may be that of Dorothy Day as recounted in her autobiographical *The Long Loneliness* (New York: Harper & Row Publishers, Inc., 1997), especially in Part 2 entitled "Natural Happiness," where she finds herself drawn in so many directions at once, earnestly looking for and trying to recount a meaningful tragectory. Her common-law marriage with Forester and birth of daughter Tamar Teresa stands squarely next to Augutine's lusty, tortured, anonymous but faithful passion for his own beloved that issued with Adeodatus. In regard to the latter, it takes little active imagination to interpret the following as an instance of genuine but socially disfigured love: "Meanwhile my sins multiplied. The woman with whom I habitually slept was torn away from my side because she was a hindrance to my marriage. My heart which was deeply attached to her was cut

In all this the diarist declares he has chosen "the religious" (222). But in context what exactly does this mean? That is an interpretive question. It seems a matter of faith, but having faith in some specific sense; faith for this life, his own and hers; faith that they might be happy together, cut from the same cloth, and stitched into a quilt made for two and sewn out of a common language. Were it possible that she saw the full difficulty of this affirmation, embraced the mess and risk of it with equal courage, then he could meet her with a corresponding childlike existential freedom and loveliness. But as it stands in his imagination, a year prior, he had to leave her charm "in abeyance" (222). "If I attain a common point of departure along this road," he currently writes about that time, "then come, you smiling freedom from care; I shall rejoice with you as sincerely as I can, braid rosebuds in your hair; I shall handle you as lightly as is possible for me, as is possible for someone who is accustomed to reach for what is crucial with the passion of thought and at the risk of his life" (222). The detail this entry includes about reading a sermon out loud to her is telling is this regard. Overcome with emotion for the theological material in her presence makes him question what the true source of inspiration might be. Is *she* the source, or the content of the sermon, and how might these be related? "Poor girl," he reports, "I wonder what she is thinking!" (222).

---

and wounded, and left a trail of blood. She had returned to Africa vowing that she would never go with another man. She left with me a natural son I had by her. But I was unhappy, incapable of following a woman's example, and impatient of delay. I was to get the girl I had proposed to only at the end of two years. As I was not a lover of marriage but a slave of lust, I procured another woman, not of course as wife. By this liasion the desease of my soul would be sustained and kept alive, either in full vigour or even increased, so that the habit would be guarded and fostered until the time I came to the kingdom of marriage. But my wound, inflicted by the earlier parting, was not healed. After inflammation and sharp pain, it festered. The pain made me as it were frigid but desperate." Augustine, *Confessions* (Oxford: Oxford University Press, 1991) 109, translated with notes by Henry Chadwick. As confessionally difficult as they are to incorporate into saintly storytelling, for both Augustine and Dorothy Day, our most tender, volatile, and ultimately personal passions play a central role as each of these authors restlessly cast about for a larger narrative that would explain and satisfy the evident enormity of their hearts and equally demanding intellects.

> She is silent, quiet, but entirely calm. That I am so overwhelmed by her—I wonder if she would attribute this effect to love. Impossible, to me that would be the most unlovely thing I can imagine. When I humble myself under God, then to believe that it was under her! No, she does not have that effect upon me. I have been able, can still bear, to live without her if only I retain the religious. But I suspect that the religious crisis is to bring it into what I have begun here. (222)

Indeed, what must she be thinking! With a potentially distracting, but directly related sense of courage, she might just be thinking: "kiss me you damn fool!" With equal probability she may be thinking: "what is his problem?" Most likely it is a combination of both. For his part, he at least admits a fundamental confusion that his whole scale of values and attitude towards life might be askew. But above the head of his self-doubt and her silence hangs the issue of earthly romance infused with religious significance that floats on the surface of the text, perhaps more buoyant as poetry than actual persons. Simultaneously young and old, the faith in question submits to erotic passion while carrying a cross, a peculiar pilgrimage of taking two steps forward and one step back, all the while suspecting that a method of travel more pleasing in the eyes of God might be to skip. Or waltz.

The Implicit Conflict

At this point the interdiction between the erotic and religious points of view come increasingly to the fore, as if YHWY and Cupid were now entering battle in earnest, while we as readers attempt peace talks.[4]

---

[4] Here I do not mean to evoke Anders Nygren's contrast in *Agape and Eros* (Philadelphia: Westminster Press, 1953). The tension I have in mind is not that between a preferential, aquisitive desire to be in the presence of some valued good, and an entirely gratuitous, theocentric outpouring of self-sacrificial benefit to another apart from any logic of desert, which is only relevant here if *both* forms of love contain poles of one another and are equally susceptible to implosion taken on their own. Rather, what I have in mind is a less analytically abstract contrast between a kind, playful, innocent delight and a keen perception of the harsher elements of human reality when it comes to what is most recognizably divine in our affective life. Within the very best of our narratives this tension frequently belies the pigeonholes of duty and desire, egoism and self-sacrifice, either personally or politically. If Christ crucified is foolishness to

Beginning promptly with what any given third party—"a stage hairdresser, a silk, wool and linen merchant, a young girl at finishing school, to say nothing of the gentlemen who write short stories and novels"—might conclude about his perplexing obsession over an imaginary guilt, when the diarist should be attending to her, *he* concludes:

> My suffering is a punishment. I accept it from God's hands; I have deserved it. In my youth I have often quietly smiled at erotic love. I have not scoffed at it, have not done a thing to hold it up to ridicule—it occupies me too little for that. I have lived only intellectually. When I read in the poets the speeches of lovers, I smiled because I could not understand that such a relationship could occupy them so much. The eternal, a relationship with God, a relationship to the idea—this

---

the Greeks and a stumbling block to Jews, this is not because Saul of Tarsus had no sense of mercy, given his experience of the law, and certainly not because Socrates had no sense that self-denial plays a role in *eudiamonia*. Jumping forward to the Renassaince, Luther and Erasmus are themselves like lovers locked in a battle in which an anxious, rhetorical *Anfectungen* fights against a patient, reasonable dialectic. On a more pedestrian level, for both Pagan and Christian lovers alike, even the most jealous of lovers confers upon their beloved gloriously undeserved blessings and the most abject sacrificial ones store up treasures that both moth and rust may eventually destroy. In any case, one will scarcely find Nygren's so-called Lutheran "Copernican Revolution" in either *Stages* or *Works of Love*, the latter often cited as a corrective to the former. My own estimate of *Works of Love* can be seen in "Kierkegaard, Compassion, and the Descent of Love," *International Philosophical Quarterly* (July 2007). What I would add here is a brief unwritten *midrash* on Kierkegaard's treatment of Peter's betrayal under the heading of an *Akedah* of Peter within the Passion of Christ itself. With *Fear and Trembling* in mind, Jesus must have had to renounce the warmth of a personal, faithful friendship even as he remained heroically, divinely open to the renewal of that very warmth after so violent a breach. It is worth thinking about each pair of lovers we encounter in the Gospels and Kierkegaard's own texts and their troubled loves from both sides: Isaac/Abraham, Agnes/Merman, Peter/Jesus, Quaedam/Quidam. Not irrelevant is that Judas is the one disciple who runs away in despairing finality, a narrative fact that has been less poorly treated in literature than in the pulpit even as *that* betrayal began with a kiss. See the section on "Our Duty to Love the People we See" in Kierkegaard, *Works of Love* (Princeton: Princeton Unversity Press, 1995). Irving Singer is additionally helpful in his chapter on Agapē in *The Nature of Love, Volume 1, Plato to Luther* (Chicago: University of Chicago Press, 1984).

> stirred my soul, but I could not grasp something so intermediate. Now—well, now I am suffering, I am doing penance, even if I am not suffering in a purely erotic way. (225)

As readers and third parties to the affair, the actual conclusion eludes any balanced inner logic since, as far as the two of them are concerned, she cannot quite believe he is a bastard and he cannot quite believe she is in love. And so we are caught between them. When we read that he thinks she lacks "religious presuppositions" and yet hates the idea of being her instructor rather than her lover, all the while longing for her to "swing herself over into the religious freedom where she will feel the power of the spirit and feel religiously assured and secure," surmising that even if his "depression" could not "fulfill her youthful, beautiful claim on life" they could at least grow old together, we should indeed wonder, with him, whether the most enviable and beautiful time of love is "when the lovers could sweep out onto the floor in a waltz" (226).

The following entry maps out the partial extent of his odd and painstaking hope that they would turn out suitable, that their happiness would be founded upon a shared spiritual trial, compared to which the struggles of Romeo and Juliet appear but child's play and whose potentially problematic internal passions were never given a chance to show themselves on stage against the inexorable external pressures that ultimately buried them. It is possible the diarist's betrothed might not be able or even interested in persevering in such a "desert of expectancy" and would prefer to marry someone else, someone more sensible and secure. The latter possibility is something he admits he wants at certain moments, and yet "at this point I have other thoughts on the matter" (227). What he displays is a perplexing mix of self-justification and desire for absolution, to be understood on his own terms and truly known in a relatively unmediated fashion and yet forgiven. This does not seem possible, for faulty as we are, every longing to connect and resolve conflicts within ourselves and between one another is so often thwarted such that our love, our very longing, becomes a vast, untrammeled question. In his own self-understanding the diarist wavers between suspecting he is either sagacious or insane, and then concludes this speculative projection with:

> Or what if she were totally unchanged, had suffered nothing in either soul or body, but she did not understand me, did not understand me entirely; what if the heart in the young girl's breast did not beat violently as it does in the breast of the faithful one; what if the blood of youth did not rush to her head as it does to mine; what if it coursed calmly in the inexperienced girl and not as it does in the cool soul of the sensible person; what if she did not understand my suffering and its degree, did not understand my chilling composure, the necessity for it; what if the word "forgiveness" between us were to become earnest, the earnestness of judgment, and not a ball we both hit in the game of erotic love while fidelity jubilated over its victory; what if she did not entirely understand that there is only one way to be zealots in our day and to preserve romance of soul in the nineteenth century's risible commonsensibleness, and that is to be just as cool outwardly as one is warm inwardly; what if she did not understand, did not entirely understand, that it is infamous to help by half measures and that it is being faithful to reject illusory relief; what if, when the hint came from heaven, the sign for our happiness, what if she were out of step and could not follow it—what then, what then, what then? (227–28)

The diarist keeps reverting, sinking deeper into himself, alternating between a wish for her release and his own desire to remain together, all the while entertaining various possibilities of fresh unhappiness. For example, her own love might be a mere self-deception, though deadly, and in proud defensive return she might refuse to admit this and thereby retain whatever dignity might remain on the books. What is crucial in this passage is how his visionary hope for their love is that they share a similarly intense, lasting romantic sense that survives the inevitable Lenten period of waiting until things work out, in, with, and under the obstacles any great love typically faces and endures. Just as he waits for a mere "hint" from heaven for a "sign" endorsing their happiness, the diarist merely hints at what these obstacles may be. One clear obstacle he has in mind is their potential need to forgive one another for grave infidelity, although the crimes he imagines remain obscure. Given the surrounding language, I doubt he fears literal, sexual infidelity so much as he fears a chilling, commonsensical attitude towards romance far more deadly than the seventh commandment announces and the spirit of which hovers above it like a holy ghost, itself waiting to pass judgment on the literally faithful. Infidelity can take many forms, and not all of them receive the rightful amount of press. For every guy that runs off with a secretary, there are a hundred that keep paying the bills and just stop caring, erecting ships in a bottle after hours, sailing who knows where. For his part, the diarist seems a bit careless himself. But he is willing to risk all, even his own dignity, because he evidently cares so much. After a long dash of thoughts, he writes "—if only I dare, I will not be ashamed of her, I will calmly say: I have lost much, very much, or more correctly, I have had to deny myself my dearest wish. Should I be afraid of confessing an unhappy love [*Kjærlighed*], should I change myself and my opinion of her because she changed toward me?" (228). He follows this train of thought with a couple biblical references, one having to do with temporal demise, the other with the foolishness of faith itself. "What is a human life, after all—it is like grass, withered tomorrow—perhaps I, too, shall die tomorrow. If a fool laughs at me, what does that demonstrate but that I have acted wisely?" (228). Intimately linking these alternately dark and foolish thoughts, he dares to hope for salvation "beyond and before God," stating his wish for them both to be "blessed" "beyond all measure" and passing all understanding, ending with: "Sleep well, my beloved, sleep well: stay with me in my dreams, stay with the lonely solitary, you heavenly perhaps with your ineffable bliss" (229). The marriage proposal here joins the stark contrast between ultimate redemption and the fragility of entirely mortal emotions. Putting them together, a year later, at *midnight*, he is still sidling along next to her in bed, haunted but dreaming, and laying down his pen. The following *morning* entry reports how reticent and calm he has tried to be, and to that degree feels innocent. This report is paired with a meditation on how his reflective tendency renders him "trustworthy enough and like a seasoned fighter who guarantees victory" when looked at directly, but "a deserter by profession…for whom it is impossible to be true to anyone" when considered sideways (229). We suspect he hates the fact that he must think everything out, and in the same vein betray the one he loves. If only they would kiss, without reservation, and then, with corresponding passion, sing compline together.

Divinely Sanctioned Deceit or Self-Deception?

2 February *midnight* begins with an apparent *non sequitur* about the coincidence of theology and anthropology, about how our personalities, made as they are in the image of God, essentially shape how we conceive our maker. What he specifically has in mind is how YHWY in particular sanctions sagacious deceit so long as it is aimed at another's welfare. Either humanly or theologically speaking the diarist claims there is nothing universal about this viewpoint given that, for his part, he "cannot think of God without this poetic vigil over the honest invention of a troubled passion" and therefore harbors self-doubt about his own projection (230). On the other hand, Christ himself withheld information from his own disciples until he judged they could withstand the truth. This peculiar overlap of theology and anthropology, however, has everything to do with his relationship to her. Sagacity and deceit might be justified if God is on your mind, but entirely demonic if the urgent motivation is moral self-insulation. But in this case, her welfare and interest are what finally preoccupy him. Weirdly, as readers we cannot neatly distinguish piety from condescension, or either of these from genuine affection for his beloved. Theology becomes anthropology in the sense that the diarist can no more assure himself of divine self-transcendence than he can of romantic self-eclipse. His love for her therefore becomes a middle term, a lock and key barring the bedchamber behind a temple curtain, torn from inside out. All of which leaves him wondering whether he loves at all in the first place, whether the language of ordinary human affection is on his side or whether the deafening silence of his reservation is essentially depraved. What he cries is "Do not dampen my fervor, do not put out its fire; it is still something good even if it must be purified. Let me never learn to bargain; I still must win, even if the method is vastly different from anything I can imagine" (232). What he does imagine is that she straightforwardly loves him, un-problematically, while his own inner life and outward orientation "cannot coalesce into a conclusion" (232). And now his own sleep is disturbed, because he cannot tell—largely to himself and mostly to her—whether he is restless due to being in love or not being in love.

As with our analysis of comments made by Judge William in light of *Fear and Trembling,* so here the nocturnal rumination bears a corresponding resemblance to points made by Johannes de Silentio. The diarist even uses the same phrase—"the teleological suspension of the ethical" (230). As with Abraham the ethical principles in play for the diarist involve both deceit and something resembling filicide and how committing it may be either justified or demonic. Simultaneously admitting and then overturning Hegel's criticism of a purely formalist Kantian account of dutiful principles as spelling evil as much as good, the diarist invites us to reflect on the latter possibility *against* happier Hegelian resolutions. Casting both eminent philosophers to the wind, and like Abraham, the diarist invokes a set of paradoxical but nevertheless higher, divinely sanctioned principles: sacrifice without killing, lying without deceit, loving without losing, each of which seems impossibly unreasonable, but humanly necessary, for our own good. While it may be true it is better to have loved and lost than not to have loved at all, the diarist emphasizes just how difficult this prospect feels along the way and the sheer suffering the judgment call implies. One need not be either a neo-orthodox nominalist or a Feuerbachian anthropomorphist to simultaneously realize our limitations and tremble before the opportunities these afford and thereby know God by knowing something about ourselves and vice versa. The diarist will return to surmounting this heady theological impasse borne within our own souls later, but at this point the text is interrupted by another related literary insertion.

This second interpolation is a liturgical soliloquy that relays the story of a leper who concocts a salve that symptomatically turns the disease inward but renders one no less contagious. What seems tempting about this particular balm is that it allows one to enter the city gates undetected and take revenge on the priests, a route his fellow leper actually takes to the detriment of his spirit, having traded external acceptance for internal death, purity of skin for self-hatred. In contrast to such a ruinous choice, Simon, who invented the salve, stays behind in the desert, out of human contact, and yet interrogates himself with a series of questions, using us a readers to serve as his jury while posing them to YHWY as the ultimate judge:

> Does not an artist hide in order to be a secret witness to how his work of art is admired; why cannot I part company with this loathsome shape and only secretly witness people's abhorrence? Why must I be condemned to carry it around and display it, as if I were a vain artist who insisted on hearing the admiration in person? Why must I fill the desert with my shrieking and keep company with wild animals and while away the time for them with my howling? This is no exclamation, this is a question; I ask the one who himself said that it is not good for a person to be without companionship. Are these, then, my companions, are these the equals I am supposed to seek: the hungry monsters, or the dead, who are not afraid of being infected? (232–33)

The point is not about physical contagion, but rather about interconnected loneliness, the sympathy and compassion that occurs when two remain at a distance, incalculably indebted to one another, neither knowing the emotional harm they might inflict, with each fearing the worst but hoping the best. Artistically, the powerful lotion in question protects no one and cannot in the end serve as its intended ruse. As a writer, a poet, what the diarist has concocted is a remedy no actual leper could literally employ. Hence the several layers of irony when Simon thanks the God of Abraham for allowing him to invent an incredulous solution that solves nothing, expressing gratitude he was never tempted to use it, just after announcing he will throw the rest of the salve away and pleading with the same God that he might forget the formula. On one level this is a bit of literary play, but thematically the point is about how we long to be known and understood while being unable to speak what we most deeply feel when the poverty of our own expression is met with illicit usury by some crowd of moneylenders bent on twisting the meaning of our passions into something profitably grotesque. The tip of this particular literary arrow is at once aimed at God, at himself, at his beloved, and then at the clergy, which ends with the snarky but pointed ellipsis: "Whenever in the course of the year there is a sermon about the ten lepers, the pastor affirms that he, too, has felt like a leper—but when it comes to typhoid…" (234).

The anxiety this fictitious leper-turned-writer feels about his use of artistic power to both guard and display the purity of his heart in a palette of potentially repulsive misunderstanding is echoed by the diarist in the following *morning* entry. In this passage the leprous impression and inner significance of his feelings correspond to an erotic-religious *gestalt* between the diarist and his beloved, though of course this is only reported from his side of things. At the beginning of this report she apparently relishes the "seductive food for pride" displayed at some dinner party he associates with being "adored...by someone who scoffs at everything else" (235). At its social center such apparent pride emerged more clearly in mixed company, which "happened in such an unbecoming way that the people present were startled by it" (235). What happened exactly? He does not tell us. Did she shoot him an explicit glance, a disarming wink, or perhaps ruffle the hair on his neck for all to see? We don't know. All he writes is that in itself it was "a trifle" and that a "young girl is allowed much leeway—such a thing may only be playfulness" (235). What we do know is that she has already witnessed him overpowered with religious sentiments and deliver witty but snide commentaries on matters of supposedly high culture. However, her allegedly trifling playfulness and his cool ironic outlook overlap. The flirt and the critic somehow both figure into the peculiar romance between them. He does not want to be taken for a mere "adoring lover who worships a goddess" and she, presumably, wants to be taken seriously. Just after the sentence about a young girl's leeway he writes: "If only I were reassured myself, but I am afraid of worse conflicts. And if it were something other than playfulness, then I sense a colossal misunderstanding" (235). Notably, if it *were* something other than playfulness, then she would be serious, completely and even scandalously serious. That would mean her perception and attendant love were real, all the way down. We also know from the report generally that he abhors the thought of being mistaken for a mere seducer with an intellect as sharp and alluring as it would be emotionally tone-deaf. Purportedly, she is a pretentious flirt, he a seductive critic, each a mixture, in mixed company. All this external posturing may be rather disconcerting for us as readers, but for the diarist it threatens to break out in "erotic bickering about which one of us was somewhat extraordinary" when for him the "religious is my principle of equality," which has never fundamentally caused him to scoff at anyone (235). He seems to assume the elevated purity of her thoughts and feelings, and then suspects himself of free play, even as he interpretively explores the reverse. In conjunction, the religious principle of equality presupposed in relations between everyday neighbors asserts itself even more urgently between lovers, since the intimacy of the latter demands a more direct and ethically warm reciprocity from the fire that produces both the heat and light in any relation worthy of our devotion and delight. Amidst all this dialectical alteration where do they, and we, stand? Consider how the whole entry concludes: "Far from asking any extravagant tenderness of amorous affection on her part, I merely want her to express herself a little more so that I can see what is taking place within her. Despite all my endeavors, I really do believe that she regards me as a very sharp critic, and this stifles her freedom of expression" (235). Among other passages this one articulates the ambiguous trajectory of simultaneous belief and doubt from within a singularly longing heart. What the diarist intimates is how a religious ascent and romantic descent are interchangeable between those who are most truly in love. Yahwistic Agape and Socratic Eros have perhaps never been brought so close between two covers, alternately human and divine, and quite problematically incarnate, a baffling mixture of *mysterium tremendum et facinans* and elastic bodily attraction. This may very well be why the aesthetes preferred not to have women at their banquet. In terms of the present dinner party, I for one can only hope the actual fare was just as sumptuous.

A Pivotal and Possible Harmony

The *midnight* entry of 7 February is pivotal for our understanding of the ethical dissonance and possible harmony between religious and romantic ideals at the heart of "Guilty/Not Guilty?" Beginning with the passing operatic image of a dying whale lying still at the bottom of the ocean spouting jets of blood, this passage opens in earnest with an "objective" report on the relationship as if from a mere observer. We are told the point of this exercise is to "drain off the comic aspect of the affair," and having "shaken the foolishness," "drag and lift tragically the same affair as a burden" (236). The report opens with the supposition that "for her God is very much like what one pictures as a kind elderly uncle who for a sweet word does everything the child wants, just as the child wants. That is why one is so very fond of this uncle. One also has a certain unexplainable awe of God that does not become anything more" (236). Furthermore, she "loves a person more than she loves God. She swears by God, she beseeches in God's name, and yet with regard to the religious she is only romantic in the little multiplication table, and with regard to the religious she is *valore intrinseco* [according to intrinsic value], only an ordinary dollar" (236–37). In all this she apparently has no conception of "resignation, infinite resignation, the relationship of spirit, the absolute relationship of spirit with spirit," and therefore lacks "religious presuppositions" (236). In regard to pious sensibilities, as on other topics, with youthful nonchalance she "presumptuously says the first thing that comes to mind," all of which is charming in a feminine sort of way (236).

At this point the reader gets an initial sense of why such an "objective" report would not help the diarist. For one thing, the whole account is distinctively one-sided and vastly more presumptuous than anything we have actually heard from *her*. However, what he assumes, or imagines about her, seems to be a foil for articulating a stark, opposing point of view the diarist tellingly describes in the third-person:

> [H]e is just the opposite, he is religiously constructed; his romanticism has the magnitude of infinity, in which God is a powerful God, and seventy years a stroke of the pen, and a whole life on earth a period of probation, and the loss of his one and only desire is something for which he must be prepared if one wishes to be involved with him.... (237)

What seems to make this equally imagined third-person diarist an opposing helpmeet to her is that he is aware that the potential loss and corresponding sacrifice of a this-worldly, temporal desire is something for which one must be prepared. Far from being a kind, old, doting uncle, God (or the created order put in place) may require a harrowing form of endurance in the face of unforeseeable deferral. On the other hand, the diarist-opponent is not exactly her one-dimensional opposite. While the task may very well be to endure a thoroughgoing period of probation, to endure in his own case means "not to disturb for himself the only love that is happy, not to forfeit the only admiration that is blessed, not to lose out on the only expectation that endures, since the task, after all, is to endure" (237). The implication of this higher form of romanticism is that he explicitly cannot simply dismiss her swearing by God as childish naiveté: "when his [perspective] is so constructed, it follows that if a person is capable of bringing her relationship with him under a relationship with God, then the schoolchild's 'by God' becomes absolute—he is bound both in time and in eternity" (237). While he surmises that she lacks his compunction in swearing by and therefore holding God to a specific, temporal, and seemingly arbitrary passion that no mere creature should presume God is required to honor, the diarist nevertheless writes that even so, for himself, he must "by virtue of his relationship with God honor the claim down to the last farthing" (238). Her dialectic, so he claims, is simply that of desire, of the pleasant and unpleasant, without feeling "religiously bound," while his, presumably, is compounded by being doubly bound, to both her and his God (238).

We should absorb how potentially deceptive and misleading this report turns out. In imaginatively positioning himself from an objective point of view between both her and the God of Abraham, his and her actual positions split into one-sided halves, each with a separate but corresponding dialectic internal to itself that would give even Aristophanes a run for his money. And indeed, there is initially something "profoundly comic in this misrelation" (238). By way of illustration, the diarist cites the case of a Pharisee.

> Imagine an individual who is speaking with God in prayer and now it occurs to him to speak as follows: I fast three times a week, pay the tithe of mint and cumin. It is altogether comic, like the man who lay in the ditch and thought he was riding horseback. In other words, the Pharisee thinks he is speaking with God, whereas from what he says he is speaking with himself or with another Pharisee. (238)

The example becomes funnier still if, for instance,

> a saloonkeeper were to stand in church and talk this way in prayer, saying: I am not like the other saloonkeepers, who give only the prescribed measure; I give generous measure, and in addition that extra at the New Year—he is not thereby a hypocrite, but he is comic instead, since it is clear that he is not speaking with God but with himself qua saloonkeeper or with one of the other saloonkeepers. (238)

While certainly amusing in light of how laughable manageably circumscribed piety can become, this is the very comic dimension he seeks to "drain off" in order to tragically lift and drag the same affair as a burden. As far as the Pharisee and saloonkeeper are concerned, they could be in all humility holding themselves to sacramentally recognizable practices while the diarist entirely cheapens their endeavors by insinuating every pitch within human affairs merely occurs in a little league game. The diarist admits as much at the outset by writing we are indeed permitted to swear by God and that in doing so one could be either "of the truth" or a hypocrite (238). That the diarist is additionally all too aware of how potentially ridiculous such an ambiguous outside perspective makes *him* appear is confirmed by the dire fashion in which the objective report concludes:

> Therefore, one should never appeal to God for help with a wish, because one thereby binds oneself absolutely. That is, if the wish is not granted, God and I are not therefore quits, by any means, for that, after all, must be left to God, but I am obliged to hold to my word. I must at all times firmly maintain that it was and is my only wish, so earnestly, so eternally my only wish that I dared to give it a religious expression. In other words, if after the passage of some time I come with a new wish and promptly send for God again just as fussy parents send for the physician for nothing, what then? Then I have made a fool of God and also made manifest that I am a comic character who, far from being a hypocrite, assumed that *to pray to God* was the same as petting papa on the cheek and saying: *Bitte, bitte* [Please, please]. (238–39)

In turns out all this posturing and appeal to higher religious standards *vis-à-vis* her supposedly one-sided dialectic of desire and its pharisaical analogues caves in on itself insofar as the issue of swearing by God and external measurements of piety is really about standards of faithful expectation in wishing for the tangible salience and warmth of human goods in this life. Does one have the humble courage to appeal to God for help in granting such wishes? For if a wish does not come to fruition one could either stick to the wish, earnestly facing the forces of creation and holding God to an equally binding oath, or give it up and change course. In the latter case, one becomes not so much a hypocrite as a comic figure, as if a second-best alternative could dry the tears of unrequited love. Clearly comic is how the one who brings a wish to God confers a more than ordinary or simply fortuitous significance upon that desire, the content of which one then promptly gives up when fortune fails to smile upon it. Better, less reckless and less morally and psychologically problematic, would be to leave God out of it, which implies we best not place all our eggs in one basket. Take care, the diarist intimates, for the degree to which one invests, to that same degree the renunciation will have to take on an eternal significance; if, that is, one remains consistent, faithful to the content of earthly life and its meaning.[5]

The investment at issue here is not a monetary tithe and correspondingly one-dimensional sacrifice this might involve for any given saloonkeeper. In this case rendering to Caesar is no simple, divinely sanctioned civic obligation, but a positively charged matter of personal identity far beyond whatever is tax-deductible. And the terms of that possession are by no means secured through simple ownership and subsequent exchange. To receive the gifts of a life rich enough to be called truly human and to be willing to give them up is a drama on an entirely different scale. So by the time we get to the *bitte, bitte,* any breath of laughter is cut short by a choke. The tragic dimension is now in full swing. It is clear that, as a case of someone with a romantic wish, the diarist is casting about between an immediate erotic attachment and a safely spiritual form of regard, and that God somehow becomes a middle term threatening to break up the party, a threat the diarist seems to accept by ironically putting God and the forces of creation at a distance, without daring to swear lest he must render to *her* what Caesar could not even begin to evaluate. Nevertheless, the analogy to the Pharisee and saloonkeeper is arguably, however unfairly apropos, since once again they too might be holding to a genuinely sacramental vision of concrete embodiment and expression. A tithe of mint and cumin might be ambiguously ridiculous as a proof of piety, but how do things stand in regard to the diarist's love for *her,* a love so intimately bound up with renunciation? Should we laugh at the diarist because he is obviously expressing a failure of nerve in a divine tongue and to that degree is no more speaking with God than is the saloonkeeper? More than one reader

[5] Mark 10. 29–30.

has suspected what we have here is a pathetic lover burnt into ashes by his own lack of properly vulnerable nerve.

This passage continues with an enunciation of the pain of this particular and entirely subjective self-perception given the possibility that she may not share it. "Can one human being, then, not understand the other; is there, then, no equality in the religious?" (239). For his part he agonizes over how even if

> everything turns out all right and she really does help herself out of her misery or never was so deeply immersed in it, for me the religious nevertheless is so much the true meaning in life that it terrifies me if she is healed only in temporal categories. If one does not have this type of concern, it is easy enough to retire into empty, glittering glory, like a chosen one; but if my, if you like, high standard has disturbed her life, then she in turn holds me with her, if you please, lesser standard; she with her lesser standard is a mighty sovereign to me, because without her I am unable to complete any view of life, since through her I sympathize with every human being. (239)

The "religious," then, is not some aloof stance, some posture and perspective beyond the content of ordinary longing and aspiration, but a formal and nevertheless emotionally felt acknowledgement of what that very content embraces. Remarkably, such a religious vision fits with his not wanting to be some extraordinary, otherwise talented or important personage, but rather "a rank-and-file soldier, indistinguishable from all the rest" (240). And arguably, what makes him so believably authentic is the waffled report he provides after the so-called objective report:

> What will save her, as I thought at first and still do is a certain healthiness of temporality. I am convinced that even in the most crucial moment, when I made the separation between us, she did not comprehend resignation. Either she believed: now I shall die and then it will be over, but that is not resignation; or she hoped altogether spontaneously, but that is not resignation; or she picked herself up internally by virtue of her natural healthiness and was stimulated precisely now to take hold of temporality—but that is not resignation. (240)

But then what *is* pure and authentic resignation? Evidently it is a prerequisite, a precursor to a certain "healthiness of temporality"; it is the ability, the humble courage to acknowledge and own a desire, to be a faithful steward of one's pain, to stand firm against odds and yet believe. The diarist honestly cannot tell whether a genuine faith borne of a simultaneously sacrificial longing has appeared on earth, in either his or her own self, or more importantly, between them. All he knows is that he made the separation and drew the distinction. And we, as readers, are left to put it together for ourselves. If the "religious" is supposed to be a unique existential stage distinct from esthetic and ethical forms of habitation, then we must immediately call in a construction crew armed with planks, chisels, caulk, and paint, and for the love of God, offer them coffee and brownies during lunch break. We might speculate at least one of the workers will need a beer as another keeps twisting the tip off a screwdriver, while yet another repeatedly throws up his arms chanting *Agnus Dei* in some sort of Scandinavian accent with ladders all around.

Artistically Conversational and Counterfeit Feelings

17 February *morning* lays out the task and difficulty of their love in an everyday conversational sense. He begins by admitting he "cannot attain enough freedom from care to express love more erotically" and then hopes he has not rendered the affair far too big and serious in her estimation, adding that "all religious moroseness and severity" is foreign to his nature, "especially with regard to her" (241). Then follows an account of his ability to handle and pleasurably receive the trivial charm of small talk, which he manages to endow with a significance that seems to both surprise and gratify her. Somewhere in this proclivity he finds "some qualities" that could make him into an excellent husband: "I have a sense for insignificant matters; I have a memory for trifles; I have some talent in introducing a bit of meaning—all of which is very good over the passage of time" even though he suspects his overly reflective, inclosing reserve might cause him to wane in the conversational drama of a life together and that as a partner he would end by merely becoming "something by halves" (241). The sheer significance he places on handling "insignificant" matters and the romantic impulse behind them sets the reader's imagination to sail. For example, what do, or would, they actually talk about? Perhaps she makes a polite comment about the well-groomed improvement in the local conservatory, which he then

transforms into a piquant remark about the lilies of the field, a reference which jolts her just enough to dryly retort: "*really*, I *do* suppose you think Easter should be an annual rather than a perennial celebration, culturally speaking!" Momentarily confused, he might wonder about the virtues of any given lily relative to an evergreen, perhaps laugh, and then shut down altogether. How might one prosaically sustain such poetic banter over the course of a lifetime? The implicit answer is that it will require an attentive carelessness that spells a "freedom from care." In any case, the following purely formal passage invites some such charitable gloss:

> My reflection instantly seizes upon what she said, a little modification, and I have transferred it over into my sphere, and in this way the conversation goes by turns. Then she says something in her spontaneous way, a little modification, sometimes just a change of tone, and I am satisfied by the remark and have enjoyment over it. She cannot understand how such a comment by her can amuse me so much; however, she seems really gratified out of joy over the intimated high spirit that prevails in the conversation. She finds satisfaction in expressing herself, and then is surprised to see her remarks as the object of so much attention; I understand some level of reflection, add to it, rejoice over her—and thus we are both gratified. (241)

Surely one can neither account for nor dismiss this as anything other than an elaborate tease between a pair who can hardly remain reserved in each other's presence. Not even the birds of the air are so free, so fragile, or more unpredictable. As audience members we might witness such scenes and indirect dialogue as actors ourselves, trying to read a script replete with stage directions written for someone else, but nevertheless someone related.

Switching immediately to the present of the next day, *midnight* a year later, he has seen her on the street appearing pale. Given his anxiety over maintaining his "ecstasy" in the black light of "countless reflections" over time, and in conjunction with inadvertently learning from a local friend of the family physician whom he awkwardly presses for information that she is feeling quite well despite unspoken social alarms on all sides, he concludes his cavalier, though suspicious attempt at gaining an objective report by simply citing the torment one feels upon observing "a phenomenon where the phenomenon itself changes in relation to the observer" (242–43). Given the subatomic, astrophysical quantum analogue, the particles at play in this scenario have just as much to do with him as with her. In a new twist of subjective plot, we find she at one time "wanted to be something extraordinary—an artist, writer, or virtuoso, in short, to shine in the world" (243). This feature of her subjectivity sets sail his own imagination. An unhappy event, he continues, could be the catalyst for such inspired productivity, but he doubts any talented evidence of such artistically sublimated passion in her that would issue in such "enormous claims on life" (243). Of course, it is possible that some "catastrophe" could transform an otherwise untalented person into a poetic soul, but for his part, such a possibility is something he cannot understand since in his own self-estimation he confesses that from earliest youth he had "lived in the continual contradiction between seeming to be talented in comparison with the particular individual and secretly being convinced that I was good for nothing" (243). The reader must ask whom he talking about here: her or him or us? We know she lost her mother prematurely but benefits from the mollified warmth of a surviving father. All he feels he can offer is a tortured sense that everything dies in the end, which is and is not exactly a special leaven for poetic genius. First he sells her short, then he downplays himself; and we sit stunned and reflective. What does seem true is that pain and confusion are providentially productive, quite apart from whether they make one "shine in the world" or whether calculated ambition ever really amounts to anything. I suppose we would like our deepest values and actions somehow recognized, but part of the pain may lie in courageously knowing that a nameless hand held on an anonymous sidewalk is itself a justification for our existence. The issue here is about the objective validity of one's feelings, about whether our inspired passion can withstand the test of time by lurking outside oneself in the mirror of public estimation. Artistic productions are typically allusive in this regard. There is no real, imaginative act without an actual, but otherwise invisible muse. That tenuous strain is common to love itself in how intangible yet embodied the whole affair invariably is. Truly prompted feelings and their demonic expression ethereally intermingle. What the diarist is desperately trying to capture is the thoroughly spiritual and eulogistic nature of love through the fourfold polarity and interplay between artist and muse, each of them giving and taking with the left and right hands of subjective inspiration and objective tangibility. He does so by simultaneously toying with and casting suspicion on both his and her talent and what might be admirable about either of them. The bizarre confusion this engenders appropriately explains why we cannot tell whether the subject at hand is her, him, or us, and adding to these, publically recognizable talent or the reliability of loveliness in itself. It all morphs in the following paragraph:

> I am free and independent, unemployed, the servant of no man, of no other woman, of no conditions of life. I lie along the shore in my boat and wonder whether some phenomenon will show up out there. If she could emerge that way as an object of admiration, that would suit me fine, it would be the happiest existence I could imagine—secretly to see her admired, secretly to stake my last thought and my last penny so that the admiration could be jubilant. How impatience already boils within me! I can coax people, I can lie, demonstrate everything, flatter, squeeze the hands of journalists, write articles day and night myself—and admiration, after all, is for sale for money and for sagacity. I give up everything; it would be my happy fate to work secretly for her. And when it is achieved, when pain has energized her soul, when fortune and favor and flattery compete with each other to adorn the honored one, when her soul swells to the point of overweening pride—and she then passes by me triumphantly, then I shall dare to look calmly at her, my gaze will not be able to disturb her, for life will certainly have vindicated her against me. (243)

This may be an underhanded parody of Judge William's tribute to an aging actress in a long footnote when he is supposed to be lauding the beauty of his own spouse, but to render things even more veiled and confusing, the diarist confesses to fancifully considering whether it was his actual beloved behind some anonymous novel at the time, prompting him to "set everything in motion to convince people it was something superlative" given a tenuous bit of literary gossip as to the gender of its author. The purpose of this whole reflection is to raise and then leave unsettled the fundamental question: when we cannot straightforwardly distinguish whether the subject and direct object of the very question are separate individuals or one flesh, who is imaginatively, artistically, immortalizing whom? On the street, discerning whether another is pale, and knowing what this may or may not amount to, is very hard to read, as is the vain humility he reports a year earlier when with self-ironic honesty he draws the patently false distinction between bowing before *her* and exclusively genuflecting "before the relationship and the ethical task," as if she, or we, could not tell either how different these are or how facile the distinction ends up in the first place (244). All of which in his mind still amounts to a "vast misrelation" between them, the very sort of misrelation that pulses in the heart of any of us as we attempt to feel out the peculiar wound of a magnetically separable whole that is the common bond of any genuine romance.

20 February *midnight* continues the series of meetings that occur on Hauser Square near the city center of Copenhagen, the particular polis that serves as the backdrop to this specific engagement. The meetings themselves occur in the light of a confidential left-handed message delivered through a grapevine full of thistles meant to situate the recipient in a spot where she is left with qualified information intended to cinch and gauge her emotional interest with unlimited interpretive leeway, as if maieutically sent by the hidden God of Isaiah. As encounters go they are ambiguously orchestrated, doubtlessly tangoed by two, but *his* aim is clear enough: "She must be stimulated so that she does not get listless and become neither one thing nor the other, neither grieve nor win" (245). On the other side of the same coin he breathes as if he serves two masters:

> I do everything to work her loose, to wipe out everything between us, and then I also discipline my soul so that it may keep itself at the peak of my wish, so that if its fulfillment were ever possible it might be just as much aflame at the moment she is lost to me forever as it was when everything favored our union, as it was most intense of all when she knelt at my feet and pleaded. (247–48)

Given this aim at keeping love alive by trimming, drenching, propping, dusting, blowing, misting, covering, and otherwise replanting that love with fastidious care, the apparent content of the confidential correspondence can seem ethically ruthless, even downright ridiculous. In a darkly amusing reversal of everyday priority he writes concerning the correspondence: "Everything is correct, especially the names and years and days—the rest for the most part is fiction," after which he announces with apparent full conviction that

> she herself cannot possibly have a reliable conception of me and of our relationship; I have confused the affair for her far too much for that and changed it into a witch's letter that can mean just anything. Everything must be left up to her, and on no account must she have an authentic interpretation from me, for then she would never be healed. That she might be able to find herself completely again is my greatest wish for her, and I shall risk everything for that. Just a single reliable word of instruction from me would be enough for her to preserve in secret an impression of me that she must not have. (246)

Then follows a speculative, insecure ruse:

> My peroration in these two months, my definitely not brilliant but nevertheless true-to-character departure, was calculated to make me seem a depraved person. This is the primary interpretation. Such an interpretation has the effect of instantly making her suffering totally autopathetic, free of all sympathy, with the result that her suffering does not become at all dialectical to her, as if she had any fault, something for which to reproach herself. (246)

Such as it is, on the surface this strategy seems to be a kindly circumspect though not entirely laudable way out, as if one could seamlessly gain moral exoneration by taking upon oneself an illusory guilt in order to put someone else's self-examination at ease by playing the villain. But that is neither his intention nor the heart of the matter. The actual villainy, the real outrage he fears, lies in the "almost cavalier kind of sympathy" he nevertheless supposes he might illegitimately proffer and elicit by striking such an unbelievable pose and circulating such a blatant forgery of feeling (246–47). Suspended right next to what she will think and feel, what ethically irritates him is how third-party readers of the confidential communication might react: "I bet a hundred to one that all three of them after reading it will say, 'Well, he is nevertheless not as bad as I thought, he is indeed not entirely without concern.'" (247). If we had to locate the pivotal point of anxiety beyond which healing and rest remain a vivid longing, it would be the place where he can neither fathom nor accept how all his responsibility and panic over holding someone's heart well outside the emotional safety of its own cavity could appear so namelessly harmless and meet with such thoughtless unfeeling simply because it has no popular or pragmatic texture. What is truly frightening would be that all it takes is a little sympathy, that the human heart is as readily replaced as it is easily cracked, like the bricks that built Babel, born not only of a single tongue, but a narrow vocabulary. Little wonder then that in the next paragraph he seeks rest, not quite banishing all scheming thoughts:

> I concentrate all my thoughts on her, on my concern and on my wish. I refuse to be disturbed by anything, but I also wish to do what I regard as my duty. If it can be right to be a fool in the world for the sake of a good cause, then it presumably can also be defensible to be scheming, or rather I am afraid of a belated misgiving and regret if I have left anything unattempted. I do not think much of schemes, not because I do not calculate everything to the best of my ability but because the matter is so important to me. (247)

The indirect tactic he employs thus unravels from within, and is clearly intended to do so, not only for him, but also for her, and for us as third-party readers. The so-called confidential communication may not be the only way he could accurately signal his own feeling without either letting go or stringing her along, but since that is the aim, a more direct, alternative approach would implicate him just as responsibly. In fact, the explicit form of the diary itself by no means circumvents the morally peculiar position he finds himself in and seeks to authentically acknowledge. We should keep in mind it is with considerable anxiety that Taciturnus pulls it up from the bottom of the lake in the first place.

What is notable about the 28 February *morning* entry is the simultaneous reference to the future as recounted in the past: "I shall reach the religious with her" (248). Even a year later he recalls, "[a] few days ago there was a man who said of us that we were a properly engaged couple. Obviously, we are that indeed: she by virtue of her seventeen years and I by virtue of the artificial leg I use" (248). This ongoing temporal distention is an integral part of the religious itself, which calls for courage and perseverance against the ravages of time. At *midnight* the same day we get a finely detailed description of how their continued trysts on Hauser Square maintain a causal pattern of orchestrated chance. For his part, he realizes his "machinations are more or less futile," that for her part "she still does have strength," and that (a week later in the *morning*, a year earlier) on any given day a youthful optimism makes him rush to meet her even as her circumspect reticence gives him pause (250). The unanswered question is how this inner courtship might land itself safely on a domestic shore. "If it would always be like this, if I were capable of always being this way, no matter what it would cost me, then it would be easy to marry" (250). One thing that does not receive a lot of press is how the impulse the diarist has in upholding his moral obligation can only be explained in romantic terms. Most readers chastise him for breaking the engagement and are then outraged he would even attempt to musically finish the movement in another key. It simply sounds too dissonant, too disjointed and cruel. All of us harbor assumptions about when things should appropriately end, and these often reflect our mood and level of courage in any given moment. But then again, all of us have occasion to remember, revisit, and revise, hoping against hope that the needle bumping and scratching at the center of the record will one day land in a groove on the other side. At these other moments, any sense of unrealistic moral integrity is invariably colored by a particular longing, a desire to repair, embrace, or simply acknowledge a heartbreakingly glorious, undead past.

The same evening of 5 March our diarist pens the third of his narrative interpolations under what turns out to be the harrowing title of "Solomon's Dream." In truth, dreams can take on a tricky reality, so much are they a product of the imagination as they reflect ordeals undergone or explored in the light of day. The apocryphal one dreamed here in reference to I Kings 3:15 occurs one evening after Solomon inadvertently witnesses his father David writhing alone in penitential despair, which the son initially mistakes as mortal terror in the hands of a physical insurgent. After realizing there is presumably no courtly guard one can call for help in less mortal cases, Solomon goes back to bed. What Solomon then dreams is that

> David is an ungodly man, rejected by God, that the royal majesty is God's anger with him, that he must wear the purple as a punishment, that he is condemned to rule, condemned to listen to the people's approval, while the righteousness of the Lord secretly and hiddenly passes judgment upon the guilty one. And the dream intimates that

> God is not the God of the godly but of the ungodly, and that to be singled out by God one has to be an ungodly person, and the horror of the dream is this contradiction. (251)

Waking, Solomon is seized by the thought that to be chosen by God, to stand in the magisterial lineage of Israel, means that he must share with his father not an assumed, blessed legitimacy but a fundamental, secret guilt. According to the biblical record, it was the Lord who visited the son in his dream, granting Solomon his request for wisdom to rule well and discern good from evil over against a wish for long life, prosperity, and military prowess, a dream which occurs just before Solomon pronounces his well-known verdict concerning two harlots quarrelling over who was the true mother to the sole child that survived the night after both had given birth. Cutting the child in half is Solomon's initial famous proposal. Against this familiar backdrop, the diarist writes in passing that while this proposal enabled the prince "to separate truth from deception," his dream remains "less familiar" (250). This should be our clue that something more internally complicated is going on than a simple external separation of truth from deception, which some attention to the psychology of the two mothers will bring to light. Both mothers *know* whom the child in question *belongs* to. But *neither* of them knows what to make of the proposal presented by the confusingly wise king. The actual, biological mother clings to her fortune, while the other who suffered irreparable loss is willing to trade the truth at all cost out of a comparably equal and desperate longing. So they arrive at the table of justice. The former, actual mother is willing to suffer her own loss at Solomon's judgment for the first time by saving the child's life, while the latter is evidently willing to totally relinquish a child for a second time. The official version of Solomon's wisdom is that the true mother wins. Why? Because she more or less only relatively relinquishes her hold on fortune by letting her child go, thinking of its potential well-being beyond her invested attachment. That troubled resignation is the moral center of gravity that gets all the press. But what about the second mother, the one who under cover of darkness held to her wish, her longing, and then in witless desperation, traded truth for deception, and became willing to perform an equally grave sacrifice twice? As the diarist tells it, the secret behind Solomon's celebrated judgment is the unspeakable thought that one could hardly choose between these two, and that the two mothers represent an earthly host of lacuna, gaps which remain in the emotional fabric of our lives given the cruelty of fate and our whole and halfhearted attempts to face and control it. The chalk circle in question here concerns moments in a personal history where nothing adds up, no amount of moral math makes it come out right, where every choice implies a remainder in which each option implies an outcome relentlessly standing in the way of a rival good. What is striking about "Solomon's dream" is that according to the diarist the legendary Israelite judge became wise but not a hero, a thinker but not a man of prayer, a preacher but not a believer, and ends an unrepentant sensualist crushed and yet unraised, staggering through life, tossed about by bold infatuations, amazing fabrications, and ingenious explanations, and only helplessly helpful to those around him (252). Split in this way, it is as if Solomon became ceaselessly exhausted by a choice whose result was a kind of spiritual anhedonia, ecstatically wavering between simplicity of feeling and tortured reflection. All this is prompted by witnessing his soldier-musician-turned-adulterous-psalmist father figure, David, brought low, a sight so fraught with guiltless anxiety that the son in his own way never recovered but seemed to realize, quite on his own, that he had every capacity to throw a spear point-blank, quell anger with a harp, or fall terribly and problematically in love. The net result was that even the Queen of Sheba was stunned by the incomparably touching texture of Solomon's mere words and who, need we say, doubtlessly had plenty to offer herself. Thus the "less familiar" story behind Solomon's famed wisdom is having been an unwitting witness to the internal agony of a predecessor's supposed divine right of kingship. Although the external lineage is that of father and son, evocative in itself, the internal message is about what many witness, and dream about, when we try to make judgment calls concerning our talents and failures relative to what we see happen around us. What the diarist seems to draw from this, wise or not, guilty or not, is a palpable autopathetic sympathy that he desperately wants to *share*, in both senses of the term. It is possible the net result is not "Guilty" *or* "Not Guilty" but "Guilty" *and* "Not Guilty," neatly entitled "Guilty / Not Guilty?"

The following Wednesday the diarist surmises his beloved had received the confidential correspondence because she failed to appear on the street at the inexplicitly appointed time. She might have arrived a bit too early or late. He cannot tell. This speculative unknowing becomes a pretext for him to meditate on his own suspended state, emotionally as well as epistemologically. If he could only move on in sad recollection and from that protective distance, like one deceased, embrace the painful aspects of the affair while recalling the beautiful, then he would experience a resolution of sorts. But this he does not dare since the wires are still electrically live for him and perpetrating such a deception about *that* seems not just unconscionable but personally inauthentic. Still, "in the middle of the action, the play is far from over" since for him "the recent past is so far from being an epilogue that the engagement was rather a prologue and the play began when it was broken" (253). Having evoked the theatrical trope, he admits nothing is really happening—at least not "visibly and externally" (253). It is as if he is trying to write lines and give stage directions for the intermission during which not only the minor characters but also the major ones continue to live their lives. In this particular production, which may very well start to bore readers, if not to death then perhaps to their own life, the "action" occurs solely in the peculiar interior life of the diarist. Such would be true of someone like Othello as well, although on stage his lethal activity will likely get most of the press, as it typically does Abraham. Akin to his Shakespearean or Abrahamic counterparts the difficult time our diarist has expressing himself should come as no surprise. Nevertheless, we are enjoined to listen to him:

> What is all this for? Why do I do it? Because I cannot do otherwise. I do it for the sake of the idea, for the sake of meaning, for I cannot live without an idea; I cannot bear that my life should have no meaning at all. The nothing I am doing still does provide a little meaning. Any other attempt to forget, to begin all over again, to clink glasses with a friend and drink *dus* with a congenial person is impossible for me, although I well realize that my life would then be regarded as having deep meaning. Perhaps there is something wrong with my eyes, but I have never seen a friendship in which the one fired up the other to risk the utmost for an idea that has a bearing on personal existence. But I certainly have seen that—because the other (οετερος) [Please

> WRITE OUT WORD—{should be "ho heteros"] does not have the modesty about oneself that everyone has in his innermost being for a period—I have seen that their association taught them both to haggle and not take the world too seriously. Only a relationship with God is the true idealizing friendship, for the thought of God penetrates to the point of separating mind and thoughts and does not arrive at an understanding through chatter. (253)

What the diarist longs for and is trying to articulate is a religiously colored romance and romantically infused faith with the sense that our lives actually mean something, something global, even unearthly, and that this significance involves another particular embodied individual and not someone to simply and amicably raise glasses with in facile intimacy. Rather it involves someone who tears us apart, someone who with their tongue and sword divides parts of ourselves that have sagaciously congealed, severing what we know or thought we knew from what we have secretly felt, or intended and left buried. That a human relationship and a divine idealization overlap in that account is par for the course. In contrast to both Simon Stylites and the bridesmaids of the gospel, the diarist lies awake with this thought and passion, not for the sake of a remarkable ascetic show or to simply keep a lamp filled with oil and win the right to slumber in the meantime, but to stay engaged against the horrific backdrops of either empty or noisy stage-productions, each as perilous as they are mute. The greatest threat is a lack of salient significance, where everything appears either trivial or useless. As a test of perception this requires confirmation from those with eyes to see and ears to hear.[6]

A Rhetorical Three-Way Street

A week later he still cannot definitively tell if she has received his indirect correspondence, but this uncertainty gives way to the definite realization that he is fairly unable to direct the traffic on this particular two-way street. As far as external evidence goes he garnered news that her father has planned an uncharacteristic jaunt to a country manor, which sets his imagination on edge, thinking she might just give up and

[6] Proverbs 20:12, Ezekiel 12:2, Matthew 13:11–13, Mark 4:11–12, Luke 8:9–10.

choose a lot away from things, "drugged in the analgesic relief of quiet sorrow" and there remain decisively offended (254). It turns out the whole trip was over an economic affair concerning a farm for rent, which the diarist finds out after speeding a hundred miles in sixteen hours and impetuously assaulting a horse-driver twice his size who promptly threw him to the ground along the way. The reader of course is not sure whether to laugh, cry, or roll their eyes at this Dostoevskian escapade. But the hand inside the glove of this tragicomic snapshot is how it will all appear "in the eyes of the world," which he hastens to add is "but blindness" (256). The diagnosis he floats is a muted echo of part of the Young Man's speech (42). In that speech the imaginary protagonist in question speaks eloquently, enigmatically, hilariously, and unknowingly about love, with veiled eyes, like Socrates before Phaedrus. Reflecting on the purported contradiction between involuntary passion and free agency, the Young Man likens the phenomenon of love to a man who jumps into a tub and "as he somewhat confusedly surfaces again grabs for the bath rope to steady himself" but then "mistakenly grabs the chain of a shower" (42). The diarist transposes this tipsy commentary into the earnestly evaluative key of how his own troubled and paradoxical passion will no doubt be received. In the eyes of "the world" he is presumably a scoundrel, and yet this verdict could qualify him as heroic, honored, and esteemed. In a rather mixed rhetorical declaration the diarist says: "Let it choose between an abandoned girl who bows her innocent head in sorrow and seeks a hiding place in the country so that she can grieve—and an actor in the theater of life, a brazen fellow who keeps his head up and defies everybody with his proud eyes—the world's choice is soon made" (256). What choice does the world supposedly make so soon? The answer is by no means rhetorical, but contains a genuine question:

> A man is given a lifelong fine for an accidental injury, but I, I have no verdict pronounced on me. Condemned! I incite people against me, and they shout, "Bravo!"; I wait for them to kill me, and they carry me in triumph. I tremble, I doubt whether I have the strength and the courage to bear the world's verdict, whether I do not owe it to myself to place myself in a better light, but I do not falter, and I pull the cord to the shower—and the world's judgment is utterly favorable. (256)

What judgment indeed will the world, the reader, deliver, given that he has apparently "not found ten men who are capable of judging rigorously?" (256). He does not actually know. In a deadly serious parody of what appears to be a comic shuffle between Pilate and Herod, he only hopes for leniency untouched by bombast. And in the midst of it all he wrestles with "you," with "despair," with "merciful God"—the references seem interchangeable—only to relax his pen and confusingly burst forth with: "I rush out there, I win her once again, I give up everything in order to challenge with gold all the splendor of the manor house, I have a wedding, and I shoot myself on the wedding day" (256).

Throughout the *morning* entries in March the diarist reports "no new symptom." Symptom of what, we might wonder? Anger, offense, failure of nerve, despair, love, any sign of the impractical investment he both longs for and fears from her and in himself? During this period there is simply no news about "whether in the spiritual sense this is growing weather and the beautiful flower is sprouting in secret or whether stormy weather is brewing" (257). All we can do is reach for the bath rope, or shower chain, depending, and wait for grace, for confirmation or any word from without, any comic dispensation serious enough to provide meaning worth both living and even dying for.

In mock self-consolation akin to someone unwilling to reinvent gunpowder for the first time, the diarist finds himself in an odd position regarding religious prototypes. Distinguishing himself from sober teachers with official posts, blockhead preachers performing an entrechat in the pulpit, and pious enthusiasts whose company perfectly pagan native Americans would fear as much as they did orthodox Spaniards, the diarist is uncomfortably nestled between the textual sheets that tell tales of the simultaneously tragic and comic exemplars, heroes, and saints who populate his imagination. Strictly in his own voice he declares: "I am really no religious individuality; I am just a regular and perfectly constructed possibility of such a person. With a sword hanging over my head, in peril of my life, I discover the religious crises with a primitivity such as if I had not known of them before, with such a primitivity that if they had not been discovered I would have to discover them" (257). Born into an interpretive community that includes both the father of faith and the son of God, he finds he is nevertheless quite alone, understanding very little except that everything depends on personal "appropriation," a willingness to hold the knife and love that hard, come what may. In his case he lurches away from simple-minded enthusiasm and suspects he has thereby placed God that much more at a distance and is therefore left only with the nascent sense that his romantic involvement, with all the ambivalence surrounding it, forms a test, a religious ordeal. The issue is whether figuring into the deep gladness of a fellow creature separate from oneself is a drama requiring repentance from the beginning, as if the very meaning of communion, sexuality, parenthood, springtime growth, music, every practical or artistic achievement, large and small, including breaking bread, basic husbandry, and marriage itself, implies death along the way. An inseparably Trinitarian God might even pause to ask such a question, with a Christ on the cross beseeching the father and promising a Spirit, a Christ all-too-human and all-too-divine and ostensibly leading a bunch of sheep. No wonder then that the diarist longs for an Archimedean place to stand outside his hard-felt, tortured, and foolish passion. Gasping for breath, he writes:

> No! If I had not believed that I had a divine counterorder, I never would have retreated, and as soon as this order is revoked I shall choose my wish again. God forbid that the effort and the tension weaken my wish before this is allowed! My counterorder I can understand, for it goes through repentance. A repentant individual who is able to take a whole lifetime to recant cannot advance. This is a very simple protest against marriage. I have neither visions nor dreams to guide me; my collision is quite simply the collision of repentance with existence, a collision of suspension with a present actuality. Until it is resolved, I am *in suspenso*; as soon as it is resolved, I am free again. This is why I am doing all I can to keep myself at the pinnacle of love. As soon as she is free, the religious crises are my task. (261)

The origin and status of this counter-order are indeed mysterious, indelibly written on the soul of a personality implacably sensitive to another's freedom, feeling, and self-possession, and without knowledge whether it really *is* a matter of life and death. He cannot repent of the potential pain he has caused, nor does he apologize for his own tears, as ridiculous as it may seem; but he does intimate a severely grave emotional upset on her part would awaken and sever him from his "lethargy of depression" even as he sleeplessly "conjures up anxieties with which no pen dares to become involved," haunted by a conscience that "gives a start of alarm and terrifies with optical illusions" (262). A charitable way of reading all this waffled rumination is to say not all sacramental ways of thinking and experiencing the ordinary elements of our inner life follow a visibly coherent pattern. Our attempts at constructing and enacting such a pattern often amount to sending a couple gargoyles, scraped off with the shingles from the roof of a bungalow at one time shared and wings broken off in the mail, to a divorcé out of mixed compassion and genuine protection. We are all priests dropping the host on the floor where seeing-eye dogs of the congregation become irresistibly interested. Ostensibly, that is what the host—the body, the bread, the blood, the wine—is there for. Syrophonencian or Canaanite, any mother with a daughter suffering from a demonic psychological malady knows this.[7]

The 25 March *morning* entry circles back to the topic of youth and old age under the heading of an Aristotelian question about happiness to reconfirm the sense in which the diarist and his beloved are at once a joined and severed pair, sharing between them the existential poles of *eudaimonia*. On the lower end of the spectrum happiness consists of being a pure and innocent sixteen-year-old girl with nothing to her name other than a confirmation dress and hymnbook. Added to this innocence is the ability to dance, with the proviso that she "goes to a ball only twice a year" (263). This relatively unproblematic marriage between aesthetic and religious values takes a complicated turn when that same youth, "sixteen summers old," "sits busy at her work and still has the time to steal a glance at him, at him, who owns nothing, neither a chest of drawers nor a tall cupboard, but is only a copartner in the shared wardrobe, and nevertheless has a completely different explanation, since in her he possesses the whole world, although she possesses nothing at all" (263). In bold contrast, our vision of happiness turns suddenly dark and cold as we turn to consider the "unhappy one," the "rich young man, twenty-five winters old, who lives across the street" (263). Between

[7] Matthew 15:21ff and Mark 7:24ff.

these upper and lower poles, it seems that when love strikes true, it awakens the soul from its dreary slumber only to make one painfully aware of how the very poverty and plenty of desire is our greatest treasure, easily lost, often squandered, and always incalculable. It makes one feel simultaneously young and old, naïve and jaded, elatedly impervious and entirely vulnerable. Given this paradoxical state of affairs it comes as no small terrible surprise that the diarist wonders why nine months in the womb were enough to make him an old man, with eyes wide open enough to see the qualitative import of life only during twilight. Whatever the economic or emotional case, the faithful lover or charitable reader, and all those with eyes to see, are supposed to perceive that a person sixteen summers young and someone twenty-five winters old can actually be the same age. This may take only three months or a lifetime to figure out.

Dreams of a Common Language

Alluding on 27 March to the illicit union of Ixion with a mirage of Hera that gave birth to a race of monsters and sentenced the former to a fiery wheel in Hades, the diarist defends the legitimacy of embracing a theory, a cloudy interpretation, "as a means of exercising, to unbuckle the soul in it so as to give one's energy new elasticity" (263). Although this vaguely sounds like a nocturnal emission it occurs at the conscious tip of a pen. What he is sorting out is whether and how what he imagines about her embodies a real form of passionate faithfulness, whether and how his midnight thoughts, his morning memories, his mere words committed only to a page, constitute an actual entangled embrace or a potential rescue, if there really is a prospect of her drowning, as the ensuing imagery suggests. In a following paragraph, he actually illustrates the ethereal substance of the very longing contained and released in carefully chosen words. "What a strange power," that paragraph begins by exclaiming, "a single word has when, as in this case, it does not accommodate itself in the context of a speech or a sentence, so that one pays attention to it only in passing, but without linguistic connection it stares at one with the incitement of an enigma and the assiduousness of anxiety!" (264). The single "word" hovering without apparent reference at the opening of this paragraph splits apart and lands in an overall multivalent context. That word itself could be *murder, love, guilt, death, hope, sorrow, forgiveness,* or *possibility,* each one fully loaded, every other cartridge a blank. Whatever it might be, the singular word he has in mind is no doubt directed at her, but requires so many other words, each of them modifying the other, that taken together give rise to multiple interpretations. One reading that haunts and depresses the diarist is the one in which it is

> as if there were another kind of real truth in this word, as if I were floating on the rush-fringed lake one quiet evening, as if I heard her scream, and I took to the oars—and I saved her life, but she never became a human being again. Anxiety and pain and perplexity would have slowly picked at the lock of consciousness until despair managed to dissipate the lovely nature of this lovable womanliness. (264)

This is one version of the story he wishes would evaporate or take flight in order to signify another, more hopeful and elevated series of implications. However, even as he tries his best to express a heartfelt thought, he finds himself having to break it down into smaller explanatory parts only to end in the position of a teacher insulting both parties. The problem is that any meaning, any set of references, must be shared by a common understanding. But since any communication is hardly ever unmediated—another way of saying there is no such thing as a private language—words pose a fundamental threat even as they make possible a meeting of distinct minds, just as severed as the original beings in Aristophanes' tale. With this anxious dream of a shared vocabulary swimming around in his head, the diarist contrasts his horrific dream with being in her actual presence:

> And yet if I were just sitting with her, just that I dared to be in her presence, that I dared to do everything even if it is nothing—that would still be a relief, a relief that, like a smoldering, is an uninterrupted dull pain but not so much a suffering. Then she would confuse everything; she would believe that as before we were sitting in the boat on that lake we sailed together, and then we would exchange, if not winged words, then expressions of madness, and would understand each other in madness, and speak of our love as

> Lear wanted to speak with Cordelia about the royal household and ask for news from it. (264)

What the reader should notice about this passage is how words from afar and silent presence are two sides of the same coin, prompting a similar anxiety, and arising from a similar longing for an often elusive full communion. What brings us together is the same thing that easily divides us, whether the model we have in mind is a printed lexicon or actual body language. Furthermore, the reference to Lear should remind us that a blessed reunion might only occur, or result, in a fresh and original prison occupied by two alone in which we revert back to the inarticulate and weepy condition of childhood Augustine describes, and so impressed Wittgenstein as he kicked away the ladder of his Vienna circle.[8] The paragraph in question ends with the ultimate cessation of any communication altogether.

> But to be separated from her! And if she died—then the one who was nearest and dearest, perhaps the only one who had a whole lifetime, be it short or long, to mourn for her, he would be the only one not seen among the mourners or, rather, he would be prevented from riding in the carriage when the funeral procession followed her to the grave, even though he would know as well as anyone that one who is dead is the most powerful of all! (264–65)

Opening with a startling, decontextualized word, about which the reader keeps guessing, this section ends with graveside silence. Between the strength of a single word standing apart like a dark horse and the sheer power of death, the weakness of love ideally joins the mute absence of meaning with a clear present of understanding; it makes a house into a home, turns a sleeping arrangement into a bed, swings a porch into a paradise, each word granted flesh. What the diarist suspects is that the average reader may have a small sense of how a Eucharistic host on the tongue and sexual union are so similarly related or how much pillow talk is for no one else's ears, a sense that almost drives him literally out of his mind.

---

[8] Augustine, *Confessions*, Book I:8; and Ludwig Wittgenstein, *Philosophical Investigations* (Oxford: Basil Blackwell, 1968) 2ff, translated by G.E.M. Anscombe.

The rest of this entry articulates the sorrow he feels, perplexing in part because it seemingly cannot be shared. He has language enough within, "as the heart invents it," but thinks of himself "as if mute" and "disabled," all the while oddly craving "the eloquence of a mime" (265). What he suffers from is what lovers of any depth typically experience: the inability to heal those rifts that regularly emerge between creatures so closely knit and yet carrying around separate inner lives. These fissures can be sexual, psychological, moral, or spiritual, usually in spider-web combination. Such fragmented insecurities and subsequent wounds often do not come about as a result of any clear intent to establish painful breaches, but neither are they mere accidents of fate occurring outside the pair. Rather, they internally occur within each of us as individuals, fraught with a mutual responsibility the other simultaneously assumes and endures at whole dollar expense. No wonder then that the diarist finds himself distinguishing between autopathetic and sympathetic forms of suffering, a distinction that ultimately folds in on itself.

When we suffer autopathetically the pain arises from within; the pain is ours alone and we are prepared for it. The diarist is able to steel his will against it with clear and knowledgeable acceptance, and thereby knows where he stands. In contrast, when suffering sympathetically, his report is that "I have to use all my power, all my ingenuity, in the service of the appalling to reproduce the other's pain, and that exhausts me" (265). Putting the two forms together, he writes that when "I myself suffer, my understanding thinks of grounds for comfort, but when I suffer sympathetically, I dare not believe a single one of them, for I cannot, of course, know the other one as accurately as I can know whether the presuppositions are present that are the condition for its effectiveness" (265–66). This brazen self-confidence and uncoordinated self-doubt make him approach and flee as if his weapons were but straw, and his straw a sword, a pen, and plowshare all rolled into a singular inexpressible tear. If and when she gets "free" of this affair, he would not be without sorrow, but shall, he concludes, have peace, as blessed and soothed and happy "as the weeping willow when it is swayed by the evening breeze" (266). Of course, we cannot quite believe this; but neither does he. What remains, "at present," is a fundamental fear, a fear not of the world, nor of her loveliness, but a fear of an "unhappy responsibility, an unhappy understanding with the eternal meaning in life" (266). An echo of the previous *morning* entry, the unhappiness in question here indicates a summer of discontent with what we would, but cannot, orchestrate between ourselves and a beloved. And so he and we along with him are left reading an invisibly written reconstruction of a legal boundary dispute that only an experienced lawyer could fairly interpret, as it were, after the facts: "Guilty / Not Guilty?" In this kind of case, there is here not so much the banality of evil, as Hannah Arendt diagnosed in the case of Adolf Eichmann, but its true origin, borne of two innocents otherwise doubting themselves and trying to move forward.

On the *morning* of 2 April we witness the bubble of autopathetic-sympathetic introspection burst from within at the diarist's own poke. Prearranged, he poses "a situational question to give her the chance to express her feelings" (267). What might he have asked? The text does not explicitly tell us. Perhaps he coolly inquired whether weeping willows could be considered happy despite the obvious prejudice they endure in the eyes of the world. In any case, whatever the nature of his desperately clenched interest may be, she straightforwardly declares that she does not care for him at all and cannot understand what he wants with her (267). Although the reader may find this rebuff just as hard to believe as the notion he harbors about her freedom and his peace, let alone happiness, her sharp and arguably fair reply should give rise to wild applause. Not because she told the truth, at least directly, but because they are obviously so equally decentered in regard to one another. His own reception of this rash, irritated outburst speaks for both of them. On the one hand the whole exchange highlights the lack of confidence he feels in his "view of life" such that any use of force would be crushed by her selfsame strength (267–68). On the other hand the explosive reply to his no doubt manipulative inquiry, which he received full in the face, reduced with white lightning the "ideal figure whom I embraced with the concerned responsibility of an eternal commitment" to something "so insignificant that I could scarcely discern her" (268). Between the flashes "she does open up for me a bright prospect" in which his depression "is as if blown away" such that what finally appears before his eyes is this: "by Jove, such a little miss!" (267–68). What is finally revealed by this startling diminutive is an incredibly fragile, frustrated tower of weakness that could at the same time level an entire army of inclosing reserve. In our attempt to put it all together, we could say she could not care for him less, which she evidently does; and he can do without her, which he obviously cannot. So it frequently goes.

On his part, this recollection of such a gloriously prospective downfall is momentarily overtaken, at *midnight*, by the possibility of her going mad. His exit in the guise of a scoundrel was partially intended to avoid foisting upon her the difficult task of loving a worthy beloved while losing him at the same time, a task that might very well test one's sanity. Strictly but narrowly speaking it is easier to suffer the loss of someone who turns out unworthy, but in this case the guise can only be partial on his part if he is to avoid a more complete insult while trying to preserve an equally partial honor on her part. That she probably suspects and may have been reflecting upon the difficulty of *this* task *on his part* is precisely what he fears, a prospect he neither can nor apparently desires to avoid. The difficulties all around must simply play themselves out, and no one can tell, either to oneself or another, how it will end ahead of time. This is to say, no one can tell whether the test is fair or whether it would finally crush anyone beneath the waves of over-consideration. What preoccupies him is not only the half-measured impotence of attempting to stand firm and aloof and to conversationally drop "a few hints in a joking and chatty tone in order to make her aware," but also how she is indeed reflective enough—despite his occasional characterization of her—to see through his whole procedure and therefore regain a handhold on his true feelings. Thus the worry he expresses about her sanity concerns not only the task of being unable to dismiss him as a scoundrel, but also the prospect of inciting her own honor against the thought that it is she who is unworthy in light of some extraordinary quality on his part—as if it were the case that he were especially handsome or charming, a poet, a scholar, a Joseph amidst brothers. She might have to contend with some positive comparability that vies against a truly reciprocal attraction, investment of feeling, and sense of self-worth. The temptation would be to correspondingly dismiss him for those purportedly matchless reasons. That such reasons could arise from a false projection on her part rather than a deliberate deception on his makes little difference, since what is more likely is that she would helplessly consider him a mere eccentric without a qualitative judgment attached to the thought, in which case she is equally left in a nameless scenario of curious reserve. Entertaining these imaginary ghosts that are supposed to frighten her away from reflection and back into self-possession curiously evaporate since she once remarked, no doubt with a measure of sarcasm, that it must be dreadful for him to be able "to explain everything this way" (274). This comment suggests she understands as well as he the cost of "ceaselessly gazing at the dubious interpretation of an eternal responsibility" and that the way of madness still lies open, as unprotected as are any of us against perfectly ordinary throws of thwarted affection (274).

Continuing the drama, three days after offering her an initial chance to express her feelings he "received the declaration and the last will and testament to and confirmed by—my little confirmand, for this is precisely the impression she makes on me, such a little miss" (275). What exactly she said or did remains equally unclear. The only information we have is that from anyone else he would have suspected "a bit of coquetry" and that "in her behavior there may be an acknowledgment of me against her will, for it is a kind of obstinacy" (275–76). Apparently whatever it is she "confirmed" is as much a function of our interpretation as it is of his. Perhaps she has developed her own art of indirect communication as she presumably works out a meaning of this whole affair for herself, as mixed and compelling as that affair has obviously become. If we had to give her theatrical lines at this point they might be "*spare me*," a line that would certainly contain enough dual significance to occupy both of them and undoubtedly be tragically amusing to witness an analytical linguist try to explain.

A Possibility Split Three Ways

The fourth narrative interpolation, entitled "A Possibility," is a sketch of the inner life scenario of a reserved, attractive, punctilious bookkeeper with a penchant for foreign languages and decided talent for drawing, but otherwise unacquainted with the ways of the world who "only once" had suffered from a premonition that he had "forgotten to be young and to let his heart be cheered in the manner of youth while days are still there" (282). This "intimation" that there might be something missing in his life is followed by an account of an "excursion to the woods" that "ended with un unusually splendid dinner party" with a couple fellow employees known to take pity on the naïve recluse by coaxing him to join them on various outings. Normally curbed and even elevated by his quiet gentility, but wanton as the two colleagues already were on this particular occasion,

> his shyness was merely an incitement to them, and his own painful awareness of it incited him in turn, and all the more as the three of them became heated with wine. Carried along by the others and overexcited, he became a completely different person—and he was in bad company. Then they also visited one of those places where, strangely enough, one pays money for a woman's contemptibleness. What happened there, even he himself did not know. (283)

After a period of simultaneous dejection and increased diligence, confusion and external success, the bookkeeper fell ill, "sick unto death" (283). Not unlike Adam and Eve in the garden he suddenly awoke to a half-lit recollection of what he had done, or not done, or might have done, and with that dim memory, sensed a mortal loss of innocence. Having his morally dreamlike existence shattered in this way he rose from bed one day to face the possibility of having fathered an illegitimate child for whom he must take responsibility. This potential consequence of his fall from grace—which, like so many original sins, could not be confirmed—merely crouched at his tent-flap as an indefinite cause of anxious concern that could at any moment turn into full blown despair. Meanwhile he flourished as before until the head of the firm died, leaving him a considerable fortune and the leisure to close accounts and pursue his physiognomical studies full time while daily pacing the flagstones between Børuehus Bridge and the south end of the street in unnerved reverie from eleven till noon.

The hereditary point of this physiognomic research was aggravated in the course of things by a repeatedly tactless double-entendre witticism on the part of his mother's cousin with whom he had taken up residence after his parents' death. No one could be sure, not even a married man, this older bachelor would joke, how many children he had. Thus a combination of the young bookkeeper's inclosed reserve and "the joking of the babbler worked upon the poor fellow so long that eventually his understanding became earnest about making a change because it could not go on serving in such a household, and the bookkeeper exchanged understanding for mental derangement" (285). Among the shifts in his service, and no doubt partially as a result of his inconclusive studies, the bookkeeper became extravagantly charitable to the children of Christianshavn, although this did little to allay his troubled sensibility since it only seemed as if he were "buying his freedom from the most sacred duty" by potentially giving alms to his child (286). Among the double-entendres on the table here one should include his subsequent fear of gratitude, lest it constitute a curse even as it only further endeared him to the poor.

The aggravated anxiety prompted by his elder cousin's insipid remark which drives him to take up other residence is tellingly contrasted with bimonthly visits to a local café where he had established a good-natured relationship with a sailor in his seventies, easily misled to mistake the forty-year-old bookkeeper for someone of sixty. The captain in this case showed no trace of "having been knocked around in life in any other way than as a sailor" and who as a younger man, we are told, "had in all decency been a jolly fellow" (287). While "indefatigable in telling lively stories about dance halls in London and escapades with the wenches, and then about India," his look nevertheless "had such dignity and his whole character was so attractive that one would indeed dare to vouch for his life and for his dash as a sailor" (287). Thus when the two clink glasses to their supposedly mutual and equally healthy-minded sense of lost youth, the bookkeeper found in the deception of his sixty years "a contrasting corollary of the all too heavily brooding earnestness of his mental disorder" (287). What we witness here is a second possibility for our well-off, middle-aged bookkeeper so poor in spirit: the possibility of making it through to the other side of innocence and experience with his "vitality unimpaired" and able, in the end, to raise a drink unruffled, to indeed live, pray, sing, tell old tales, laugh at gilded butterflies, hear of court news, take upon himself the mystery of things, as if he were God's spy, and generally share in a higher madness in which guilt and responsibility, blessing and forgiveness cancel each other out beyond the pale of publicly sanctioned calculation.

Between fully embracing this highly comic, alternately mature posture and remaining submerged by his overwrought rejection of bourgeois insipidity, the bookkeeper appears helplessly caught, not by just one possibility, and then a consequential second, but by multiple possibilities. Like a file, possibility works in various ways, dulling raw material that is hard and sharpening that which is soft, unlike less graceful tools, such as a hammer. Thus the narrator reports, "[e]very new possibility the unfortunate bookkeeper discovered sharpened the saw of concern that he was drawing all by himself and the bite of which he himself suffered. It would not have helped him if someone had wanted to help" (286–87). This observation can be read from both directions, couched as it is between the cousin and the sailor. On the one hand the raw material in question is indeed soft—the pliable, misty memory of choices made and unmade, of desires obscurely fulfilled and left wanting, of possible selves namelessly embraced and turned down. Were the material more substantial, the guilt more clear, the need for forgiveness more circumscribed, a certain edge could be filed off by the prospect of roads yet untaken. On the other hand any suspense lacking a definitive result, infused by adolescent confusion, can become razor sharp, both terrifying and deadly in its own way. Read together, the sailor's jocular poise represents a higher resolution of the cousin's sinister double-entendre, although the ambiguity remains.

Part of what is so telling about this sketch is how the vaporous narrator reports secondhand conjecture and inside knowledge side by side with such ironic authority. The rumors, we are told, are so privately held that our storyteller has heard only one; namely, that the bookkeeper had once been in love with a queen of Spain, a rumor so delicious it is difficult to believe but hard to dismiss, although it does nothing to explain his more obvious attention to potential orphans (279). What we have here is a narrative about the kind of isolating insecurity we typically carry within us along life's way juxtaposed with a partial map of our vain attempts at humble self-knowledge as we try to salvage a genuine, but mediated sense of ourselves amidst the morass of interpersonal failure. The mood is at once detached and tender, pathetic and humorous, all above and below and finally beyond the heterogeneous froth of "aims and goals that prompt the inhabitants of the capital to such noisy and busy activity" (277). As a last word and testament the narrator finally joins the elder cousin at the bookkeeper's funeral and, in earnest jest, notes "his having no family to inherit whatever fortune he might have left behind" and laughingly mourns "his not having married and left children" (288). The reason the diarist inserts this story is probably to invoke the difficulty of taking responsibility for wrongs committed when all we intended to do was embrace good things, and the corresponding difficulty of not quite apologizing for it. Possibly.

Perhaps with the poor bookkeeper, his insufferable cousin, and haplessly jovial sailor in mind, the next evening on 6 April the diarist cites the facile dinner party banter of a couple of clever ladies who along the way let fall hints that a broken engagement certainly would be forgivable if the girl in question were several bulbs short of a chandelier. Such light-minded insight would be fair enough if the insight these ladies had in mind was the emotional intelligence of knowing the awe and responsibility of falling in love and feeling the particular worth of a singular commitment. However, what they insinuate is the snobbish street-smart wisdom lacking the interiority of endowing earthly pursuits with a lasting significance and the devastating wit that levels everything to an inside joke for all those collectively immune to genuine laughter. In contrast, the diarist is more than willing to seem a prude, to seem "the poor manikin who could not manage to love more than once, the straitlaced bungler who was so narrow-minded as to take seriously that beautiful phrase about the first love and could not regard it as a coy cliché that experienced and at least half-experienced young women banteringly toss around among themselves at the supper table" (291). Striking such an ambiguous pose the diarist lets us in on the truly comic by revealing his inner appreciation of not only "how loathsome but also how ludicrous it is that falling in love, the ultimate in earthly life, is supposed to be nothing more than an invention of sensuality, being in heat as the animals are, or a game of wittiness and a partnership of clever people!" (292). That the matter at hand is a question of emotional intelligence is indirectly signaled by what any given reader, any given lover, any mere observer, person of faith, or lackluster philosopher might in fact find laughable, merely silly, or positively nauseating in the talk during such a meal. No doubt nervously enclosed within himself, the diarist impetuously subtracts the true content from the surrounding speech and erupts with: "When falling in love—that is, the eternal in falling in love—is absent, then the erotic, despite all possible cleverness, revolves around less than four marks and eight shillings, revolves around what becomes nauseating because spirit *qua* spirit wants to have an ambiguous involvement with it" (293).

There are several ways to read and feel the nuance here, and it is easy to become dizzy, to become sick on either the rich or fast food of urgent, uncanny attraction. Apart from the armchair, lima-bean thesis that humans are no different than dogs in heat, we are faced with a choice about what is more nauseating: (a) the middle-aged staff sergeant who sticks his fork in your dessert and, with twisted jowl, blurts out "give me a break" when you confess, in useless explanation, "your daughter is a shade tree amidst all things withered and pointless"; or (b) the lover who maintains an unhappy affair so as "to become happy in the highest sense by means of it," a stance that would award him for a singular act of courage with only a second-order iron cross, but would at least exempt him from having to "munch in unison on the scraps of falling in love, and drool life away in a marital association" (294). This choice might not so feverishly detain us if it did not pose such a questionable either/or. As for the diarist, he is as irritated and enervated by the ladies' clever banter as the bookkeeper was by his elder cousins' insufferable statistical quip. A day later this awkward dictation of hilariously sobering fare still leaves open the possibility that one might take a broken engagement with absolute seriousness without becoming an equally thoughtless, humorless prude. If he were not so flummoxed during the dinner the diarist might have roundly silenced everyone by floating the thesis that anthropomorphism cuts both ways by turning God into a dog and us into a specimen so remarkable that neither Feuerbach nor Darwin could make head or tails of it. I for one choose to believe that at least one of the ladies present would have found that funny, although the name-dropping might be equally insufferable.

An Engaging Christological Pair

The entries for 7 April form an interesting pair, to say the least. We find in the *morning* that the diarist's betrothed breaks off and breaks off and yet does not break off, while at *midnight* he has organized his life a year later as if he were married. "My table is set for two; coffee is served for two; when I take a drive I always ride as if I had a lady beside me" (295). He even has "a complete set of furniture in readiness at a secondhand dealer's" in the event of a sudden change of theatrical scene (295). What these designs frame is the middle of the action, beginning with a declaration of war on 8 April and lasting until 4 May, when he penultimately introduces "that terrible word into the course of conversation," a period when the past and present are so proximate and so far apart even though the entries are equally spaced all along from January to July. In an intervening sequence sure to prompt nervously outraged marginalia, the diarist sketches a scene in which he arrives meticulously dressed, with a hop and a skip, "hat in hand in an easy conversational stance" and "in passing kissed her hand obligingly and with polite stateliness, and hurried into the drawing room" where he knew "there were guests, since it was a family festivity" (296). Some lady at the gathering invited the two for the following evening. Jumping in against the usual protocol, he accepts the invitation for both of them, which she could not refuse without appearing foolish. Then, in parting, he tells us that "having said good-bye and already halfway through the door, I suddenly turned around and said to her: Oh, by the way, you know what—shouldn't we break up? Thereupon I swung around and waved good-bye" (296). "Immeasurably bored" as he was on the following day for the appointed gathering, he nevertheless managed, as on other occasions, to "slip in quotations from her" (297). In the face of this particular immediate invitation for the next evening, it took just a look, and then: "'Good Lord, my dear, can't you remember? It was just yesterday—no, wait a moment, I don't want to be too insistent—it was four days ago, exactly four days—can't you remember' etc. She knows very well why four days were mentioned" (297).

Given the testimony of the diary he may be referring to the veiled declaration of 5 April, about which we know about as much as any other third party. Far more revealing is his declaration that she "understands me very well, I can certainly see" (297). Yet in a wavering mood active with hope "that this childhood disease is soon over and there is still such a good understanding between us," he "ventured to read aloud to her from a devotional book," which, needless to say, "makes the whole affair even more strange" (297). Along the way he ominously ruminates that an elder wisdom would advise against making something sacred appear ludicrous, which he is at pains to avoid given how to him she is both divine and something less. Rather weakly he insists he never once plagued her with some ideal demand and "merely wished her to sit still while I concerned myself only much too earnestly with the relationship" (297). No doubt a third party might "find it dubious" he can be as he is and yet "also want to be a religious person" (297). But then again, if it is true, spiritually speaking, that "it is with an individuality as it is grammatically with a sentence"—that one consisting "only of a subject and predicate is easier to construct than a periodic sentence with dependent and intermediate clauses"—then it could indeed be true that "she is receiving more justice than if in an erotic relationship I presumptuously wanted to be the one doing the admonishing" (297–98). Put otherwise, if what he knows for sure is that she already understands him "very well" and yet hopes that the "childhood disease" of unmediated romantic longing between them might land on a more settled shore of mutual "good" understanding, then it is indeed better to mix in his own confusing, playful, unnerving coquetry with her potential frustration, sinister as this might seem, than don the elevated role of spiritual advisor. After all, what is worse: a platonically bald nincompoop or an aesthetically volatile suitor? As readers, the test of our sensibilities is whether we can see beyond the available opinions of either playful seduction or devotional reading and acknowledge the kind of mad piety that honors an incarnate mess instead of merely inhabiting the wasteland of "simon-pure solemn earnestness" (297). As part of this mess the diarist claims he "must always have the redeeming equality"—as startling, tragic, ridiculous, wonderful, or bastardly as this seems—trying as hard as he is to write down and presumably live out the role of genius-hero-saint who takes upon himself unwarranted guilt. And as weird as *this* posture seems, what he says of her potential defiance applies to the reader: "here it is the esthetic idea that judges between us"

(298). Though maddeningly unclear, it seems the "esthetic idea" is whether flesh and word can ever Christologically congeal into a seamless, acceptable whole in a manner that accurately embodies and subsequently signals the higher point of view of a genuinely religious perspective and stance.

While striking a kerygmatic pose, however, the manner of the diarist is that of an ostensibly private writer with a conspicuously romantic soul imbued by a vivid and lugubrious imagination. One might think a truly apostolic composer would have better material to work with: for example, the author of John's gospel. But even in that case the form and content, the flesh and word, are at once both already words, while the first miracle, the first sign worth mentioning, consists of Jesus turning water into wine at a random Canaanite wedding having been reluctantly prompted by his mother. Stepping more closely outside *Stages*, the same "author" who wrote *"Guilty/Not Guilty?"* later took pains under other pseudonyms to distinguish between a genius and an apostle only a few years after claiming Mozart's *Don Giovanni* as an unsurpassable musical incarnation of pure, unmediated, amoral sensuousness, while in the meantime yet another author insists there is no essential difference between a first-century follower of Christ from one following after. In this latter, intermediate text the God-man is likened to a king so enamored with a lowly maiden that he could not help but take upon himself the guise of a fellow servant, not as a cloak but in reality.[9] Disciples, readers, and beloveds more generally cannot help but wonder, or be volatilized. In any case, the news we receive by catholic immersion is how the words themselves, scratched in pen and typeset, really do signify how the curried waltz of our splintered lives, eloquently wafted by the braille of the aurora borealis, set down in vinyl and played in the background of a sumptuous, tinkling feast, really do rise and fall in the very image of a creator who fashioned thought and feeling out of clay

[9] See Kierkegaard's "The Difference between a Genius and an Apostle," in *Without Authority* (Princeton: Princeton University Press, 1997); "The Immediate Erotic Stages or The Musical-Erotic," from *Either/Or I* (Princeton: Princeton University Press, 1987); and "The God as Teacher and Savior," in *Philosophical Fragments/Johannes Climacus* (Princeton: Princeton University Press, 1985). All edited and translated by Howard V. Hong and Edna H. Hong.

and made us originally one. All of this is to say that the "esthetic" idea is so grammatically interlaced with a "religious" one that any "judge" between them must morally waver like an unsteady lover cast between scoundrel and saint, each of these sharing at the hinges of their triptych the elements of heartbreaking affection and offhand offense. It is no surprise that such a volatile mixture could prompt defiance on her part and elicit scant apology on his, all the while resulting in considerable agony for both, altogether a tender and bitter crèche of incongruously soring dimensions.[10]

Peace Talks in a Strange Country

Fourteen days after apparently receiving his enigmatic "confidential communication," during which time the armed struggle between the lovers waxes and wanes, dramatically fueled in part by ghosts perceived in "random comments, in poetry, in mystifications"—often the thin gruel tortured affection weakly feeds on during such times—two incidents stand out as moments of involuntary confession and real peace. The first occurs after she hears an exaggerated account of his being unmasked and wounded during a fencing lesson the same evening he failed to show up as promised. In response to an imagined mortal threat she anxiously arrives the next day to check in. This leads the diarist to surmise "bloodshed, the tension between us or our thrust and counterthrust, and then perhaps a little love combined to keep her sleepless" (299). When chilled by someone's emotional impudence there is nothing like a broken bone to suddenly heat up our truest feelings and level the playing field. Which is exactly what the diarist reports:

> She looked at me now and then in such a way that I understood she had something to tell me, but then I talked about the dangerous wound and about the oddity that it was a mask that had fallen off. Then she laughed, even though there was a tear in her eye. Then I said, "Yes, you may well laugh at me for being unmasked that way." Then she said, "Oh, that's silly—you know very well what I mean." "Yes, that I should challenge him again and say: The whole thing

---

[10] Relevantly, Walter Lowrie translates the subtitle of "Guilty / Not Guilty?" as "A Passion Narrative."

doesn't count if the mask falls off." And then we talked of other things. (300)

Rarely have such fine lines been drawn between anger, insecurity, understated love, and a declared truce.

The second incident occurs in church, a place of particularly disadvantageous interrogation for the diarist. Farsightedly she catches his eye, and nods. He quickly drops his own and "leafed through the hymnbook as though I had lost the hymn and by this movement managed to shake my head" (301). Looking up, the two exchange another glance. Seeming to have understood the meaning of his first gesture she nods again, this time "as if she, giving up hope, were asking only for an admission" (301). Having found the hymn, but considerably flustered, he lustily joined in the singing, lifting and sinking his head along with his voice in a movement "resembling that of one who is bidding at an auction and says 'Yes'" (301). Perhaps no criminal on record has so willingly and yet so involuntarily confessed that, yes, he loves her still, and yet cannot explain himself. This confession, which erupts a year after her own tear-filled laughter, and could be just as easily dismissed, is followed by an extended meditation on the possible outcomes of the affair given the common challenge of coordinating the longing, disappointment, and corresponding sense of guilt and innocence inherent in any life infused by romantic ideals. But before this, the pastor "entered and separated them," after which they left the service by different routes, he by retracing the way he had come with steps more anxiously than a "Pythagorean" (301).

In the mediation following these unguarded revelations the diarist highlights the terrifying "misrelation that I already feared in that dreadful two-month period: that we would jointly sorrow over an unhappy love affair" (301). What haunts him in particular is how different their sorrow might be, a difference that corresponds to the juxtaposed feelings evoked by ancient and modern tragedy. On a spectrum, ancient drama emphasizes the pain of objectively fated, external conflicts while modern tragedy typically accents the private torture of subjectively borne and often incommunicable inner responsibility. Stretched to their limits "what solidarity is there," the diarist wonders, "between guilt and innocence, what kinship is there between repentance and an esthetic sorrow over life, when that which awakens repentance is that which awakens her sorrow?" (301). To make sense of the oddly gendered characterization that follows this set of questions, the first thing to remember is that such a misrelation is relative. The tragic element is cancelled in both modern and ancient cases if either individual responsibility forms a Pelagian enclosure or external tempests render human conflicts indistinguishable from natural disasters. In cases of personal love the whole spectrum may apply short of these extremes and the salient interpretive question becomes how the relevant actors think of themselves. Between defiantly appealing to powers beyond oneself and recklessly accepting full and absolute responsibility each of us must problematically take on simply being involved without being able to clearly assign guilt or innocence *en medias res*. At the outer limits of this spectrum Christ stands as a supremely innocent figure, guilty before all, for everyone and everything, a fact which raises the puzzle over whether the gospel is tragic or not.[11] Rather confusingly, the diarist insists it would be "unethical for her and for me to sorrow jointly in this way" (301–302). What he assumes is that she inhabits a different locale on the tragic spectrum and rhetorically asks how, assuming otherwise, she could "ever come to sorrow religiously when she must leave undecided an ethical issue such as my behavior toward her, when it is indeed over its result that she wishes to sorrow" (302). On these heels he intimates that were she to venture a religious movement she would be lost to him. Even stronger still, he muses that, "A woman can have passion as strong as or perhaps stronger than a man, but contradiction in passion is not a task for her, such as the task of simultaneously giving up and preserving the wish. If she works purely religiously to give up the wish, she is transformed; if the moment for its fulfillment ever did come, she would no longer understand it" (302).

[11] See the section entitled "The Tragic in Ancient Drama Reflected in the Tragic in Modern Drama," in *Either/Or I* (Princeton: Princeton University Press, 1987); and Hegel's *Aesthetics, Lectures on Fine Art,* Volume II, chapter III, section C, division C (Oxford: Oxford University Press, 1975), translated by T. M. Knox. Prompted by the essay from *Either/Or I,* I have borrowed the Christological formula from Dostoevsky's narrative and point of view of Father Zosima in *The Brothers Karamozov*, Book VI.

Like other suspect, gendered assertions we encounter in the diary these suggest a larger common issue somehow split between them. With resounding echoes of how Judge William claimed women properly reach the altar of resolution without reflection, so the diarist imagines various, apparently thoughtless outcomes on her part. Admitting he is perhaps "talking quite foolishly," chief among these outcomes is a failure on her part to make a genuine religious movement of infinity and therefore become not positively awakened by an eternal decision but end "weary from futile wishing and weary of the futile act of renunciation," gently slumbering on into eternity, and after some time had passed "woke up and belonged to life once again" (302–303). Considering her getting over him in this way—which falls short of the monastic suspension he nevertheless fears but which is presumably the only realistic and humane possibility that could in his mind set each of them free—simply gets him all turned around. What he describes as "an illusory resignation's slumbering on into an eternity, a relaxation, while time passes by, until she once again opens her eyes and is awakened to new life," is contrasted with the categorical consolation of "genuine religiousness" he seems to entertain for himself as an ideal (304). Yet he looks with distain upon these "dubious" options, since if she did gain "the eternal" in this way, he would "in her eyes vanish like an atom, as an occasion, like the sale of Joseph…but then neither would there be any question of a new love affair" (304). And so *in one of the most revealing* passages in *Stages on Life's Way* as a whole, he disparagingly writes that "what she will be healed by is a life-wisdom permeated with a certain religiousness, a not exactly unbeautiful compound of something of the esthetic, of the religious, and of a life-philosophy," which makes his own categorical caveats sound like a clanging cymbal when in fact he quite desperately believes otherwise in spite of himself, fully admitting that "anyone busily engaged in judging others *in concreto* rarely remains true to the category" (304). To round this out he states that everyone who wills something indirectly judges those less willing, all the while knowing "that even if a person has only one step left to take he may stumble and relinquish his category" (305). All told, fully admitting this, in the tremendous half-light he resolutely maintains he simply cannot "escape…and be rescued by nonsense," which in this case means he is doubly bound by patronizing self-accusation, along with all its crippling and ennobling effects.

This entry continues with an insistence that "my thought is my life," combined with the power she still has over him and the humor and delight he otherwise longs to offer. To fully appreciate how remarkably and genderlessly dialectical the text finally is, we must absorb the following:

> Long ago I crossed out differences, but that which sustains life for me is that in willing there is an equality of all human beings, that on this point one dares to require the same of everybody. And yet how she has prevailed, just by a slight suggestion, upon me to be—as a third person presumably would say—decent about that dubious resignation. And why? Because I, in turn, am unable to exist intellectually unless she must be able to exist in the same thing. From that it is clear how dangerous it is for a thinker to be in love, to say nothing of being married and having daily arguing from a woman. Should he perhaps be neither the one nor the other, or should he perhaps be both?—Yes, it would be a male who came up with such a life-view, who relinquishes to a certain degree, and then in turn comforts himself to a certain degree. But no! Be quiet, you passion that wants to provoke my mind to rebellion, even if it may have its reasons, for what I demand of myself to the point of despair, not as something extraordinary but as the right thing—this I cannot bear to see confused with something else, I cannot haggle. (305)

Although a cursory reading of the tone here implies he cannot haggle with a softer, feminine point of view, he is doing exactly that and moreover concludes it would be a male "who relinquishes to a certain degree, and then in turn comforts himself to a certain degree." The central issue here is the tragic posture his reflection casts by assuming "all the responsibility" and then in self-consolation hopes a more "dubious kind of resignation" lacking "infinite reflection" preserves her own beautiful integrity (305–306). What he laments and agonizes over is not primarily a difference in gender between them but the level and degree of complication to which any sensitive soul could succumb and the humble courage it takes to stand firm, the courage to love despite a poverty of inner resource, which can be as lonely and fruitless a gesture as putting pennies in the temple treasury. And so he simply wishes she had been in love with someone else before he got involved, which would allow for a backdoor "new alliance" (307). Of course such an alliance would be as perplexing as his own passion since he only imagines a reawakened first love on her part would be "supported by the self-reproach she must feel at having preferred me," while the episodic memory of this preference might teach her to find the original love "more beautiful than ever" (307). However, this possibility is a vapor with which he cannot really commune, cannot actually embrace, share a meal, or dispel a nightmare. Nor, presumably, could she. After all, what kind of solution is it to prefer a first love in the form of sloppy seconds, temporal sequence aside? Indeed, the very pen that prints such a possibility is a bit of steel with ink and not a bird bearing a leaf, and as such offers a "splendid" but extremely "weak" hypothesis, like the foam of thin beer that "vanishes instantly" and can only be sustained between midnight and two in the morning, after which authentic passion beyond deceitful spiritual trial requires some sleep (308). Much more substantial is the vision, illusive as it remains, of the two of them healed by "a life-wisdom permeated with a certain religiousness, a not exactly unbeautiful compound of something of the esthetic, of the religious, and of a life-philosophy" (304).

Behind this nocturnal rumination lurks the daydream of Abraham's binding of Isaac, the silence and solitude of simultaneously giving up and holding on to a desire for felicity in this life, here and now. The difference between the scenario in *Fear and Trembling* and the one we encounter in *Stages* is that we are no longer talking about three days and part of a fourth—which did indeed include time to chop the firewood and sharpen the knife—but an ongoing incomplete year of expectation and fatigue, literally months of mixed resolve, ironic aggrandizement, ominous self-doubt, and rather obvious romantic longing, all of it more familiar but no less equally rare and paradoxical. One could say that in *Stages* the Abrahamic guiding assurance becomes a horizontally receding vision we perhaps might follow with fascinated reticence. On the *morning* of 15 April, after this most recent night of turbulent rumination, "the weather turned out fine, even clear" (308). What he recalls in particular is the fencing incident and how fortunate it was "that death came between us," how he did "dare to believe that I am loved," the very grammatical tense of which should baffle the heart of any reader (308). That incident still on his mind, two mornings later he recalls with elation how the anxiety she felt that fateful evening left her more unguarded than ever, but nevertheless happier, a memory quickly transposed into the *midnight* thoughts of the following day, each a variation of 14 April. What the diarist more clearly delineates here is how his truest wish, "the culmination of the divine frenzy in my soul"—deeper than the desire to see her set free and in love with another, and awaiting only his own unbound courage—is to have and to hold her affection (310). Perseveringly keeping sadness at bay he "will not call back the night watchman who stands on the look-out for expectation" (311). Like Abraham, he feels correspondingly suspended.

On the *morning* of 20 April he notices/recalls a pattern in the scale of her devotion and the chill of his reticence, and reports it in the way an investigative journalist might later tell the real story of a court case buried beneath the facts. Like such stories, this one also has the tone of intimation masked as discovery, all the while including a new *corpus delicit*. Starting with the latter, she sits him down in a chair, backs away a few steps, then approaches, and falls on her knees. In the next instant he grabs her, lifts her up, and anxiously looks around the room for potential witnesses, thinking "I do not know how much I would have paid for the certainty that no one had seen it, or how much I would have paid not to have seen it myself!" (312). The overall pattern he detects, or thinks he detects, is an irreconcilable conflict between her sad, flirtatious, and vaguely demented bliss "at having found the right expression for her passion" and his own "inclosed reserve" (312). What is particularly revealing in this entry, what it actually intimates, is how he concludes he has gained complete power over her with her having "none whatsoever" over him and therewith delivers the guilty charge of spiritual seduction on himself, all of which is belied by the fact that her direct and impetuous display of devotion "has put a frenzy into my blood, a confusion into my mind, an anxiety into my inclosing reserve, a despair into my resolve, and above all a buzzing into the ear of presentiment" (312–13). Based on this it would seem seduction is a two-way street and that its power cannot be either neatly assigned or divided between the spiritual and handheld sort. True romance is indeed "like" such a "tale of seduction," a tale distinctly uneasy to tell, full as it is of helplessly sad, flirtatious, demented bliss. No wonder then that the next day he was sitting in a café reading a newspaper when he suddenly burst into tears. On other such occasions he becomes similarly dizzy: "my thought cannot quickly enough grasp anything firm in the hodgepodge, and it seems to me as if I were a murderer. There is nothing to do then except to reject the idea with supreme effort as a religious spiritual trial" (313). But at this moment, in that café, reading whatever bit of news was on the docket for the day, he definitely could not help himself. That is exactly what it is like to feel something and not know, to inhabit a wordless story yearning for expression.

On the *morning* of 24 April he feels like someone who has arrived in a strange country of people with other customs and who speak a foreign tongue. The reason is because she seems at ease and with genuine faith to accept her love happily despite the conflict between them. Unlike encountering a dismissively self-enclosed national pride, this has the character of an apparently illusionary absorption with him as a person. "She is loveable and busies herself with her love like a child who shifts for itself but is merry and happy at its pastime" (314). What is striking about this characterization is that she lacks both naiveté and malcontent. "But the conflict, my changed behavior, the intervention of death, transforms her nature; she is displaying a lovableness I sadly admire and that makes me an enthusiast to her" (314). What he explicitly concludes in this particular travelogue is that she must be somehow tone-deaf to both his lower proclivities and higher aspirations. But what higher motive could a foreign national intimate than to love another for what they are in all their complex mixture of difference and simultaneously acknowledge, celebrate, and romantically gush over a tenderly felt similarity? It is as if *she* has become his Abraham, the one who simultaneously loves God and loves him, simultaneously devoted to an ideal while embracing a mess that is as provincial as it is common. If that is what she represents, if that is what she *is*, then of course he loves *her*, or at least should, given his own point of view and what mobilizes his passion. The problem is that he lacks belief and is paradoxically absorbed in his own illusion that she might not be this person or up to the task. The divine madness in all this confusion amounts to cherishing the subjectivity of one we respect and being enamored by their fragility, full and empty as they are as an imperfectly incarnate image with Trinitarian proportions. Or to keep with the regional imagery, it seems like a mixed marriage, wherever one is from.

Patience, Quick!

The seamless brevity of form and content delivered on 25 April *midnight* will no doubt enervate the sensible reader with a mixture of gall and amusement: "Patience!" (314). That's all the diarist writes, which might make one throw the entire book against the wall, or out the window, depending on whether we should keep it.

Having urged such patience upon us, not to mention upon himself, and most of all on her, he continues meditating on the confusing height and depth of his cherished standards relative to her devotion. Normally he is not awed and humbled by others, nor is he arrogantly preoccupied with what stage they are at, since so much of his energy is spent on figuring out his own degree of separation. She, however, interrupts all this fastidious tracking by happily tossing bread in all directions, as if the path were as obvious as the clues are irrelevant. That he therefore finds himself "*obliged*" to love her is a veritable sign in the overall mystery of being unable to "sacrifice" the principles of his breathtaking spiritual existence (314–15). One of the central ironies here is that she has apparently made such a sacrifice with ease and thoughtlessly confident joy, inhaling what he exhales along the way, while Abraham breathes all on his own with elegant double-movements as he mounts Moriah (315). That the existential issue shared but split between them is further imagined by the entry of 28 April. Reflecting on the tension between the two of them and her lack of resistance leads him back to the conversation with himself that what he fears the most, the citadel into which God freely enters and internally interjects, is not a thunderclap, but a whisper. The point is that she enjoys a share in such immanent dialectical power by surrendering, leaving him, as well as his reader, to take up a full half of the dialogue. Somehow what is most divine is directly related to an inner subjective individuality rather than revealed in external, universally secured, socially recognized mores. Both an Abrahamic figure and the romantically oriented individual share a Socratically daemonic conscience, while in the present scenario, we have two such subjectivities displaying a delicate and stormy set of elective affinities.

Having introduced the resonance an esthetic characterization of anomalous romantic individuals might have with religious heroes, 29 April *midnight* calls our attention to an explanatory fabrication of the diarist and whether or not "I could give a more lenient conception of myself" (316). This fabrication, within scare quotes, oddly split between the first and third person, goes like this:

> 'To a certain extent I was a corrupt man, yet not totally bad; I had my good sides as well. I certainly have loved her but lacked earnestness. And then there was my instability, which cannot hold firm to a resolution. I certainly did regard her as a charming girl but still did not find in her the spirit with which I could become happy. It is therefore beautiful of her to resign herself to her fate. It is magnanimous of her to be reconciled to the girl who some day will captivate me with a greater power: for this much is sure, that if he finds a more brilliant girl, he will find no one who would love him in this way. This he himself must certainly admit, and, as far as that goes, he certainly has also repented of his conduct, even though he is too proud to undo anything.' (316–17)

In its own bizarre way this masqueraded third-person self-description is arresting partially because it is so apparently obvious and so patently misleading. The reader should be in no urgent need to hear that in such an explanation "every sentence is meaningless and also untrue" (317). On the contrary, if *we* had to characterize him in our own scare quotes it might go something like this: A socially enclosed, ethically oversensitive, erotically reserved, religiously dark, easily bored, bookish, depressed, idealist egalitarian with an imagination bent by a sense of possibility and obsessed with meaning who therefore harbors grave doubts about whether he can be a decent husband by contributing to someone else's happiness. But he is also one who falls desperately in love and earnestly longs for reciprocal affection and understanding, simultaneously hopeful and despairing about this as a realistic possibility, all of which goes against the grain of his overall personality and gives rise to a restless frustration that gets filtered by a creative distain for ordinary novels of everyday life and other romantic comedies, all the while displaying conspicuous doubt whether or not he as an author has been rendered in the image of "an eternal and righteous God" who "originally produced the ethical" or "a bungling tailor" who "slapped something together"' (317). To continue with *our* characterization, now including his own, inside the text but outside the internal quotes, he is terribly sensitive to and downright afraid of being a playwright who confounds our perception of "all existence" by delivering clever lines to an audience made up not of human beings or "the demented" but "dazed June bugs" (317–18). He would rather be portrayed as hypocritical and corrupt "or even to the point of nausea ensnared in self-deception" than come off as a sleepy, naïve hero baptized with the name "Caesar Alexander Bonaparte Appleorchard," composed and endorsed as such with corresponding satirical bombast by the then popular author "Scribe" (318). Alien to his surrounding culture in this way and frequently a second, third, and even fourth theatrical set of persons to himself, he falls on his own tortured face in a manner that would make even the most cavalier postmodernist marvel. In point of fact he may be just "as chivalrous as anyone," but can tolerate neither the thought of her "religious individuality in the proper sense" nor take "advice from flesh and blood" (318). All of which begs the question about where to put him, how to characterize him. His own suggestion is that we rank him with Pericles, who reneged on a law banning citizenship to children not born of Athenian parents after all his own legitimate offspring died of the plague. In *that* case, the people dealt gently with Pericles because they believed the gods had taken revenge on him for his initial, overly principled stance, according to the "moving" authority of Plutarch the diarist is anxious to cite, bookish as he is (318–19). It is not incidental that he chooses this example over the one Brutus Johannes de Silentio cites in *Fear and Trembling*. In that case Brutus resolutely upholds the sentence of capital punishment against the fate of his own son.[12]

---

[12] Plutarch, *The Lives of the Noble Grecians and Romans* (New York: Modern Library, 1975) 211, translated by John Dryden and revised by Arthur Hugh Clough. Kierkegaard, *Fear and Trembling/Repetition*, 58.

May Flowers and April Showers Followed by a South-Pawed Birthday Lectionary

By the end of April and beginning of May the diarist reports she is "no longer effervescent in her expressions of devotion" and moreover "became exasperated over an inattention" (319). For him to comment on such wavering is naturally a case of the pot calling the kettle black since what he reports is that "[f]rom the very first time I saw her, during all the time she was my preoccupation in the form of hope, I have been able to imagine her dead without losing my composure" (320). However grave this sentiment might sound, the basis for his form of detachment is and apparently has been "the eternal," forever present and "supreme" (320). Needless to say, a more oblique form of detachment on her part mirrors this explicit, protective stoicism on his. What ought to hold true between them is a mutually self-conscious awareness of the infinite distance that inhabits the free bondage of love, a perpetual sidelong engagement. What he doubts is whether she is on the same page, and whether this kind of internally fissured partnership is viable to begin with. If not viable, then it would seem a married individual is indeed "a pasha with three horse tails" (320). Short of such romantic attachment undertaken and haunted by a religious descant it might be that personal intimacy mostly amounts to a bizarre patriotic façade. That he cannot conceive of the matter differently, and that his "premises" result in a "lifelong sentence" usually reserved in the popular press for engaged couples, is a verdict he is willing to bear, and bear alone. "Whether it applies to two or one, I dare not say; the verdict upon me is the more certain. But is it not unreasonable to make two people unhappy when one is enough?" (320). More centrally, he is unsure whether she imagines his own death as vividly as he does hers and still wants to take part in the dance—to make love, have tea, share a life—while nevertheless willing to give it all up. Most of what he notes are the creepy, ominously silent, and correspondingly bombastic bargains and half-measured thoughts that typically emerge in the middle of such romances.

Perhaps in light of or against such half-measures, on 2 May he wonders if he harbors a secret anger against her. The direct expressions of feeling from her haunt and perhaps annoy him. In his overwrought estimation the whole matter would be less aggravating if her straightforward and pain-filled declarations were by common knowledge nothing more than "some nasty belches, some little hiccups, brought on perhaps by too much reading of novels, that these thoughts of death were dreams, not like those of Shakespeare's Juliet after having taken poison, but like Wessel's Grete after having eaten peas" (321). All this belies his claim they do not understand one another, a clear cover for the inestimable fear that what he earnestly respects could appear ludicrous and he himself might become a laughingstock through her jeering "with the same words" concerning how the current veil of tears looks in the light of eternity (321). Gnawing at the edges of the whole document are not only thoughts about our final mortality, but the very temporal ruin of our vain attempts at faithfulness along the way. Such are the stunning sentiments that crush his consciousness and somehow simultaneously raise doubts about the faithfulness and reciprocity of her own pathos even as they helplessly drive him into the hands of a living God. It is not without great irony, therefore, that he cites a drunken woman on the street mouthing a corresponding cry in that she can get up all by herself and has only God to thank "and no one else—no, no one else!" (322). Apparently it is all right when a nameless intoxicant jeers with the same lines, but not when an actual intimate drums them into your ear. But romantic connections often imply exactly this kind of confessional inability to cross the great divide of shared affection, colored as it is with the purple possibilities of lent, even at the beginning of May. What angers and frustrates him, we are led to surmise, is that her frail, incidentally feminine, and soberly sly self may just well be the help he so desperately needs. Directly paired with this enervation, to be humbled and made erect by YHWH directly is correspondingly inglorious. It is as if Cupid lent the God of Abraham an arrow and said "try this." Indeed, it has only been a week since the diarist wrote: "Here I have been humbled. And who is it who humbles me? It is a young girl, and it is not by her pride, for then we could have managed all right, but by her devotedness" (314). Quite possibly YHWH has been firing arrows at random from the beginning and is still a better shot. Around this time the diarist introduces "that terrible word" into the course of their conversation (322). A separation between them is immanent. And with *that* prospect on the horizon:

> What I am suffering inwardly where everything is confused and shaken, what I am suffering at the thought of her pain, at the thought that I probably will never recover from this impression because my whole edifice has been made to reel, my view of life, of myself, of my relation to the idea has failed, and I shall never be able to erect a new edifice without remembering her and my responsibility—that is my share. It is a lion's share, or more accurately, the sorrow is so great that there is abundantly enough for both of us. (323)

The appropriate commentary here is to say he is autopathetically split, which is not something one could claim about every confused lover.

Following this passage is the penultimate narrative interpolation about the tyrant Periander, the external details of which Herodotus and Diogenes Laertius deliver, but whose interpretive center of gravity is drawn from one French archbishop Fénelon, already anticipated in the entry of 18 April. Against the suggestion by Herodotus that there were two Greeks by the name, one wise and one tyrannical, Fénelon says of a singular Periander that he always spoke as a wise man but acted like a lunatic (310, 323).[13] The story the diarist picks out from the details handed down is how Periander could never finally overcome the split in his character to the point where, even in arranging his ingenious suicide by ordering two men to kill and immediately bury the first person they encountered in a prearranged secret passage, and thereupon ordering four others to do the same to the first two, and still eight others the same to the second four, posterity knows neither where Periander is buried nor what to make of him. He could not recover and rest even in death. What prompted the mad rift in Periander's personality remains open. Was it the rumor that he had penally culpable relations with his mother; was it the Machiavellian advice he received from his fellow friend and tyrant Thrasybulus who suggested that, to an absolute ruler, even a friend is suspicious; or was it that in a fit of jealousy he kicked to death his beloved Melissa who had borne him Cypselus and Lycophron?

---

[13] Herodotus, *The Histories* (New York/London: Penguin Books, 1972), translated by Aubrey De Sélincourt and revised with notes by John Marincola. Diogenes Laertius, *Lives of Eminent Philosophers,* Volume I (Loeb Classical Library, LCL 184. Cambridge MA/London: Harvard University Press, 1925), translated by R. D. Hicks.

Whatever the reason, whether it was "the infamy of disgrace for the proud prince, the temptation of the significant cryptic words for the ambitious man," or "the anguish of guilt for the unhappy lover," it surely could not have helped when the younger, sensitive, and talented Lycophron found out about his mother's fate from grandpa and thereupon emotionally stonewalled his father (326). Dated on Kierkegaard's birthday, and entitled "The Reading Lesson," this whole section seems to be about the kinds of smoldering, un-christened passions that conspire to divide ourselves and the kind of unity we long for but cannot manage to secure, a phenomenon that has always puzzled moral theorists, whether Socrates or St. Paul, Mencius or St. Augustine. In the present context we have ample reason to think the diarist is incredibly sensitive to how the tone of his own actions do not harmonize with the texture of his thoughts and is desperately trying to see his way clear without drowning in the waters of inner conflict. As a lectionary reading, this one is darker than "A Possibility," but nevertheless retains a final ambiguity in that Periander, like the bookkeeper, tries to acknowledge, express, and make up for an innocent guilt very much his own.[14]

Dress Rehearsal for a Trip to Mt. Moriah

The three *morning* passages of 6–8 May all settle on the motif of how imagination theatrically plays against reality in the form of a dress rehearsal. So far, the diarist informs us, things are going "better and

---

[14] In an alternative, psychologically doctrinaire approach to these portions of *Stages,* Joakim Garff writes: "Against the backdrop of Quidam's misery-filled love life, the six inserted pieces, individually and collectively, tell us that the crisis must be traced back to the father, who because of *his* guilt ruined the son's innocence, thereby depriving him of the immediacy that is the precondition of natural love. Even the title 'Guilty/Not Guilty' is thus split between two characters, a father who was guilty and a son who was not." *Søren Kierkegaard, A Biography* (Princeton: Princeton University Press, 2005) 352, translated by Bruce H. Kirmmse. While one need not strictly oppose bowing down with Freud before the ancient dispute articulated in Exodus 34:7, echoed in Numbers 14:18, reversed in Deuteronomy 24:16, and then played out in Ezekiel 18, Jeremiah 31, and then John 9, Garff's interpretation makes restricted sense of the specific surrounding details of the text.

better" since in this particular act she "seems tranquil" at the prospect of separation even as his "hope is like an overcrowded lifeboat on a stormy sea," both of which make him wonder how things will sound and appear when it actually comes down (328). He cannot speak for her ahead of time, but nevertheless pretends to, saying that she "seems to understand...that what was too coarse as a jest must be in earnest" and is "not without vehemence," which is "good" (329). For his part, here is what his troubled imagination delivers:

> When the merchant stands at the furthest tip of the harbor and watches his ship and its cargo in distress and, concentrating his mind on the loss, goes away saying to himself: It is your own fault that you did not insure it—I wonder if he really would be happy if a sailor came running after him and said, "We can see the ship again; it has not gone down!"—and the merchant turned around, and the sailor took the telescope to look out there and said, "Why, now it is gone again!" (329)

However real this train of thought may be as an ill-suited simile, what we find he actually writes in a letter to her is the following: "In order not to keep on rehearsing what must nevertheless happen, what, when it has happened, will certainly provide the strength that is needed—let it then have happened. Above all, forget the one who writes this; forgive a man who, even if he was capable of something, was nevertheless incapable of making a girl happy" (329–30). Thereupon she shows up at his apartment while he is out and leaves a corresponding note, "composed in passionate despair," beseeching him for God's sake, and for his own sake, "for my salvation's sake, in memory of all that binds me, in the blessed name I rarely mention because my doubt has kept me from appropriating it, even though for that very reason my veneration for it is unmatched" (330). Biographical notes from the Hongs suggest this desperate plea includes a veiled appeal to Kierkegaard's own late young mother his father got pregnant when she was still a maid in his employ. But the literary content is relevant enough: it would be the death of his beloved to be without the diarist. What does he conclude? "So, then, I am wedded to her" (330). Such a conclusion might seem strange if it were not for the fact that she presumably knows how complicated a personal history can be and chooses to play a card whose face conjures every ambiguity that nails him to a homesick sense of himself. Combine this with the provincial sense of honor he feels on her behalf for appearing outside his apartment without a chaperone, together with the nagging thought that she may have safely fled the scene unnoticed and was yet "desperate over not being good enough" (331). In the light of such veritable complications, it makes sense that "the terminus of our separation has been postponed" while the "whole affair has taken on a terrible shape" and that a "religious point of unity is nonsense" if he is "the guilty one and she the one who suffers" (331). This state of wedlock, incongruously filtered through the theater of his circumspect imagination is not one he is intent on fleeing. Still, without entirely heading for the ditch in some bourgeois neighborhood, he cries yet one more time:

> Take complete control of me, then, you formidable passion, you forger who are truth's changeling but in the deception are not distinguishable from it. Brace me up for two months; that is the time, not one day more, but punctually and conscientiously that long. Change all the agony in my breast into foolishness on my lips, all the pathos therein into nonsense when it is uttered. Take away, take it away, hide every trace, every look, every feeling, every hint of a feeling that could please her, hide it all so well that no truth glimmers through the deception. Transform me; when I sit beside her, let me sit like a nodding mandarin, with a thoughtless smile on my lips, reeking of nonsense. (331–32)

Then reality momentarily sets in. "I went to see her. She was relatively more calm than I had expected" (332). The drama here is about what we cannot control, what we confusingly wish for, and the variable impression we give of ourselves out of a mixture of compassion and self-deception and otherwise cannot imagine. Having inadvertently headed for the roadside while agonizingly maintaining Victorian appearances, he interjects that while "secret lovers need to be circumspect in order to conceal their understanding with one another," the two of them "are lovers openly and yet it is necessary for us to conceal *our* understanding" (332). These italics form a skeleton key. The lock, we are led to assume, is not only *theirs* but *ours*, as readers, if we have the nerve and wherewithal to open it.[15]

---

[15] The manuscript of *Stages on Life's Way* was written in the autobiographically unresolved midst of Kierkegaard's own experience. Søren met Regine in May 1837, proposed on 8 September 1840, and the two were officially engaged two days later. On 11 August 1841 he returns the ring, and officially breaks the engagement on 11 October. Two weeks later he left for Berlin. In July 1843 he learns of Regine's engagement to Frederik Schlegel. *Either/Or* was published in February of that year, and *Repetition* and *Fear and Trembling* in October. Between these publications, on 17 May 1843 the journals report he has "just begun a story entitled 'Guilty/Not Guilty;' of course it would come to contain things that could amaze the world, for I have personally experienced more poetry in the last year and a half than [is contained in] all novels put together, but I cannot and will not do it, for my relationship to her must not become poetically diffused; it has a completely different reality [*Realitet*]. She has not become a kind of theatrical princess; so, if possible, she will become my wife." *Søren Kierkegaard's Journals and Papers,* Volume 5, *Autobiographical, 1829–1848*, 5664. This is the same entry that contains the often quoted, "If I had faith, I would have stayed with Regine." *Stages on Life's Way* was published in April 1845. On 3 November 1847, Regine finally marries Schlegel. Near the end of June 1849 Regine's father dies, an event which prompts renewed thoughts of reconciliation on Kierkegaard's part. During this time he finally commits to private paper a series of facts and interpretation concerning the events of eight years prior, and awkwardly proposes a written correspondence with Regine, *through* Schlegel, which the latter promptly and understandably rebuffed. But until 17 March 1855, the day the Schlegels left for the West Indies and Regine sought out Søren for what turned out to be their last meeting, the two regularly exhanged looks in church and intentionally met on the street, often every day, for stretches of time. Kierkegaard's journals lose much of their characteristic sense of humor after the publication of *Stages* and the ensuing scandalous altercation it provoked in *The Corsair* and again after Regine's actual marriage to Schlegel. This is not to say Søren could not have imaginatively projected open possibilities on an actually settled past, but this is historically not the case. The upshot is that whatever interpretive judgment the reader is tempted to offer about *Stages* as a self-contained literary production should not be unduly colored by how things experientially unfolded after November 1847 in Kierkegaard's own recapitulation, which happens to include a continued fear of her passion and terrifying ambivalence over the possibility that she might "repent" of her marriage. Perhaps fortuitously, perhaps providentially, but certainly existentially, there is neither a fictional nor historical *result* that could serve to let us off the hook of judging *in medias res*, both literally and literarily. A truly tempting parallel between Kierkegaard's life and work at

In the meantime he must brace himself for a "last battle" and "reign of terror" not knowing whether her theurgical appeal to the most sacred figures that populate his inner life is meant as a cheap shot or an earnest disarmament. "Perhaps," he surmises, "it is such a ferocious skirmish that she did not know what she should think up to use against me and so she has used this" (332). Perhaps. Perhaps she knows which blade cuts the deepest. Perhaps she thinks less of God and more of illicitly cherished but buried mothers; perhaps she thinks more of God and less of his rhetorically adorned self-abuse. Put yet otherwise, perhaps she thinks more of the welter and waste out which we have been creatively born and asked to artistically fashion ourselves, and less of some lifeless platonic lump of clay posturing in the form of an absolute. Perhaps. In any case, the "ferocious skirmish" that would predictably flummox him

---

this point—if one must be drawn—is that both *Stages* and his actually imagined life contain neither the corrected outcome of *Repetition* nor the ideal resolution of *Fear and Trembling*. In *ad hoc* support of this thesis, when in February 1846 Johannes Climacus provides his glance at Danish literature as a lead-up to Kierkegaard's long, inconclusive (it turns out) postcript to the pseudonymous authorship, *that* author speaks well of making literary use of "a love affair, which is always a usable theme in relation to what it means to exist, even though *philosophice*, in relation to rote reciting, it is folly," especially when such a use places the accent on a confusing and problematic suspension of the ethical rather than a definitive, cavalier breach. Søren Kierkegaard, *Concluding Unscientific Postscript to* Philosophcial Fragments (Princeton: Princeton University Press, 1992) 265ff, translated by Howard V. and Edna H. Hong. Later, in 1849, but in direct relation to the midnight entry of 7 February in "Guilty/Not Guilty," we could consider the following passage from the journals: "This is why I am so indescribably happy in the midst of all my sufferings. My imagination almost swoons to think of the millions of possibilities that God has at every moment. I do something wrong. I am aware of it at once. What is to be done now? My gloomy imagination instantly perceives the possibility that this little mistake can ruin everything. But then, the very same moment, I say to God: *Bitte, bitte,* I made a mistake; but even if I am a pest, an impudent pest, O God, make something good out of this very mistake. And then (God who has millions of possibilities at every moment), then the circumstances are combined somewhat differently and, so it is. This very mistake proves to be the right thing. That is how I pray to God. And that is how I get more joy out of this mistake than out of the most proper thing I ever did." *Søren Kierkegaard's Journals and Papers,* Volume 6, *Autobiographical, 1829–1848,* 6514.

gives way to the comment: "Be that as it may, I must respect it" (332). We might be tempted at this point to simply say, "No shit, Sherlock." Be that as it may, what they both might also have in mind is that the father of faith had two wives, one a fertile insolent handmaiden, the other a jealous barren half-sister, and two equally cherished sons, all four of whom he had to give up, two to the wilderness, one by his own knife, and his first love Sarah to an equally inscrutable natural death.[16]

Such biblical overtones help make sense of the diarist's diffuse proposal, which may as well be addressed to us as third-party readers as to her, although equally addressed to himself:

> What I shall venture to do now is to pull myself away from her, if possible, scramble her image of me into sheer inanity and utterly confound her. Every counterargument will be respected. I know very well what these will be. All sympathy for me will be wiped out, and she must also be run weary in reflection. In all human probability she will then be over the worst suffering with me and, humanly speaking, will not be inclined to begin all over again the moment I leave her.—One becomes almost calm when it is a matter of acting, even if what one will do is the most desperate and in the most difficult form—namely, in the form of time and duration. But if I cannot be calm, then I might just as well not begin this work. (332)

According to Johannes de Silentio's official report, it was of course Abraham who had gloriously contended "with that crafty power that devises all things, with that vigilant enemy who never dozes, with that old man who outlives everything—he had fought with time and kept his faith."[17] But even that author presents several alternate versions. In one of those versions Abraham reveals his aim to Isaac with a gentle gaze epitomizing fatherliness, but unable to tolerate his beloved son's alarm and confusion, "turned away from him for a moment" and

> when Isaac saw Abraham's face again, it had changed: his gaze was wild, his whole being sheer terror. He seized Isaac by the chest, threw him to the ground, and said "Stupid boy, do you think I am your father? I am an idolater. Do you think it is God's command? No, it is my desire." Then Isaac trembled and cried out in his anguish: "God in

[16] Genesis 16–23.

[17] Kierkegaard, *Fear and Trembling/Repetition*, 19.

> heaven, have mercy on me, God of Abraham, have mercy on me; if I have no father on earth, then you be my father!" But Abraham said softly to himself, "Lord God in heaven, I thank you; it is better that he believes me a monster than that he should lose faith in you."[18]

Without exactly displaying a star of faith, this version is at least understandable, and may even positively reveal a form of the paradoxical passion *via negativa*. In any case what it helps illuminate is how the diarist inhabits his own story from within and the strange and gentle lack of confidence that softens the edges of his otherwise acidic courage. In fact we catch an introductory glimpse of the more truly humble form of courage de Silentio lauds that same evening of 8 May. Exactly a year after he sent his letter, this entry ruminates on the quiet, secure, ordinary stillness of a *midnight* hour that "seems to be the most subtle fraud of existence" (333). Unlike the "eerie, ominous, secretive" silence of a "closed-up house" or that same soundless echo "among the graves," this "vegetating stillness" annoyingly rings in the diarist's ears with the sense that down in the village "pretty Marie" too "had a love affair; now the pain is over, now the musician scrapes away on the violin, and Marie is dancing with a new lover" (333–34). What seems "foreign" to his soul in such "dabblings of the finite" is the prospect that his beloved might quietly get over him rather than perish of hateful distinction. Accommodating himself to such a pedestrian attitude and possibly sending her "a more lenient" and presumably retrospective "explanation" is frankly "abhorrent" to him (334). Whether one is Abraham or anyone else, leaving behind the impression of a mad scoundrel and idolater is simply the flip-side of the incomprehensible regret of unapologetic abnormality. And so the diarist sits, transforming all this ordinary peace and quiet into a shivering, deserted, infinite stillness that, at the tip of his pen, is "more copious than successions to thrones and world events" (333). But then—the story keeps going—four days after exorcising the unnerving quiet of those "who go about their business all week long, keep up their account books, shut up shop, and go to church on Sunday," he unexpectedly runs into her outside the royal urban gardens (333). Having only thirty seconds to get their

[18] Ibid., 10–11.

bearings, he detects a gestalten movement on her face wavering between "suppressed pain" and "the beginning of a smile" (335). Apparently being more a patient than a doctor himself, he can only observe that she "looked vigorous" though "somewhat pale" (336). We are led to believe that dacrygelosis expresses a veritable pinnacle of human feeling, an exceptionally faithful mixture of resignation and hope. This all might be only in his imagination, but now it is in ours, uncommonly fake and incredibly real, a mixture, in its own way, of Abraham's fatherly gaze and terrifying half-measure, at least according to one version.

On 16 May, a year later, he goes at this all again by getting some fabricated third-party letters into her hands via a friend he does not trust an inch and is therefore an unwittingly reliable mail-carrier. Penned in three different kinds of ink "for safety's sake," the content of this indirect correspondence is conveyed with equal indirection to us (338). After she has "presumably" received such letters he rehearses the various explanations he might give of himself and how they would likely be read. For instance, if the diarist were to say that his desire was too large to be spent on one woman or that he was tired of her or that his pride prevents him from repenting of his decisions, then he can imagine being understood, even celebrated as "just like everyone else and like the heroes in French poetry" (339–40). In contrast, if he were to say, "She was the only one I have loved; if I had not been sure of that when I left her, I would have never dared to leave her," or that "nothing, nothing would so satisfy my pride as to dare to undo it," then it would be off to the loony bin with him and even provide grounds for deportation (339–40). The range of these explanations once again echoes de Silentio's alternately faithful and unfaithful accounts of Abraham's inner posture during the *akedah*. From the perspective of socially acceptable sanctions the diarist, like Abraham, stands apart, animated by the paradoxical passion of resigned desire lovingly prepared for loss that is out of sync in any age and ill-suited to serve "a whole nation, the human race as a whole, all future generations" or even "a little circle of contemporaries" (340). The diarist is neither a tragic hero nor "a model of virtue, a bright normative human being," since the latter is "for one thing, very embarrassing—and also very dubious" (340). While de Silentio's more positive characterization of Abraham as one who knows "how beautiful and beneficial" it is "to be the single individual who translates himself into the universal, the one who, so to speak, personally produces a trim, clean, and, as far as possible, faultless edition of himself, readable by all," the diarist diffidently says of himself that he only serves "the participants" of social conformity "by being a scoundrel" (340).[19] Falling short of Abraham's ideal confidence, and certainly lacking the pretense of apostolic authority, the diarist simply assumes "that every human being is essentially assigned himself" (340–41). Nevertheless, what de Silentio says of Abraham remains comparable to the central existential position of the diarist: "the true knight of faith is a witness, never a teacher, and therein lies the profound humanity."[20]

But in the present case there is also a shift in nuance. Although like Abraham the diarist is unable to explicate himself in seamless moral terms, he feels forced to deceptively break his own silence by delivering half-truths that stretch, bend, and twist Abraham's entirely accurate and perfectly ambiguous response to Isaac's question about where the sacrifice will come from on their way to Mt. Moriah.[21] At much more equivocating length the diarist writes:

> My explanation that I repent but cannot undo what I am guilty of doing is nonsense. In other words, if I cannot give the reason why I cannot undo it, I should never speak of repenting, but least of all give my pride as the reason (i.e., that I do not want to), for that is actually to make a fool of her. Therefore I have never represented myself as repenting before now, although I do indeed repent and have repented that I entered into that relationship and find my humiliation in not being able to undo it, precisely what my pride desires, since it is crushed because I, who have had an almost foolhardy conception of willing, must wince because there is something I will, will with all my passion, but cannot do. Why I cannot (which is due to my relation to the idea, until either this is changed or I am), I cannot tell her in such a way that she can understand it, but for this very reason I have never said that I repented. Thus there was meaning in my conduct. But to repent and to give pride as that hindrance to the expression of repentance, since, on the contrary, it ought to be the object of

[19] Ibid., 76.
[20] Ibid., 80.
[21] Ibid., 115–20.

> repentance, is high treason against God. How anyone can understand it and find it plausible, I do not comprehend, but in return most people presumably say the same thing about my view. (345–46)

Part of what this "explanation" expresses is the sense in which, far from being a "world-historical" character like John the Baptist, or Abraham for that matter, whose exemplary appeal and stories are graced by harrowing but nevertheless edifying, discernable outcomes, the diarist is merely "an existing person" in the middle of his own action with his suspended "crises of realization" along the way (342–43). Neither he nor the reader knows what the result of all this suspension is going to be. The diarist is riddled with a fragile sense of unrepentant responsibility de Silentio in part relieves Abraham of by delegating that potential part of Genesis 22 to several alternate versions in the obsessed imagination of an anonymous man who had heard the story as a child, but then grew up, and erstwhile slips it back in later by contrasting Abraham with a seductive, guilt-stricken merman.[22] The point here is that the three days and part of a fourth de Silentio officially comments on is extended throughout any given year of life lived along the way. Amidst these layers, this passage includes one of several references to the diarist's relation to "the idea," which sounds abstractly platonic to the point of complete inhumanity. However, the thick description the diarist provides of his emotional scenario suggests that what he longs for more than anything is to recognize in his temporal experience a significance and eternal meaning that can withstand the miasma of ordinary time. His beloved both represents that ideal and falls short of it. We could blame him for that, for holding on to such an ideal, and holding her to it. We could also blame him for settling, for thinking a pastoral relationship with a "fine" girl is our common, realistic lot. But romantic ideals typically divide us against ourselves in this way and often render us ridiculously conflicted, as hard as it is to tell a respectable match from a fling or a faithful devotion from sloppy seconds. It all amounts to a kind of madness, perchance divine. Whether the diarist is actually playing the part of Abraham or merely acting may

---

[22] Ibid., 9, 13, 94–101.

be a function of a sublimely theatrical ruse to get us thinking for ourselves.

Speaking of theatrical ruses, in the 21 May entry the diarist meditates on how absurd it would be for him to seek a confidant since his pain is far from "rich in incidents, in changes of scene and setting," and therefore must seem incredibly boring (347). Interestingly, he considers whether an exotic journey abroad would help pass the time and have the added benefit of fostering further ambiguity as to his real state of heart and mind. But what he actually hopes is that their paths will continue to cross in town, "because she benefits from seeing me; she thereby has the opportunity to reassure herself that I am here and living as usual and that I am not in a foreign country—and possibly thinking of her and possibly being homesick" (347). The ironic similarity in this contrast is in fact considerably more than boring, but at once sickening, heartfelt, tortured, and honest. His reader, his potential confidant—if that is what we are—should be awakened by the further ironic thought that prayer might be more popular if permission to do so cost something. Of course prayer by its own nature prefers solitude "and being as secret as possible in order neither to be disturbed nor to embarrass others by its emotion" (348). Striking a similar chord in an adjacent minor key he writes: "Falling in love is not beautiful if one looks to see if it pays, and even if one sees that it pays exceptionally well, it is not a happy falling in love" (348). As for "her, her!" (and us) we would do well not to seek "finite consolation" (349).

Several weeks after he breaks their engagement the two are still seeing each other, sharing things, including laughter, which the diarist declares "the best method of exploration" (349). Such laughter on her part exhaustingly gives way to "pleas and tears" while nevertheless retaining the turbulent sentiment that she would rather have "all this" than not see him. For his part, he tries to remain calm and chatty when in fact he feels "jabbed where the most delicate nerves are" (349). Each in their own way is trying to maintain, and sustain for the other, a tragicomic perspective that is the painfully ennobling hallmark of romantic ideals as we plumb and gauge the whereabouts of our truest feelings. Unable in good conscience to either recollect or forget her, the diarist describes the depressed enthusiasm that marks his life and places him at such odds with ordinary ways of inhabiting the world (349–50). Tellingly, he feels trapped by the very arduous idealism that has made him "unhappy but also indescribably happy" (350). To make sense of this paradoxical inner state of affairs, we must consider how little he can tolerate his own apparent self-importance, how much he "wanted to have the power to be able to express myself in the universal any time I wished," and laments that his "life is religiously structured and is so far back in inwardness that I have difficulty in making my way to actuality" (351). Against this backdrop he wonders what kind of honor his life will retain in the end. As the greatest of external goods, honor is both terribly valuable and dramatically secondary.[23] To depend on another's recognition and then renounce all rights to expect it is a particularly revealing psychological strain both public and private souls continually face. It makes the diarist feel at least as disgusting as Richard III and equally intent on proving "despite language and all the laws of life, that he could be loved" (352). Thus, whatever honor he can reasonably expect is relegated to that which might be found in "a new heaven and a new earth" (353).

This minor theme of honor as an unstable good and its attendant promise of stilted happiness are carried back in time on the *morning* of 30 May, covering familiar ground. What he cannot imagine is that the two of them could form a happily married union. The reason for this skepticism is based on his depression and the ensuing task of concealing it, a grave reticence that presumably makes her unhappy. In turn, this inability to imagine an authentic form of felicity given the limitations of his temperament is then foiled by her presumed lack of "freedom of thought in relation to another view" (354). Along the way, he is incensed by the prospect that she might settle for a "morganatic" relationship (355). A true marriage must be fully reciprocal, based on "mutual understanding" (355). It is that or nothing. His position on this is quite inflexible, which is why—if her inability to imagine and existentially inhabit a deeper, fully problematic bond is accurate—his own vow would be meaningless. A simple passion would constantly clash with a complicated one, and therefore precisely "in that which should bind us together most intimately, I see a divine protestation against the whole

[23] Aristotle, *Nicomachean Ethics*, lines 1095b 25 and 1123b 20.

thing" (355). It is much more than a rhetorical question to ask: "Is one merely to ask about carrying through one's passionate wish and ask nothing about the idea; is one merely to believe in one's passionateness and have no faith or confidence that the person one loves can mean well, as they say, even though he does not have the same meaning?" (355). Behind this question lurks the doubt that he is wrong about her altogether. Or to articulate the faithful side of doubt, behind this question lurks the baffled confidence that she knows as much and better, revealed in a following series of rhetorical questions, replete with doubtful answers that shower confetti on his agony:

> What a strange and wonderful creature is woman, and what a strange power is love! I cannot stop loving her, and yet her fidelity is of a dubious kind. Is it love to love the way she loves at this time, is it an art? No, it is weakness. Is it beautiful? No, it is unfree. Is it a power? No, it is a weakness. Is it fellow feeling? No, it is self-love. Is it faithfulness? No, it is a subtlety of nature. And yet when it is a woman who does it...No, I do not believe I would like this in anyone else, but when she does it, she does it in such a way, or I look upon it in such a way, that she loses nothing in my eyes. (356)

Behind this passage, which parrots a sentiment one of the banqueters might express, is the ineffable sense that "she is the strong one and I the weak" (356). While this is immediately qualified by "inasmuch as I am always fearful on her behalf," he could just as well have directed each of his questions at his love as he did at hers: Is it involuntary, weak, and selfish? Is it beautiful, powerful, and artistic? The rhetorical answers are evidently yes and no.

By the beginning of June a year later, these "dialectical difficulties" have not abated but rather intensified to the point, hard on the heels of a religious infinitizing, where what he imagines and even wishes for her is that "she might be intensified in her temporal existence, become something great and exceptional" (357). Of course this would only make things worse for him, since it implies that his own failures, far from ruining a purportedly innocent purity of devotion on her part, might at least be partially responsible for bringing about a kind of perfection he had been looking for in her all along, which is itself its own kind of betrayal. In that case he very well might think of himself not as the faithful bear who comically mauled his master to death as it drove away a fly, but tragically as the one who painfully restrained his own power and in so doing made everything less needlessly dangerous (358). But such comfort would come at the terrible cost of last chances lost.

Pariahs and Changelings

The retrospective *morning* entry of 5 June invokes a perplexing reference to an "erotic arrangement" outside of wedlock as a possible solution, "of which there are examples" (358). This thought seems inspired by Johann Georg Hamann, an adult convert and professional failure who lived and wrote outside official channels back in Köingsberg where Immanuel Kant helped him land a job as a low-level civil servant in a tax office, and who had fallen in love with a proper Katharina but was denied her hand by her stilted and unreligious brother. It was there that he is reported to have faithfully lived with a woman outside wedlock and by whom he had four children, all deeply cherished despite their occasional distraction to his peripatetic and avant-garde scholarship respected by Goethe, Hegel, and Kierkegaard alike. What apparently impresses the diarist about such an example is the very option of twisting the ethical bond away from social norms and placing it squarely on two individuals standing solely on their own conscience, which would assume and even require a kind of religious responsibility to sustain the outlandish dimensions of such a romantic breach of protocol. The diarist is not convinced his beloved is up for that version of inner authenticity. However, nor is he correspondingly interested in some "more exceptional girl" and finding "ever-new joy some other way in the world" (358). The public dishonor of "circumventing the wedding, whether she is willing to put up with it or not, whether she could depend on my fidelity or not," he concludes, "is an outrage" (358–59). Even so, while he refuses to "become a knight" at the cost her becoming a pariah, and even though their current status places them both in such odd straights, working as he is to at least leave her own honor intact, this alternate possibility nevertheless occurs to him (359). Perhaps what he is exploring in this passage—about her, about himself, about us—is whether any of us have the nerve. Thus it is no surprise when he ends this section with: "If there were one person to whom I could turn, I would go to him and say: *Bitte, bitte* [Please, please], put a little meaning for me into my confusion" (359). We have heard the diarist plead in this German before, variously bowing to God and now at the feet of a fellow human being (239). As it currently stands, and despite all comic relief, he is "succeeding so uncommonly well at jabbering and drooling that at home I have to make the opposite motions lest for me, too, it end with the whole thing disintegrating into nonsense" (359). Jabbering aside, in its own way the example of Hamann may be an indirect addition to the strikingly similar but opposing commentary of Victor Eremita and Judge William on whether marriage is something more sacred or profane, about whether a couple's first meal should consist of the Lord's Supper or a casserole. Presumably, the one fare without the other does not a marriage make.

After reporting this vaguely appalled fascination with an alternative life of unofficially sanctioned faithfulness, the final literary interpolation that follows tells a story about Nebuchadnezzar, the great king of Babylon. In it the king has a terrifying dream that he would be changed into a beast of the field, driven away from all human society. Although the original tale comes from the apocalyptic book of Daniel, the diarist characteristically makes it his own. According to the original, when this transformation into a beast occurs the biblical account does not record the inner thoughts and feelings the king had while undergoing his metamorphosis. According to the diarist, during the change Nebuchadnezzar still knew himself but, unrecognizable to others, could only bellow like an animal. Frightened and confused, the king agonizingly dwells on the strange power of this foreign Mighty One—The LORD God, YHWY—who is able to subdue him in such a fashion though this God has no throne, no armies, and indeed not even a street address. There is no confirmed material threat that this Mighty One might either completely conquer Babylon or even magnanimously leave him a political portion to contemplate, and yet in this god's hands "kings' brains are like wax in the melting furnace, and their might like a feather when he weighs it" (362). Once restored to his normal state of self-consciousness Nebuchadnezzar immediately summons all his wise men to explain the secret of this cunning power of Israelite origins. But they all prostrate themselves before the great king and declare the whole thing a fantasy, an evil dream. Apparently, he had a dream within a dream. And yet the experience was real enough and had lasting effects. Interestingly, according to the biblical account, on a previous occasion when this sort of thing happened Nebuchadnezzar even demanded his interpreters not only explain his dreams but also report what those dreams were in the first place. Without any special powers of his own, Daniel was the only one who could perform the task. Why and how? Because the Mighty One—whose very inscrutable power required explanation—had revealed it to him, and by that same power rendered the faithful Israelite immune to both lions and the furnace.

What we should make of this story in the context of the diary does seem like a task of explaining a dream we must first describe on our own. If we can, we can expect honor and reward. If we cannot, we shall be torn limb from limb and our houses shall lie in ruins, at least according to the book of Daniel. Less apocalyptically, let us venture the interpretation that the diarist earnestly hopes that neither his love affair nor the obscure divine interruption of it is just the meaningless dream of an overactive imagination. To be locked away within oneself bellowing like a crude beast longing for gentler words really would be terrifying. But romantic idealists who nevertheless cling so vigorously to reality often feel this way, whether they are feeding on bread and wine or dandelion greens.

A Pond, a Duck, a Book, a Girl, and a Guinea Pig

7 June opens with the description of "a little pond in a peat excavation" that was an important source of imaginative development within the diarist as a child. Replete with a willow tree whose extended branches served as a raft in harbor from which he could "gaze down into the darkness" and the fascinating activity of a particular wild duck whose cry and flight from the surrounding woods "awakened dim memories in the heads of the sedate ducks," prompting them to beat their wings and "fly wildly along the surface," this whole setting is then compared to the importance of a single, even poorly written book that if read with passion can deliver "as much as there was in yourself" (363–64). Both the pond and the book, each one as revealing "as antediluvian discoveries to the natural scientist," are then compared to her. "I gaze

and gaze so long at this girl—until I draw out of myself what I perhaps would otherwise never have come to see, even if I had seen ever so much, for this would not imply that my inwardness had become transparent to me" (364). The common thread sewing all these references together is the way in which our tactile selves forge a fragile bond with our moral and spiritual sensibilities. As an adult, given his background and proclivities, she affects him in an equally particular and arbitrary way:

> If she had been unusually gifted with spirit, she would never have affected me in this way. She is quite enough for me when it comes to responsibility, and again the responsibility is mine, and yet it is she who in this responsibility brings my inwardness to consciousness. I was far too much and far too definitely developed for her to be able to influence me by means of communication, nor was she equipped so as to enrich me spiritually with new content. But in order ultimately to understand oneself, it is a question of coming into the proper situation. To this end she has helped me in terms of responsibility. (364)

On the surface it would seem she is no better than a bad book, but above that she is a wild duck, a true echo of the divine call he confusingly follows. A page later this gives rise to an extended meditation on the tragicomic contradictions of human life it is our task to inhabit and embrace without completely falling apart. That task consists of being earnest, properly compounded by a sense of humor. In a mood similar to what prompts Socrates at the end of *The Symposium* to suggest true playwrights are equally adept at writing comedy as well as tragedy, the existential aim is "to endure contradiction, but also keep it at arm's length in freedom" (366). In contrast, "the point" of a purely immediate existence is precisely not to acknowledge life's contradictions, which amounts to a "bigoted earnestness" that "always fears the comic" (366). With dramatic irony internal to *Stages* as a whole, the diarist insists upon a lived unity of the comic and tragic that results in neither an actual Hegelian synthesis nor "a new kind of literature" (366). Rather, he articulates an authentic earnestness that "sees through the comic, and the deeper down from which it fetches itself up, the better, but it does not mediate" (366). Thus "the comic purifies the pathos-filled emotions, and conversely the pathos-filled emotions give substance to the comic" (366). As a concrete example of the contrast in question, he writes "anyone who could in truth make a hypocrite a butt of laughter will also be able to crush him with indignation. But anyone who wants to use indignation and does not have the corresponding *vis comica* will readily degenerate into rhetoric and will himself become comic" (366–67). As for "a new kind of literature," this agility at making light of hypocrisy without resorting to prudish indignation sounds like constructive criticism relevant not only to how one should properly inhabit the world but artistically represent the task. Arguably the potential impotence of literary productions and our lived, existential compulsions share a common problematic itinerary, which can be handled either well or poorly in either case. For his part, the diarist simply must not forget her since "[o]ften enough my fractious understanding has wanted to whirl the whole affair into laughter for me, but out of this very whirl my tragic passion has developed more intensely" (367). In his own commentary on the diary he himself has composed as an imaginary psychological construction, Frater Taciturnus will return at length to the literary correlations of this existential venture, as if, really, we could separate the two.

In the midst of this extended meditation on tragicomic unity, whether proposed in life or art, the diarist confesses he is "aware that I am very far from being a paradigm," "model," or "prototype," but at best "a sample human being…who could be needed in a crisis, a guinea pig life uses to feel its way" (365). On the one hand this suggests he stands pathologically apart from notable moral exemplars. On the other hand, a Socrates, a Diogenes, Simeon Stylites, Abraham, or Jesus, as individuals, do serve as prototypes in their very exceptionality relative to socially accepted norms. And they do so with problematic disruption. The main difference between these classic examples and the diarist is that he is as apologetic about his own ascetic tendencies as he is shy about his erotic ones, and is therefore the bastard kin of a perennial renaissance, trying hard to juggle a re-appropriated set of priestly and prophetic chainsaws. In any event, what we should notice in the diarist is a corresponding regulative ideal that does not issue in a neat synthetic unity of personal orientation but could nevertheless serve as a representative paradigm, at least "in a crisis." The question then becomes whether human health is not always in some sense critical. If so, the guinea pigs might then provide an authentic litmus test. Stitching this whole entry together in terms of a penultimate draft of himself, the diarist supposes—or perhaps merely hopes—that he has "indeed maintained earnestness in my relationship with her," and concludes at length:

> If it had not been this way from the beginning, if I had not step by step perceived the comic and under its surveillance kept the tragic to myself, then in all probability, if it so happened that she became another's, either a certain passionateness (which for all its vehemence is not earnestness) or laughter (in an un-warranted way in its separation from the pathos-filled) would have gained the upper hand over me. Now that the situation is reversed, it is indeed comic that I am the villain and she the one who wants to die. But this blow I can certainly bear, for my pathos is saved from the very beginning. My pathos does not stem from her or her vehement outburst—it is my soul's inwardness. This is why change cannot play games with me; I hold firmly to the idea, and the comic from the outside has no power over me. That I have believed everything, every word of hers, as earnestly as is humanly possible, that I feel myself bound by it as tightly as a person can feel it, is not at all comic. ...Indeed, if I had believed it only because of her, because she said it, if I had believed it out of confidence in her reliability, then I would be comic and in a certain sense would already have been comic. But I have believed her because she stood in an ethical relationship to me; therefore it was my duty to believe. On my own initiative I have given her words the weight of eternity for me because I respected the relationship; I have not established my life on her word and gown. (367–68)

Part of what is amusing about this passage is how *seriously* he takes himself. But it does not result in a straight comedy, since all along the way he insists he remains immune to laughter because he has explicitly not relied on any definite knowledge of her own subjective stance in regard to their courtship. He has simply taken her at her word, and if she says she will die apart from him, then that is what he must believe. The humor here is not the sort that produces chuckles. It is far darker and circumspect, far more nervous—or at least ought to be—particularly because he evidently *does* rely on her subjective reliability, about which he cannot possibly remain agnostic. And also because he himself is so vehement about his own unaltered passion, just short, of course, from establishing his life on her public vow and wedding dress.

Faith remains the cornerstone that holds the parts together, love the mortar, and hope the color. The mortar, of course, is the greatest of these, and most in need of repair over time, but they all remain essential to the architectural structure of our foremost commitments. Such a pair of lovers should make us simultaneously laugh and cry; for what, really, is the alternative? There is nothing particularly funny about love, the lengths to which we will go, how we refuse or get over it, or not, along with the unconscionable jealousies, strange protections, and ridiculous hopes it involves. Yet we laugh, and simultaneously sit on the edge of our seats, gripping the hand next to us, blessedly assuming there is one to hold.

Meaningful Third Parties

On 11 June, *midnight* in the present, the diarist crosses paths with his beloved on the street coming and going from some errand. He was otherwise occupied with a third party, but took the opportunity to gather what impression his unacquainted companion took of her emotional state. The diarist jocularly explains that one of his "diversions" is "to pay attention to people's exteriors in order to draw conclusions about their interiors" (368). The third party was dismissively annoyed by this preoccupation of his. But the idiocy of pressing his cohort in this way runs so counterclockwise it actually makes sense as a riff on how much or little we can tell about another from an external point of view, beginning with their manner and visage. For starters, he relies with obviously feigned relief on the phlegmatic appraisal of this unfamiliar, ostensibly impartial passerby with his offhand opinion that she appears just fine. Throughout, the external point of view in this passage refers not only to what may be visible to the eyes but notable to a casual, unwitting observer. Each of them, it would seem, are unreliable, and each of their perspectives raise a corresponding question about whether and how our senses can deceive us. Having correct vision, whether we are near or farsighted, suffer from stigmatism, or must make use of either a telescope or microscope is one thing. Whether we are in a position to perceive that someone is suffering from the throes of love and properly evaluate such a condition in terms we could all understand is another. The alternating confidence and hesitation that each question shares give birth to a doubtful child the diarist predictably adopts "on the sly" (369). For readers, as well as lovers, this adoption is par for the course for all those who have moments when, while loathing interpretative uncertainty, in the end playfully handle such an odd, unwelcome, glorious progeny unexpectedly placed on our doorstep to feed and clothe and watch grow up. Par for the course, that is, if we have the ears to hear and eyes to see.

On 12 June he reports that the day before, a year earlier, they were at a party where one of the ladies present commented that engaged people typically become thin. As third-person readers who have some inside information about what is transpiring, we can well imagine just how close to home this might strike. The scene becomes immediately more comic and correspondingly awkward when a gentleman responds that in recompense one generally takes on weight after marriage. Then, in an effort to change the operatic tone of this untimely exchange in order to put the relevant party at ease, the diarist mentions a known acquaintance whose name was enough to provoke laughter, retorting: "He has been married three times and is thinner than I am" (371). This whole sequence is a disquieting example of tragicomic perception. Starting with an observation that calls to mind the difficulties of love in all its suspended glory, continuing with an ironic quip that pops the very bubble of that thought and ends with a vaguely pathetic counterexample that combines the two sentiments several feet short of a Hegelian resolution, we are left feeling rather exhausted, with almost too much perspective, given the scale of what we are supposed to see, acknowledge, and absorb. The way this scene pans out, "[p]eople deigned to laugh; she had time to collect herself" (371). Although these are acceptable outcomes to a purportedly casual dinner conversation, the "torture" of it "is ruinous to both body and soul" (371). This final unvoiced comment is written to us as an indication of how delicate our feelings are and the sheer courage it takes to face them without either dropping our guard or throwing in the towel. For his part, the diarist delivers his lines "as lightly as a heavily armed person can," which is not very well. As a conversational maneuver, in person and then on the page, this exemplary repartee indirectly answers a question about how to redeem a situation *without* making light of it, a talent for living well with another that may very well lay beyond our aggregate power.

In conjunction with the issue of whether any of us display much of a talent for welding an Aristophantic bond, the entry as a whole is vigorously preoccupied with an allergic fear of meaninglessness. The two great threats the diarist cites are the prospect of becoming her "benefactor" or "the absurdity that I am supposed to be something important and disdain her" (370, 372). That he might kick out all the existential stops, ignore his inclosing reserve, and glide along respectfully by preserving her honorable social standing or float the impression that she is simply not good enough, are equally obnoxious to the "idea" that compels him. This "idea" to which he is so dedicated takes flight above both the pedantic nonchalance of theatergoers and the sagacious practicality of its detractors. As an idea, its meaning hovers with the impressions of a complex, well-told story that never entirely distinguishes between the flow of actual events and how one might narrate them, and leaves him altogether at considerable odds with civic enthusiasm, cultured affectation, and disenchanted irony alike. As a result he feels offensive to everyone but cannot manage to apologize directly, except in secret, disclosed from the bottom of a pond locked within a box containing the key inside. That apology is ostensibly addressed to her, the one who roots his whole point of view in the earthly, liturgical seasons of birth and death, but also an indirect confession to the public, ostensibly written by Frater Taciturnus and published by Hilarious Bookbinder. In the midst of all this veiled publicity the diarist is caught, tempted by the thought that it "would be superb if she herself could be brought or if it would occur to her to break the connection, for then she would be spared the humiliation" (372). But he only partially succumbs to this temptation by merely dropping hints and dares not "speak of it with full voice and total passion," for "then she would discover how much she preoccupies me and then she would try all means once again…" (372). It remains unclear who is being either addressed or seduced here. He therefore remains bewildered, unable to repent and yet left feeling guilty. The nobility of his position shares little with the deflated chivalry of Victorian times or the unkempt egalitarianism of modern sentimentality. What emerges universal is the degree to which romantic ideals, in any era, both incorporate and transcend the limitations of the most objective postmodern and least philosophical standards of a historical imagination.

Reading the diary is not unlike getting on a city transit and sitting down next to someone who suddenly bursts into tears. One reaction would be to remain very still and discretely offer a tissue. Another is to become annoyed and offended that such a person had the audacity to rain on the morning of one's own ordinary parade. Alternatively, one could call 911, except that the relevant authorities lack a code for this kind of distress. More sympathetically, one could offer conversational comfort of some kind, but at the considerable risk that the suffering party might simply lash out and plead: "I'm sorry, but you just wouldn't understand." Surely *that* would put everyone concerned in a tight spot. Making bleary-eyed confessions is an act of unwarranted and involuntary courage; receiving them is an art. The exchange rate is so far beyond the pale that political economists all told would end mystified and equally poor in spirit. It is with this in mind that we should approach the crucial entry of 14 June *midnight*. That is, if you find yourself on this particular subway.

Midnight Thoughts about the Wedding Day

The central theme of 14 June is a pervasive, uncommon awareness of our fragility, of the threats we commonly face, and the ensuing depression that attends such self-imposed prescience. Close on the heels of this theme is how these very thoughts lead to "a religious assurance," an "eternal certitude of the infinite," followed by whether one should burden a more cheerfully oriented confidant with such melancholy perceptions (374–78). In order to unpack this perplexing confluence we might begin with the following: "If she had become mine, I am sure that on the wedding day I would stand beside her with the thought that one of us would die before evening, or with some such gloomy notion" (375). This raises all kinds of questions. Like *who* thinks this way? Why? Are they justified? Is such an attitude avoidable? Should they share this information? All these questions are genuine, and none rhetorical.

Answering them is a common project. And the various sides we take will tell us something about the diarist, something about her, as we might imagine either of them, and finally something about ourselves. Herein lies the genius of this particular literary construction. There is no single author here to tell us what to think or how to determine our proper feelings. The truths remain sunk, hidden, and then starkly raised out of the depths from one sitting across the boat from a naturalist friend who offers an instrument for picking at things below. As repeatedly noted, the *real* author of the diary does so with a large measure of trepidation.

Succeeding his initial revelation about having gloomy thoughts on his prospective wedding day, the diarist mentions an elderly woman he knew who confessed a fear of being buried alive. There are precautions one can take against this prospect, as there are against the terrifying possibilities of car accidents, carbon monoxide intake, or rape, which are more statistically frequent than live burial. All the same, although none of these happen to everyone, in the case of any pair of lovers, one will assuredly die first. This latter inevitability—"the simplest objection, one that will occur to anybody"—frequently preoccupies even the youngest of couples, quite apart from whether it counts as an objection to their most tender investment. But we can say that a lover with any amount of passion would neither choose to remain living nor deprive their beloved of a corresponding preternatural demise, since a loose end remains at either pole of such choices, only tied up by conscious agreement *in extremis*. As for the diarist, he is especially sensitive to these threats to earthly felicity and is neither willing nor able to flee from their inevitable possibility. In theological terms, he confesses that although he has "the most inspired conception of God's love, I also have the conception that he is not an old fussbudget who sits in heaven and humors us, but that in time and temporality one must be prepared to suffer everything" (374). While this view of God is startling and for some even horrific, the diarist takes solace in the implicit theodicy. Distant from the infantile comfort of a Freudian father figure, it offers "a God who would not protect me but would surrender me to the dangers of a life worthy of being called human."[24] By design our lives are fashioned in such a way

[24] Paul Ricoeur, *The Conflict of Interpretations* (Evanston: Northwestern University Press, 1974) 460.

that the very insecurity of finite happiness lends it dignity. In contrast, "most people"—apparently including his beloved, and even the anonymous woman fearing live burial—"have a fractional idea of life's fraudulence, but then along come experience and probability etc. and patch the pieces together, and then they are safe and secure and have reasonable grounds for it" (376). In point of fact, this more sagacious view of life is what the diarist finds truly frightening. Better to have developed a healthy fear of God and interior reserve that is the unique opportunity of sailors and frontiersmen:

> When the storm rages in the night and in it the hungry howling of wolves sounds forebodingly, when someone in distress at sea has saved himself on a plank—that is, has to be rescued by a straw from certain ruin, and consequently one cannot send a message to the next cottage because no one dares to venture out into the night, and thus one can save one's shouts: then one learns to be content with something other than confidence in night watchmen and policemen and the efficacy of distress signals. (379)

As for those in the urban centers so concerned with the trimmed status of their hedges or the distracting sheen of their shoe polish, they just might benefit from a stroke of lightning, because otherwise the real danger is that life might add up to this:

> He was young and still remembers many enjoyable impressions from that time, many happy days; then he was married, and everything went well, except that he once became very ill, and a physician, the first one available, was hastily summoned, and so Professor D. came and proved to be a very careful physician, and thus became the family physician; also in Pastor P. he found an earnest spiritual counselor, of whose deep religiousness and sincerity he was more convinced than of his own religiousness and therefore became fonder of him year after year. Then he became acquainted with many congenial families, associated with them, and then he died. (379)

Immediately following this inky characterization, the diarist asks the following darker series of questions: "And why should it not be beautiful to have had a happy youth and to remember it; why should it not be gratifying to have learned to know Professor D. and Pastor P.?", and then answers for himself "but if this is supposed to be the ultimate when all is said and done—then I would rather not have inconvenienced either the professor or the pastor but would rather have heard the howling of the wolves and learned to know God" (379–80).[25]

For some readers this may seem like a pathetic and exaggerated excuse for not embracing all a humane social life has to offer, starting with marriage, in sickness and in health, for better and for worse, including sexual embraces, dinner parties, and trips to the park. But here again we must coordinate the relevant players in on the action. What *he* claims is that he cannot share such depressing thoughts, for a "confidant will not think my depressing idea with the same passion as I do, and consequently he will not understand, either, that for me it becomes a religious point of departure" (375). Furthermore, he posits that to "live confidentially with another person requires either that one not have such thoughts, that one's world of consciousness end at the scarcely Greek, even less Christian, systematic board fence—the outer is the inner and the inner is the outer—or that one not have them on such a large scale that they do not retreat before what is called reasonable grounds" (375–76). To invoke William James's categories, this makes it sound like only happy souls should get married and that sick souls should keep quiet and stand socially apart, out of basic respect.[26] But what if the diarist is right that his beloved does not share his thoughts with the same passion? Or what if she cannot, or will not? Positive answers to these questions may very well constitute a "divine protest" against their union (375). This perplexing disjunction seems to imply he should find a fellow sick soul to join with, which in its own way might be tenable if it were simply a matter of linking one-dimensional personality types. But this conclusion is not one that directly invites or finally haunts the diarist's imagination. As a personal witness within the scenario what he does imagine is marrying her, and further imagines coming around to "the time of suffering before I became mature and that it was that old woman's depressing notions that plagued me." "Then," at that point, he "would speak and initiate her into it. She would really laugh now, for sure, because it would be inconceivable to her where anybody could pick

[25] This would bear an external comparison to Henrik Ibsen's *Brand* (New York: Penguin Books, 1996).

[26] William James, *The Varieties of Religious Experience*, lectures IV–VII.

up such notions" (376). He considers but then brushes off whether such "innocent laughter would be the very best cure," insisting that his depression is "continually the point of departure for a religious fulfillment" in comparison to which the "considerable power" of "youthfulness" and its attendant happiness is one in which he could only take "sad pleasure" (376). Imagining further on this route, she would presumably offer cheerful reasons against his dark thoughts and thereby initiate *him* into a "dialectic that is supposed to bind the one who for fifteen years day and night has improved himself in handling thoughts dialectically, just as the Arab handles the snorting steed, as the juggler plays with sharp knives" (377). The question for us is whether the old woman's paranoia or his beloved's good cheer is a sharper knife. Given that the diarist's "fourth and fifth precautionary measures of which she had not dreamed" seemed to help the old woman, who in fact thanked him for it, but which left him in a state of not knowing whether to "laugh or cry over it," one also wonders whether the dacrygelosis the diarist formerly diagnosed in his beloved here turns terribly south into a bizarrely self-inflicted anhedonia (376). The various characters on the table ostensibly appeal to multiple parts of ourselves, and the question behind the text is whether we are willing and indeed able to hold them together. As for the two of *them*, an authentic marriage is neither a split existential contract nor a mute agreement, but a sonnet of true minds admitting every unknowable impediment, all told.

As to whether the diarist should share his thoughts, and in what form, is no doubt vexing. But those thoughts have evidently been disclosed. The whole confusing mess has gone to press, for better and worse, simultaneously committed to both her and mere paper and left for the rest of us to keep from decay at the wan behest of Hilarious Bookbinder via the anonymous and deceased Mr. Literatus, who was the first to pass along this disingenuously composed, handwritten psychological construction attributed to Frater Taciturnus and brought to the Bookbinder's renewed attention by a suspiciously young and talented normal-school graduate and candidate in philosophy. Some readers may feel irritated by the form, others embarrassed by the content. Still others may find themselves piqued by either or both. Relevant in this regard is that the diarist's depressing ideas—his whims or sad fancies—are "reminders" of his primary love, his love for God, who sends deformed messages to his children by way of dwarves and old hags (378–80). As a disciple of divinely indirect matters he likewise communicates with us, and in an equally deformed manner with his earthly beloved. The question will no doubt persist: does he suffer from self-deceived pretension or is he just horribly thirsty for salient connections amidst a communion of saints? It is hard to tell. Perhaps the birds of the air and the lilies in the field might know, well after midnight when morning is about to break. What does seem clear is that the diarist writes as if carrying out a divine commission and, in doing so, intentionally places all these questions before the jury of individual readers. No matter how upsetting, his both priestly and prophetic mission invites us all to a sacred feast of interpretation rather than be starved by the thin gruel of one-dimensional clarity. In the end, we must admit the prospect of death and loss with which the diarist is preoccupied in this entry is the most powerful and confusing test of love. In an effort to be prepared couples often split over the level of comfort or anxiety that animates each of them and the ingredients of flourishing the other adds or excludes along the way. It would be facile to say one could be either recklessly or unduly prepared for such a grave possibility as the death of a loved one on the wedding day, for the spectrum of how we respond to the test is not just wide, but thick, and the range of color severely mixed, as is the dream-life of our emotions itself. Full of glorious ideals, petty preoccupations, and terrible insecurities as we all are, the yellows, reds, and blues, continually haunted by black and white, can just as well give rise to resentment as hope with a barely perceptible shade of difference. Needless to say, this range includes the precious pastel hues that at least some of us avoid like the plague.[27]

---

[27] An initial gloss on the question of whether one should initiate another, especially a beloved, into the full existential insecurity of human life is presented in *Fear and Trembling*, 107ff. There a decidedly nihilistic Faustian figure keeps silent, a decision actual figures like Sartre and Camus faced and handled in their own way. The diarist presents a simultaneously more romantic and religious version, full of corresponding reservations, but bent on belief. In an alternative, less sympathetic reading, Vincent McCarthy hits upon the apparent link the diarist seems to draw between his morbid inclosing reserve and more elevated religious sentiments, a link that simply amounts to a solipsitic, emotionally

Divine Juries and Human Judges

Front-loading the drawbacks of his "total individuality" and "entire makeup," the diarist asks himself and provisionally answers a corresponding series of questions (381–82).

Is he guilty? Yes, of having ventured into a relationship he later decided would only detract from his beloved's happiness. We know she protests this conclusion, which leads us to surmise he lacks the courage to believe she could handle and indeed celebrate his oddness of character. What is his consolation? That God has benevolently used this perplexing conflict to teach him his own lack of strength. What is his hope? That he can be forgiven. But this leads to other questions, the answers to which are left to us. Forgiven for what? Forgiven for not understanding himself earlier? Forgiven for understanding all too well a virtue that can become so turned in on itself in such a way that others find insufferable? Forgiven for projecting his fear and self-doubt on another? Forgiven for a lack of trust or lack of will? Maybe he needs to be forgiven for making definitive guesses about what she could or could not handle or might even welcome in light of what he would not welcome or cannot imagine handling. In all this confusion over potential guilt, the one thing he insists upon is that *her* forgiveness "is part of the divine procedure" (381). He does not seem particularly worried that God could or would forgive him, whatever his guilt, but that she, as the central plaintiff in "an intermediate court, a legitimate court," would not understand (381). The way he sees things, any possible forgiveness on her part would be like signing off on a contract when the one party can neither read nor write. In addition he assumes she is in the position of approving a petition without knowing what is even being sought. The only thing that could make the scenario worse is if they spoke different languages altogether. Apart from the distracting evocation of legal protections and judicial appeals when it comes to matters of the heart, a more central irony is that his otherwise punitive, trial-based view of God

isolated, schizophenic, macho romanticism as a faux manner of excusing himself from the relationship. McCarthy even goes as far to suggest the diarist should have simply worn his lady's colours in a Medieval courtly fashion and left it at that. See "Morning and Melancholia in 'Quidam's Diary,'" *International Kierkegaard Commentary*, Volume 11, Stages on Life's Way.

is actually trumped by her role as a chief witness. The Divine Judge suddenly appears both understanding and forgiving while she is simply given over to helpless, teary incredulity. But this mixture of love and anger usually associated with authoritative greatness is exactly what Jesus suffered as he wept over Jerusalem (Luke 19:41). The twofold implication here is a solid but tender theological brushstroke. "Forgive one another as I have forgiven you," says Christ. This requires belief and understanding—*crede ut intelligas*—which the diarist refuses to foist on anyone, least of all her. After all, as part of the Apostles' Creed the "forgiveness of sins" is the most difficult part to believe since unlike the virgin birth it literally cannot be taken metaphorically. And so once again he is caught, and pickled.[28]

---

[28] More than one commentator has diagnosed Quidam as despairingly recalictrant in acknowledging God's love and forgiveness and thereby stuck in a vicious cycle of opaque self-understanding, akin to one fruitlessly staring into a windowpane transparent in itself but lit only from within amidst darkness all about. Such critics even quote Anti-Climacus' formula for faith as "resting transparently" in the divine power that has granted the self its existence in the first place and then forms its absolute moral criterion and final redemptive benefaction. See Louise Carroll Keeley, "Living the Possibility of a Religious Existence: Quidam of Kierkegaard's *Stages on Life's Way,*" in the *International Kierkegaard Commentary,* Volume 11, Stages on Life's Way; and Søren Kierkegaard, *The Sickness Unto Death* (Princeton: Princeton University Press, 1980) 14, 82, 131, edited and translated by Howard V. and Edna H. Hong. Somehow this failure at transparency is his own fault, and presumably a chief barrier in his relationship to Quaedam herself, even though the trick in every academic sermon about objective grace and subjective sanctification is even more fundamentally about who is supposed to raise the overpowering sun that would flood the inner room of inclosing reserve and make that dark mirror and corresponding faulty image of ourselves disappear. Describing *what* exactly occurs at such a juncture is just as puzzling as positing by whose agency it comes about. For one thing, when the blaze of redemptive light shines from without, does any image of oneself remain in the glass, however transparent? One version of this story might be that Christ ideally replaces the image of ourselves in the window in a kind of total, immediate Lutheran transformation. But that is just another reflection we can only imagine or accept, from within, the plate glass still intruding with other glares and refractions perhaps more blinding, since the whole point is to know ourselves as we are known, but nevertheless presumably known *as* ourselves. Moreover, given Anti-Climacus' altogetherly apt formula in *Sickness Unto Death,* we should grant proper weight to the unsolicited demand

What he finally reproaches himself for is "the earnest words I secretly interspersed in the confusion" (383). This confession comes directly on the heels of a related irony—that he deliberately chose "not to make myself understood but to give her to understand that I was tired of her, that I was a deceiver, a muddlehead" (382). Had he spoken either to her or us directly and said "the maintenance of the relationship is my own wish," he "would not have been permitted to say more..." (382). Why not permitted? Because, as he imagines it, she would have in jubilation immediately interrupted and said: "'O dear one, you do not know how happy you are making me. It is your own wish; alas, I had given up faith in that and learned to be satisfied with less until it again became your wish, but now everything is fine, in fact, more than just fine, it is splendid—you wish it and I wish it, so every hindrance is gone'" (382). He is quite sure this would only compound a misunderstanding between them he is bent on indirectly mitigating. The shibboleth bleeding from his pen indicates that the judge, the jury, the plaintiff, and the defendant all become one, equally lost in translation. But this blur paints a picture of the common predicament in which we attempt to coordinate our most

---

this definition of faith places on creaturely life to in fact know ourselves, as individuals, *in* communion *with* another, and *under* their command, which is as terryifying and disorienting as waking up in a dreamless world populated by strange and untold figures produced by someone entirely different from ourselves. No doubt this prospect would be wonderful, and indeed liberating, since no one would wish for a pure solitary confinement as either a moral or ontological condition. But this is also precisely why a human love story is so instructive, since the terror and attraction at this level are so palpable, and the love of God, whom we cannot see, may be just another grand illusion. In fact, it is impossible to state definitively who culpably suffers from inclosing reserve, or exactly at what point. For his part, if Quidam disparagingly writes of Quaedam's conception of God as a simplistically kind old uncle, but then chastises himself for it, perhaps that is because within every self-enclosed Pygmalion there is a true lover whose halting prayers are authentic enough to be honored by Venus herself. In any case, the *rest* to which Anti-Climacus refers arguably does not imply a circumvention of the difficulty, fear, and doubt that marks the internal drama of religious subjectivity. Rather, it evokes a particular comfort amidst the difficulty, as when with eyes shimmering against candlelight an amputee and widow share a subtle joke as they pass steaming mashed potatoes during a false dinner party hosted after the war by some Secretary of Defense who can barely look one straight in the eye.

cherished ideals and desires with another's face and name that intimately calls us to respond in kind. Such is the unprofessional story of our lives as we attempt to sort through personal wounds and private affections. Trial by error is par for the course. The very madness of the project lends it nobility, accompanied as it so often is by the haunting cry of a bittern. Or in the diarist's own tongue, when it comes down to the true feeling of devotion, "the most poetic is also most ethical" (384). All of which leaves us with a common, urgent expectation of temporal existence: "that it would make it clear whether I was trapped in self-delusion or I loved faithfully…" (384). The answer to *this* question will most definitely not be located in a book; that is, unless a book can be as complicated and un-didactic as life itself. In the *morning* entry of 19 June he recounts a telling illustration of this arresting difficulty of working through matters of personal love. After a break in the text "[t]oday" she impetuously called him mad, which in a certain sense "hit right in the heart" but upon scrutiny proved a wild shot without actual aim (385). She also called him "malevolent, not good," a declaration she had also delivered the day before (385). He seizes on these ongoing claims and therewith reels off a bunch of nonsense about the split conjunction between love and respect in novels and legal contracts and actually manages to make her laugh. However, this dialogical repartee leaves him feeling depressed and alien, and five days later he jots that "[n]ot even what I am writing here is my innermost meaning" (386).

As we near the end of the diary, these rifts in the text where the past and present overstep each other become a regular feature. He increasingly bids his whole life on the wedding day, just after bidding half his life for a mere six months of happiness with her, and then settles for just fourteen days (385–86). The nonsensical talk continues between them, but at this time she is no longer laughing. He recommends she sagaciously dismiss him so that as a result "I would soon regret it and return like a whipped cur" (387). She laconically accepts this advice but then adds, "'No, I don't trust you an inch'" (387). After this exchange she bursts into tears while acknowledging it as a relief of sorts as he consoles himself that he had never averted his eyes from this sight even as he remained "completely unaltered" (387). After the outburst, the nonsensical talk picks up again, but alas "it does not seem to signify as much to her as to me" (387). What this seems to *mean* is that he cannot find a way to stay but refuses to walk away. The *reason* is our task to figure out given "the dead calm in which a lover worked and worked and almost became the beloved's murderer—not out of malice, not by accident, but in accord with his most honest conviction" (388). This conviction contains a mixture of conceit and sorrow that are the sibling rivals of her own love and anger, all of which sticks in his mouth like the sliver a child leaves in a seashore mussel after tiring of playing on its gaping hunger with a twig (388). Switching the simile, he feels as poor as the Englishman who found no one in the village to change a five-hundred-pound banknote. But then again, what he really thinks is that truly shared sympathy is a shilling that magically eludes any exchange rate so long as one does not attempt to estimate its value (388–89). Love and money mix about as well as oil and water, the one as toxic to wildlife even as it can serve as a balm, the other both a buoy and a condition for drowning. In the end, what seems important, what actually gives him comfort is how he has "trouble separating the alien parts [in himself] that I nevertheless do not really want to separate" (388). These parts include the romantically effusive, the sagaciously bourgeois, and the religiously traumatized. Put them together and one just might come out with a whole human being, one worth loving if you have the fully embodied nerve of a reluctant savior. Either or both of the two in question may or may not harbor that nerve.

Although the diarist suspects an eyewitness would find his understanding of love dubious given his action, he is certain about its pain. The pleasure he knows too, but at a considerable distance. Admittedly, the love he actually expresses is largely lyrical:

> Swiftly, through the omnipotence of being in love, swiftly like the growth of plants when they are cultivated by fairies, she unfurls, lovelier than ever—through herself, through the germinating power of being in love, and through my breath and the words that are whispered into her ear. Then I take her on my arm and dash through the world with her—this much, at least, I understand about love. (389)

Unfortunately, this very cognizance drives him out of his mind and immediately gives rise to suicidal thoughts. Tempted in this dire direction he spends the *morning* of 2 June ruminating on how, if "in a fever of delirium she betrayed what is taking place," her closest kin "would believe it was all fantasy" while he would recognize it as all too real (390). Once again, the feature of love picked out here is the necessary and often despondent role imagination plays in our more cherished relations with one another. At perhaps his darkest hour he surmises that spiritually she "is not even exhausted as much as she is beginning to become a little weary, with a little admixture of being bored" (389–90). One could surmise the same about any given reader, either *as* a reader or in their actual lives. If accurate, such fatigued affection would indeed signal a stillborn passion, an outcome as depressing as it is possible. What the diarist ultimately hopes is that in an eternal, sweet hereafter he will be healed of the starving "power of the imagination" nourished by such possibilities and that the two of them will finally come to an understanding. Short of this, time lingers on, inserting itself between them like a laconic referee (390–91).

Old Haunts

Forced by a thundershower into the café in which he nourished his early longing but had not visited "since those days of expectation," he unexpectedly saw her once again on 6 July (391). Drugged by un-prosaic recollections he sat in his old place "looking out the window now and then…" (392). Then he saw her. "She was walking with another young girl, both in a lively conversation; she was cheerful and healthy and happy. Was she perhaps coming from her singing lessons, my beloved songstress—is she going to her singing lessons again? Has perhaps only the song changed?" (392). This is the context for him to play the chorus with which we are already familiar: the perplexing rivalry between Cupid and YHWY with a bourgeois marriage holding them apart, initially accentuated by Judge William at the occasion of a christening. He both hopes and fears she has recovered, has found or re-found an actual love that would bring her back to herself, and yet wistfully thinks of him sometimes. Hanging on as best he can, he chastises both her and himself:

> She herself is partly to blame for the confusion, for she has disturbed the erotic by playing false in the religious. She refused to be satisfied with the erotic, with being loved or not loved and the consequences of

> that for her; she seized upon the religious and in responsibility became a gigantic figure for me. To be sure, war between two great powers has come about because a prince sent back a king's daughter; for me, who refused her, my conflict became just as terrible, for it was God who was her sponsor. (393)

At the feet of the gigantic figure she has become is the desperate acknowledgment that who and why we love in particular can be neither rationalized nor fully expressed. This fact, which lies at the heart of the entire romantic tradition, drives us to take ownership of emotions over which we have no ultimate control. It seems the test is to ask and finally live with a question that has no answer, a problem without a solution. To pose it is to acknowledge it, to embrace it freely, to accept it fiercely, weep over it joyfully, and learn to relax in its difficult half-light. There is nothing so threatening or so welcome, no experience so confusing and yet perfectly understandable, no ideal more worth fighting for lest we perish in the desert of a self-enclosed, mitigated thirst. Marriage lies at the exemplary center, not as a signed and sealed guarantee, not as a complete mystery that speaks on its own, not as an inviolable social contract that keeps old wine skins new, but as a middle term, brokenhearted, fully dismayed and quite terribly romantic. It turns out the form such marriage takes can and regularly does vary. The diarist's story is a flowering cactus in a desert of illusion that embodies and imperfectly represents a sincere, troubling, and heartfelt commitment. No doubt it does not unfold an entirely ideal vision. But that is because ideals make us defensive, gloriously un-centered, and generally drive us mad. Who of us could really claim we had done any better, suffered either more or less, romantically enacted it in a better or worse way, or more rightfully regretted, and un-cynically resigned and recalled it either way?

This entire discombobulated clash of values is reiterated in the penultimate *morning* entry of the diary, where he recounts going to her and "with unusual cheerfulness" proposed "that it was possible to do what she wished" (394). He went away and then returned at noon to "coldly and definitely" announce it was over between them. Her reaction to the former declaration was to accept his offer once again, but she seemed to do so "somewhat coldly" and "without a word reflecting sympathy" (394). In his mind, his feigned recommitment was an "extreme attempt to see if she, prompted by having been victorious, would not decide to grant me my freedom, when all along it was he was supposed to free her" (394). In response to the second, imperative and inflexible "rash undertaking," she only begged that he at least think of her sometimes. He promised to do so "in a casual tone" while "perhaps she did not mean much by it" (395). Given both the form and content of the diary, this may come across as not only unusual but cruel. But the ambiguous parity of meaning and intention, feeling and intimation, is ultimately moving. He supposes each of her reactions is heartless and wearily born while both his initial declaration and impending reversal appear equally disingenuous, since the *meaning* of each cancel the other. What we are looking at here is a negative image that serves as an indispensable template for a positive photograph. If we want to reproduce it, we better keep the negative.[29]

Here the diary ends with the expressed relief that it does not cover a year, as does the unrelenting church calendar, lest he suffer a perpetual "year of mourning" (396). An intentional or inadvertent irony here is that the church calendar in fact includes periods of "ordinary time" between Epiphany and Ash Wednesday, Pentecost and Advent. Whether in a liturgical or ordinary sense, one might consider this time a period of silence and rest, without mourning, a time to recover in order to begin again and learn something. The overall structure of the diary of course suggests not even a half-year, but a year and a half, which happens to

[29] Caroline Coleman O'Neill wrote a fictional account of the historical affair between Søren and Regine from the latter's perspective, about which we know comparatively little. *Loving Søren* (Nashville: Brodman & Holman Publishers, 2005). According to O'Neill's story Søren was in no uncertain terms loveable insofar as he was paternalistically haunted, socially disarming, seductively ironic, religiously abstracted, poetically engaging, and uncontrollably sad. By all this, and with full understanding, Regine was predictably and terribly rivited. However, as the tale O'Neill tells unfolds, it is not in the end about their love but rather about how she and Fritz Schlegel were to establish a separate peace in a proper marriage, apart from the scandalous forays of passion Søren otherwise displayed in both public and private. O'Neill is not alone among readers who must make their own peace. As far as it goes, Regine's own actual report can be found in *Encounters with Kierkegaard*, collected, edited, and annotated by Bruce H. Kirmmse (Princeton: Princeton University Press, 1996).

raise the ante. Perhaps the hint in all this is that Christmas might arrive in July, Easter in October, or that Good Friday might fall in any given week whatsoever. The disorder in the contrast reflects how badly we might want our inner lives to correspond to an objective schedule and how poorly this often works out, liturgical calendars aside. The way the diarist expresses this in particular is that it "would have been better if I could have remained faithful to her; it would have been greater if my spiritual existence had countenanced everyday use in a marriage, and I would have understood life more surely and easily. This is the order of rank. Next comes what I do" (396). As a result he thinks of himself as a printing error full of meaning even as the diary "deals with nothing" (397). As a diarist, or a person, he deals with nothing, not in the sense of superfluous accounts of Louis XVI sitting around between hunting expeditions, but in the sense that "it is the hardest life that deals with nothing" (387). Put otherwise, our temporal lives paint a meticulously scripted icon of a distended eternal present, full of memory and anxious expectation, wonderfully cut short and unimaginably lengthened with every story included. Which would, given time, take patience to see, hear, and absorb.

4

A Taciturn Commentary by the Actual Author

Frater Taciturnus completes his imaginary psychological construction with an address to the reader that feigns interpretive clarity not only in regard to his fictional hero but also in regard to how such a character would be received in flesh and blood. Such clarity would be a tall order to demand of any creative writer and a downright ridiculous offer for an artist to presumptively provide ahead of time. Fortunately, the present author too is fictional, full of the same arrogance, limitations, insights, and ambiguities as real people. As anyone could tell, Taciturnus begins, the character he conjures "is a demoniac in the direction of the religious—that is, tending toward it," and then suggests how "funny it would be to see [in actuality] such a spook, troglodyte, or cave dweller come sneaking out after listening secretly to people's romantic talk and claim to be an unhappy lover of the first rank!" (398, 400). Well, where are we at as readers at this point? Taciturnus' profession, of course, is not only that of a writer but also an observer of real people. Two-thirds of his readers, he supposes, will have by now thrown the book away before getting halfway through out of sheer boredom and confesses he himself has been tempted "to abandon him, and give up patience, which amount to the same thing" (398). This is all part of an overall literary construction that pushes the envelope on the supposed line between art and life while nevertheless acknowledging the reality of that very division. Our task is to remain inside the blur, to follow the train of thought, however much it seems like having a dream occurring in someone else's head. Inhabiting this world, we notice that Taciturnus has "deliberately" kept the girl "altogether ordinary" and thereby draws out a contrast to the diarist in order to "better illuminate him and teach him to exert himself," assuming imaginary characters are actually teachable (399). As irritating as it is for an artist to admit typecasting, it is ultimately for us to decide whether this is not an indirect comment on how we do in fact draw such distinctions in character just to get our initial bearings in reaction to both fictional *and* real people. All such characters—the corrupt cop, the lone ranger, the town drunk, the rebellious youngster, the overbearing mother, the transformative schoolteacher, and shall we say, the melancholy existentialist, etc.—either reveal or unravel their parts depending on how we react to them. They are the necessary literary manna that can both feed and over time sicken us, depending on how they are drawn. One distinction that immediately unravels is the way in which Taciturnus dismisses the romantic dimension of his construction, which he claims is a minor concern to him and uses it "mainly for orientation in the religious" (399).

On his internal radar is apparently some related author, a one Constantin Constantius, who wrote a comparable book entitled *Repetition* about a singularly poetic lover who broke with his beloved because he feared that if she became a wife she could no longer serve as a muse. To Taciturnus, that literary venture failed because it remained within a merely esthetic sphere. In contrast, his hero "is much too advanced for that" (403). Nevertheless, Taciturnus describes the diarist as an "enthusiast," with shades of meaning barely distinguishable from that of a poet (403). Certainly the diarist is not an esthetic enthusiast in the sense of living by immediate impulse graced only with an effusive, post-adolescent infatuation that suffers an equally immediate, depressing decay. For the diarist, the stakes are much higher and the depression much deeper. Whether this is a difference of degree or quality is itself an interpretive question. Arguably, the distinction between the young poet and the religious enthusiast seems a matter of age rather than development, designations that frequently do not correspond to one another in actual life, particularly given how the young man in *Repetition* becomes obsessed with the book of Job, not exactly typical of the infatuated youngster. Beside this, one reason Taciturnus claims the diarist would in reality be laughable is because while most of us might tolerate and even condone the feelings and words of the very young in pursuit of romantic ideals—so long as it happens "once in his life and at most for half a day"—to transpose such enthusiasm that is only useful as a quaintly social idiomatic reference into something more enduring and significant "betrays a slovenly upbringing" (401). Fortunately, the diarist is imaginary, and Taciturnus need not bother with the task of "having to argue with him or dialecticize him out of his dialectical difficulties" (403). In either case, the central characters of both Taciturnus and Constantius are animated by romantic sensibilities, and each of the authors remain preoccupied with unhappy love affairs whether or not those affairs are animated by entirely religious or purely esthetic values in their posture as legitimate "exceptions" to a settled married state. Furthermore, Constantius bears a similarly problematic interpretive relationship to his own central character.[1] It is possible that Taciturnus has intentionally misread Constantius in a flourish of earnest self-satire. All of which should alert us to the fact that Taciturnus is no more or less authoritative as a reader than the rest of us, even of his own work. Still, we do well to pay attention to what he has to say about his diarist, since it is at least plausible that

> one is able to study the normal in the aberration and, if nothing else, always learn this much, that the religious is not something to make light of as something one can easily do, or something for stupid people and unshaven striplings, since it is the most difficult of all, even though absolutely accessible and absolutely enough for everyone, which is already difficult to understand, just like the contradiction that the same water in the same place is so shallow that a sheep can wade and so deep that an elephant can swim. (398–99)

To say the least, this is enough to make one sit up straight and pay attention.

As a matter of literary fact, Taciturnus begins his treatment of the diary with an explication of unhappy love and the variation he sees in his own imaginative production, which has always been an apt topic for poetry. At the forefront of his mind is the basic relation of form and content, of what can be expressed and how to express it, but this issue is continually qualified by what he imagines people can receive and understand given what they are prepared to see and hear in what an artist has to offer. This complex configuration of literary communication burns the edges of everything he has to say. For starters, unhappy love

---

[1] Kierkegaard, *Fear and Trembling/Repetition,* 175–231.

"implies that love is assumed and that there is a power that prevents it from expressing itself happily in the lovers' union" (405). Though obvious and even trivial as a definition, the task of the poet is to select an obstacle and level of passion that are fitting. As far as obstacles go, these range from insignificant barriers to harsh realities not within the power of the lover to remove. On the other side of this coin, in terms of passion, it must be assumed that the love is real and powerful but also somehow impotent. If the obstacles and relevant passion are unfitting, the collision is entirely uninteresting and, at best, the subject of satire. For example, a lover might be depicted as tortured by a fear that his beloved might develop corns on her feet, an obstacle he is singularly unable to remove. Interestingly, Taciturnus suggests that the current generation of artists and their audiences limp on both sides, "neither believing in love as the absolute passion nor choosing obstacles of *prima* quality," and so the category of unhappy love is dropped altogether in favor of "more or less happy love" (405). In any event, in the face of unhappy love and any compelling production about it, we encounter a "duplexity" the poet must somehow resolve. The love in question must be powerful enough to potentially conquer and yet confront a barrier extremely difficult to overcome. But shall that barrier be internal or external?

Interpretively alluding to a few classic accounts, Taciturnus points out how Petrarch's great love is impeded not from within but by the fact that Laura is already wed. In Abelard's case, it is not that he feels his love conflicts with his holy orders, but that Heloise's drunken, discontented, jealous, and half-witted uncle Fulbert refuses to recognize how the erotic and religious might be consonant despite the institutionalized strictures of the times.[2] Turning to Romeo, while he inherits a family feud with the Capulets, that conflict does not stand out internally in regard to his love for Juliet, as colored as this passion may be by his initial unrequited love for the stalwartly chaste Rosaline. Taciturnus' initial point is that a poet worthy of his salt is unwaveringly focused on resolving such duplexities, and naturally refuses to do so by showing up the relevant passion as small, as if the lover in the end did not really love. There would be little drama in that. The love must

[2] Particularly compelling and insightful in this regard is the portrait George Moore provides in *Heloise and Abelard* (New York: Boni & Liveright, 1925).

appear and remain significant and irrevocable throughout. However, in such classic examples, the "esthetic hero must have his opposition outside himself, not in himself" (407). Any hindrance the lover confronts may then be resolved either comically or tragically without tainting our view of the love itself. If the lover falters due to a paltry passion, then it is not very tragic; if he conquers because the obstacle is trivial, then the comedy remains quite low. According to this initial analysis of unhappy love in such accounts, Taciturnus suggests the irrevocable passion in question remains "immediate," by which he means that it is unquestionably assumed, unexamined, and uncontested *within* itself. If there are any intimations of internal wavering on the part of the lover, then the poet must turn away from the lover and declare him guilty of not really loving. And if the poet is to proceed with his task, there must be some "higher passion" under scrutiny worth exploring. But what could that passion consist of?

A Dismissively Relevant Internal Conflict of Values

Taciturnus mentions one possible obstacle, and he does so more than in passing. "If the passion is love of the fatherland, then this must be undialectical in itself, and if the hero sacrifices an erotic relationship because of this passion, he is not called an unhappy lover but is named after the passion that is undialectical in him" (406–407). One reason this possibility is not ancillary to *Stages* as a whole is that Taciturnus interrupts himself twice to address it. Apart from the wicked stepmothers and other dragons that might stand in the way of personal love, it may turn out a hero suffers from an *externally* conflicted *internal* allegiance. In this connection Taciturnus mentions *Hamlet* as a potential anomaly, to which he returns forty-five pages later. But he could also have mentioned *Antony and Cleopatra,* whose evident personal passion is continually displaced by an equal sense of political honor, an ambition that is finally trumped when it could well have gone the other way. In that case love does indeed conquer in finally clarifying values that cannot be simultaneously maintained in a particular case. No doubt the young Octavius Caesar forces the tragic resolution, but there is enough evidence that ghosts of glories past would haunt their happy union even in a private political peace. For one thing, the very conflict within

Antony himself is a primary feature that attracts Cleopatra to Antony even as she demands an absolute, but equally conflicted allegiance; hence all the comedy amidst the tragedy, as when Antony bungles his suicide and Cleopatra softens her own with the intoxicating bites of a couple asps. For Taciturnus, however, the main plot of his critical analysis is how "[i]n our day unhappy love does not make a good show" (407). The reason is because whatever form the conflict might take, the single-minded immediacy of romantic passion has somewhere along the way become "incomprehensible" and given way to "common sense" (407–408). As an odd consequence, almost everyone is ready to stand up and applaud one another for having suffered and conquered—just yesterday in fact. This would provide exquisite material for a comedy, except that it would be difficult to theatrically produce since the audience cannot be both in their seats and onstage at the same time (408–12). Declaring the death of theater in this way, the autopsy report is that our esthetic sensibilities have not hit upon a higher passion. In apparent contrast, when love becomes dialectical, conflicted within itself, and presented as such, poetry must relinquish it. Why? Because (a) "there has been added an introduction of which the outcome is critical," (b) "there is no assurance that the outcome will be happy if only all the external obstacles are cleared away," and that (c) "in case of death there is no assurance that it will be a heroic death from love or from passion, since it might be a feverish cold of which one dies" (409). It is as if neither an available poet nor a given audience can comprehend such a love. This state of affairs marks a cultural vacuum since having "given up love as an absolute passion" and leaving behind a corpse of deadened esthetic sensibilities, vultures gather "in the shape of novelists, serial-story writers, hermaphrodites of tragicomic writers who are not sure whether they want to be writers of tragedy or of comedy and therefore are neither, for without passion there is no poet, not a comic poet, either" (409–10). One can imagine how Taciturnus might diagnose the average televised sitcom, no doubt rolling over in his fictional grave.

At this point Taciturnus returns to political passion as a possible rival and alternative to love as a primary personal orientation. However, what he chooses to point out is that the "same thing that weakened faith in love—the lack of a sense of the infinite—will also weaken faith in the other passions" (410). Nevertheless, if "politics is viewed with the passion of the infinite, it will naturally be able to yield heroes such as there were in antiquity, when people also believed in love" (410). What he ventures is that the same kind of mealy-mouthed sagacity would undermine political passion as well such that every other person becomes a Pericles and no one half the lover Alcibiades was. Political martyrs too would then become a dime a dozen as they clink glasses with one another between legislative rounds. Of course, even in his time, Aristophanes had a heyday with this sort of realpolitik, but Taciturnus assumes it is even more likely that his more advanced age would produce "a generation of armchair life-insurance salesmen" who "consider it an injustice on the part of poetry that it does not select its heroes among the worthy contemporaries" (412). No, poetry really is at an end, Taciturnus concludes, because any immediate, infinite, unquestionable passion has been met by "an equally infinite reflection" (412). Between the lines here Taciturnus intimates that patriotic sentiments are subject to a similar though more abstract torture of feeling. What we should read out of this is how our hometowns, constitutions, and vast landscapes of xenophobic failure make up a strangely mobilizing but unnerving part of our personal identity. When we are not comfortably numb each of us may harbor the paradoxical desire for both social recognition and complete independence. That conflicted desire too may be just as dialectical and a corresponding object of infinite reflection. James Baldwin, for example, is a good candidate for America's more prominent representative of someone trying his best to hold himself together both politically *and* personally. At one and the same time, being weak, talented, judgmental, despairing, hopeful, and always brutally forthright, Baldwin's novels and essays make any number of our passions seem paltry by comparison.[3] The ancient debate over whether *Eros* furthers or undermines the aims of the *Polis*, and vice versa, here reaches a pitch of sublimity worthy of death on a cross. As for the diarist, he hates it that his personal affection is so obtuse, his longing and sense of loss so distended, when his beloved may just want to lie still and feel the warmth of an attentive and gloriously thoughtless body

[3] See especially Baldwin's essays *The Fire Next Time* and *No Name in the Street*, and his later novel *Just Above My Head*.

resting in the crook of her armpit. Undoubtedly he is both drawn to and completely disarmed by this. If the question that springs to mind is whether the two of them can get it together, then one is very near the heart of the matter.

Throughout this section Taciturnus predictably talks out of both sides of his mouth when he says that passion, whether personal or political, has become "dialectical." On the one hand, this discussion is a prognostic lament over how thoroughly ironic the age has become with its disbelief in ideals in general and global sense that external obstacles are a thing of the past. Such sagacity leaves nothing worth singing about and everything a boundless object of lowbrow guffaw. On the other hand, when passion no longer encounters difficulty from without, when it no longer "collides with the world" and is in fact "favored by peace and security," then difficulty arises "because love must reflect itself in the individuality" (413). The cause of difficulty may vary. Subjective anomalies could be either serious or silly, which is partially why passion of this sort "provokes resentment, or so it seems to the individual," and correspondingly why Taciturnus says "I express myself very dubitatively and do not have the passion of my knight, but I am trying to understand him" (413). Thereupon he floats the thesis that in cases where no external obstacle obtains and yet a deeply problematic reticence remains, the task is to "constantly make double-movements" (413–14). Anyone who cannot perform this task is lucky if he has at least not lost his delight in poetry; anyone who can "also knows that infinite reflection is not something alien but is immediacy's transparency to itself" (414). What this double-movement suggests is that love may be a given, and felt absolutely, but some countervailing reserve impedes the way to a straightforwardly happy resolution. In the particulars of the scenario, he imagines the lover completely embraces the involuntary immediacy of his passion since "freedom does not at all mean that he is to give it up" but also that "in order to hold on to it firmly he uses the passion of infinity by which he could give it up" (414). It takes an agile imagination to hold such thoughts together. For Taciturnus, if one *happily* undergoes such infinite reflection "then it is something different, then it is religious; if it runs aground along the way, then it runs aground on the religious" (414). For the sake of his thought experiment he has kept the diarist suspended in order to display the double-movement at its most clear:

> Simultaneously he holds on firmly to his love, and he has no obstacles from the outside; on the contrary, everything smiles favorably and threatens to be changed to terror if he does not follow his wish, threatens him with the certain loss of his honor, with the death of his beloved—thus he simultaneously holds on firmly to his love and maintains that despite everything he will not, cannot make it concrete. (414–15)

This construction is bound to provoke any given audience member to frustratingly leave at intermission and is apparently unusable as an esthetic theme in the first place. But that is the story Taciturnus wishes to tell. Taciturnus could have just as well compared himself to the author of *Fear and Trembling*, except that Johannes de Silentio was not invited to the initial dinner party, probably because the theme of Genesis 22 was too sacred and off-putting to warrant a clink of glasses over the theme of "women." But it is fairly obvious that if Johannes were invited he would have given a speech about some young swain in love with a princess. The story there is about how one might handle a genuine but impossibly unrealizable affection. Cave into it one must, give it up one cannot. And there is no saying what external credentials bar the princess from falling for this extraordinary swain. Which in its own way is an even *more* ideal characterization of Abraham's ordeal in being willing to give Isaac up even as he fully loves the child of promise.[4]

The broad cultural diagnosis Taciturnus offers of poetic demise gives the sense that it is the end of an era, including and detracting from any lacuna concerning audience reception in its apocalyptic mood. This kind of typological, trans-historical analysis strikes us as statistically neat and organized, but also dubious for anyone who inhabits their own skin. The owl of Minerva may spread its wings only with the falling of dusk, but it stays awake all night. The "situation" of his diarist is "so dialectical" that we must not be in a hurry, "for that would result only in confusion" (415). Part of the confusion is that "for the person for whom it is true that the time of immediacy is over, for that person, too, the most difficult

[4] Kierkegaard, *Fear and Trembling/Repetition*, 41–47.

dialectical movement will become popular; otherwise I am very willing to admit that my imaginary construction is far from being popular" (415). What our author suspects is that his point of view might become unpopular due to "the many technical terms" which "scholarly windbags have in common with skippers, for example, who are unpopular because they speak a jargon and not at all because they speak profoundly" (415). On the other hand, "the terminology of a philosophy can also make its way even to the common man" even as it is "the thought, not the incidentals of expression, that essentially makes an exposition unpopular" (415). Somehow Socrates stands in the middle of this mess, since he "was the most unpopular man in Greece because he said the same thing as the simplest person but meant infinitely much by it" (415). Patching all this reneging reflection about lost immediacy and bombastic linguistic pedestrianism into a left-handed third option, Taciturnus writes that

> to stick to one thought, to stick to it with ethical passion and undauntedness of spirit, to see the intrinsic duplexity of this one thought with the same impartiality, and at one and the same time to see the most profound earnestness and the greatest jest, the deepest tragedy and highest comedy—this is unpopular in any age for anyone who has not realized that immediacy is over. (415)

But "neither can what is essentially unpopular be learned by rote. More on that later," he provocatively tempts (415). When in his own critical assessment Taciturnus suggests that, whether or not his production is well-received, it will in either case probably be for the wrong reasons, this puts the reader in a rather tight spot. In any case, amidst all this culturally prescient, artistic fallout, the task he has assigned himself is "an unhappy love affair in which love is dialectical in itself and in the crisis of infinite reflection acquires a religious aspect" (415–16). As a task he claims it is easy to see how it differs from other unhappy love affairs "if one looks at both parts at the same time" (416). Otherwise, he concludes, "one will perhaps not see either of them" (416). Those parts, so to speak, must be kept in the grease-pan for later when everything needs to be reassembled and made ready for a trip across land.[5]

A Hegelian Cross-Pollination

Before setting out on the final leg of our journey through *Stages* as we try to situate Taciturnus' problematic hero, we do well to familiarize ourselves with Hegel's characterization of the Romantic Movement within the arts, along with the seeds he detects of its own demise. Without exactly knowing the future of aesthetic production beyond the crude symbolism of prehistoric painting and the wholly incarnate but sightlessly sculpted hero-gods of the classical period, as Hegel narrates the history of art he unearths in the backyard of his own times the principle of inner subjectivity, the inviolable content of heart and feeling that cannot be neatly translated into objective form. In the ensuing predictably tripartite analysis, under the heading of romantic sentiment proper, the meal consists mainly of leftovers, of scraps only Canaanite

[5] For readers treking across such a land, one could make a stop along the way with the decidedly Quixotic thinker Miguel de Unamuno, who writes the following about various forms of physical love and spiritual loss along with their corresponding pleasures and pains: "And this is felt with still more clearness and force in the seeding, the taking root, and the blossoming of one of those tragic loves which are doomed to contend with the diamond-hard laws of Destiny—one of those loves which are born out of due time and season, before or after the moment, or out of the normal mode in which the world, which is custom, would have been willing to welcome them. The more barriers Destiny and the world and its laws interpose between the lovers, the stronger is the impulse that urges them towards one another, and their happiness in loving one another turns to bitterness, and their unhappiness in not being able to love freely and openly grows heavier, and they pity one another from the bottom of their hearts; and this common pity, which is their common misery and their common happiness, gives fire and fuel to their love. And they suffer their joy, enjoying their suffering. And they establish their love beyond the confines of the world, and the strength of this poor love suffering beneath the yoke of Destiny gives them intuition of another world where there is no other law than the liberty of love—another world where there are no barriers because there is no flesh. For nothing inspires us more with hope and faith in another world than the impossibility of our love truly fructifying in this world of flesh and appearances." *Tragic Sense of Life* (New York: Dover Publications Inc., 1954) 135–36, translated by J. E. Crawford Filtch.

women and other dogs would feed upon. Beginning with representations of the life of Christ, his lowly birth, inglorious death, and baffling resurrection, and then moving on to the purely maternal love of mother Mary, followed by the general devotion of disenfranchised disciples, some of whom suffer the abstract and one-sided fate of martyrdom, and others of whom, like Mary Magdalene, live on as shining examples of subtly converted eroticism, romantic art gives way out of the depths of a "Golgotha of the Spirit" to a corresponding agony at the heart of chivalry proper, only to die the death of romantic aesthetics in general as the principle of subjective inwardness decomposes under the headstone of purely formal individual character, freed of all earnest content, and finally rots in the soil of a show of common reality in the hands of mere compositional skill and a humorous "perversion and derangement of everything objective and real by means of wit and the play of a subjective outlook."[6] This history includes Dante's *Divine Comedy*, the miniatures of the Dutch masters, and a smattering of local satire. Short of this disarming prediction of every postmodern pop calligrapher and vaudevillian politico our contemporary media will eventually stage, there is presumably some room for a Thomas Mann or Graham Greene, a Gauguin or Rodin, before Mark Twain gives way to the depressing graphic possibilities of talk-show parody and reality television, in no particular order. His own or other examples aside, it is Hegel's general description of the romantic content of art that is relevant here.

After tending to the pure and disinterested devotional seeds of Mother Mary's love, precariously planted right next to Magdalene's fully adult erotic warmth, the easily broken reed of romantic love along with all its contingencies and collisions spontaneously sprouts. While it might be tempting to make light of this account as a veiled reference to a marriage between the virgin and harlot, Hegel writes that what romantically constitutes

> the infinity of love is this losing, in the other, one's consciousness of self, this splendour of disinterestedness and selflessness through

[6] G.W.F. Hegel, *Aesthetics, Lectures on Fine Art,* Volume 1 (Oxford: Clarendon Press, 1975) 576, translated by T.M. Knox.

> which alone the person finds himself again and becomes a self, this self-forgetfulness in which the lover does not exist, live, and care for himself, but finds the roots of his being in another, and yet in this other does entirely enjoy precisely himself; and beauty is chiefly to be sought in the fact that this emotion does not remain mere impulse and emotion but that imagination builds its whole world up into this relation; everything else which by way of interests, circumstances, and aims belongs otherwise to actual being and life, it elevates into an adornment of this emotion; it tugs everything into this sphere and assigns a value to it only in its relation thereto.[7]

What renders this romantic subjectivity so tenuous is that it often collides with differences that form a particular test of personal honor and the substantial powers these differences may represent in "the interests of the state, patriotism, family duties, etc." In addition, there are general external circumstances that may stem and block the flow of love: "the usual course of events, the prose of life, misfortunes, passion, prejudices, restrictions, stubbornness of others, and incidents of the most varied kind."[8] Showing his crucial Hegelian card, it turns out such collisions are rooted in a "contingency" within the phenomenology of romantic feelings themselves. While "love has of course a high quality in it in so far as it does not remain in general a sexual attraction but is a sentiment in itself rich, beautiful, and noble which abandons itself and, for the sake of unity with another, is living, active, bold, and sacrificing," it is nevertheless only "*personal*."[9] "In the family, marriage, duty, the state, it is not subjective feeling as such and the consequential unification of just *this* individual and no other, which should be the chief thing at issue. But in romantic love everything turns on the fact that *this* man loves precisely *this* woman, and she him." Furthermore, to give

> absolute preference to one woman and precisely to this one alone is therefore in every case a private matter of the subjective heart and the particularity or peculiarity of the person, and the endless stubbornness of necessarily finding his life, his supreme

[7] Ibid., 563.
[8] Ibid., 565–66.
[9] Ibid., 566.

> consciousness, precisely in this woman alone...appears at the same time as an idiosyncrasy and a pertinacity of personal caprice.[10]

In contrast, so-called classical renditions of love are more lively and detached, "without endless suffering, without this domination of the whole of existence or the pious devotion of an oppressed, silent, languishing heart" which apparently "lets itself go cheerfully in immediate enjoyment as in something innocent with this or that character; and the endless importance of possessing this girl and no other remains just as unnoticed as the monk's notion of renouncing the sex-relationship altogether."[11] No wonder, then, that a more modern rapport comes into conflict with "the eternal interests and objective content of human existence, with family, political ends, country, duties arising from one's calling or class, with freedom and religious feeling" since it is concerned first and foremost with its own self, "the self that wishes to receive again the feeling that is reflected back from another self."[12] Thus, this kind of chivalrous romance points in two opposing directions:

> love burgeons in noble and fiery hearts; this secular religion of the heart now unites itself with religion in every way, now subordinates it to itself and forgets it. Since it makes itself alone into the essential and even the sole or supreme business of life, not merely can it decide to sacrifice everything else and fly with the beloved into a desert, but in its extreme, where indeed it is unbeautiful, it proceeds to the unfree, slavish, and shameless sacrifice of the dignity of man.[13]

Picking out the more bleak aspects of both trajectories and gazing upon an unforeseen horizon, Hegel unfurls the romantic character that formally disassociates him or herself from anything resembling either piety or earthly love. As examples of romantic individuals remaining absurdly true to themselves in their unmediated one-sided firmness of character, he cites Shakespeare's *Macbeth*, *Othello*, and *Richard III*. These are dark and compelling but ultimately disgusting versions of the

[10] Ibid., 567.
[11] Ibid., 563–64.
[12] Ibid., 566–67.
[13] Ibid., 565.

romantic personality, exemplary maniacs in love with lies and ceaselessly scratching their own wounds. We sympathize with them only insofar as we might wish in an infantile fashion to right the world of all its equally infantile injustice against us, usually with a gun or sharp object of some kind. Notably, this whole analysis begins with the saints of Christendom and ends with a purely formal separation of character from such contra-classical figures. In the interim, the knights and heroines of chivalrous passion have yet to perish in a reversed resurrection that throws Lazarus to one side as it constructs a piñata out of his grave clothes and fills it with corn syrup. It is the middle, more complicated part of Hegel's overall narrative, and flip side of the final, purely formal romantic personage that should strike us. Among the heroes and heroines cited are Juliet and Hamlet, along with a certain King in Thule conjured by Goethe and, "in modern times," a host of men "belonging to the lower classes who are without education enough to understand national purposes and without a variety of objective interests, and therefore when *one* purpose of their own fails, they cannot now find in another a stay for the their inner life or a firm footing for their activity."[14] Hegel describes these "completely contrasted" characters as those with "substantial hearts which incorporate a totality but in their simple compactness generate every deep feeling only in themselves without developing it outwardly and unbosoming themselves of it."[15] Equivocating further, if such personages are of

> worth and interest, there must be an inner richness of heart, but it lets us recognize its infinite depth and fullness only through precisely this stillness in a few, so to say dumb, expressions. Such simple, unselfconscious, and silent natures may exercise a supreme attraction. Yet, in that case, their silence must be the stillness of the unruffled surface of the sea, concealing unfathomable depths, and not the silence of what is shallow, hollow, and pointless.[16]

However strangely attractive such characters may be, Hegel nevertheless wanly writes that "for a heart so shut in upon itself a time

[14] Ibid., 581–84.
[15] Ibid., 580.
[16] Ibid., 580–81.

must come when it is touched at one specific point of its inner life, when it throws its undivided force into one feeling determining its life, clings to it with undispersed strength, and is fortunate, or else, lacking support, perishes." As for the official, more or less immediately mediated Hegelian conclusion goes, such individuals are not finally compelling since "as a support man needs the developed breadth of an ethical substance [like the state] which alone supplies objective firmness."[17] Along the way Hegel measures this stark conclusion with the fact that "it may sometimes happen that a very common-place man, through a demeanor which expresses little but which here and there provides something half intelligible, arouses an impression of his great wisdom and inner resources, so that one thinks marvelous all that lies hidden in this heart and spirit," but cannot help but add that "at the end it is obvious that there is nothing behind his façade," and inform us that

> Whereas the infinite content and depth of those still hearts is revealed (and this is something that demands great genius and skill on the part of the artist) through separate, scattered, naïve, and unpremeditated *spiritual* expressions which, without an eye on others who could understand them, show that such a heart grasps with feeling the substance of existing circumstances; yet that its reflection is not complicated by the whole concatenation of particular interests, concerns, and finite ends, and so is clear of them and unacquainted with them; and to such a heart cannot be distracted by ordinary emotions or by the seriousness and sympathies ordinarily involved.[18]

Replete with counterpoint, not only does this analysis resonate with Taciturnus' *ad hoc* rumination about the devolving impotence of poetic production in his day, but it also helps us read *Stages* as a whole and the situation of the diarist in particular. Hegel himself is at pains to acknowledge the "substantial interest" of such romantic characters which, if that interest is profound rather than superficial, "we must at the same time come to see in them that this restrictedness of their personality is itself only a fate, i.e. an entanglement of their peculiar restricted character with a deeper inner life."[19] The representative test

[17] Ibid., 581.
[18] Ibid., 581.
[19] Ibid., 585.

case he cites is Don Quixote. It seems Hegel's dramatically reticent perspective is that folks with any romantic sense will earnestly laugh at Quixote's personal and national passions only to the degree that they find within themselves a portion of that noble lunacy. Otherwise the Don could only be the butt of bombastic jokes concerning an outdated schedule of what really matters and thereby more accurately spell the death of romantic ideals amidst a cacophony of truly absurd realism on the part of an urbane audience. As for the diarist, he is clearly in the throes of a melancholy crisis out of the ashes of which he hopes for renewal, a renewal that has something to do with *her*, something to do with his stormy, demanding, and largely silent God, and something to do with a pen scattering ink in a pattern worthy of being called artistic beyond the miasma of natural decay. While it seems clear that Hegel himself would think the diarist severely limited, entirely enclosed, and lacking legitimate, objective social aims, as a character he does fit the problematic bill of a romantic individual who cuts across the categories of discipleship, chivalry, and inner wanderlust. He shares elements of Mary Magdalene and the unnamed beloved disciple in John, Romeo and Don Quixote, and even Richard III or Faust. Although difficult to sort through, and even more difficult to assess, the horse for which he would no doubt gladly trade his kingdom is a sort of personal integrity and warmth, completely given over to idealistic longing and yet free of despair, as mad and un-political as it is erotically divine. Although he might plausibly precede Maugham's protagonist Charles Strickland in *The Moon and Sixpence,* we should probably stop short of claiming the diarist as simply a precursor to Andy Kaufman.

A Half-Empty Overexposure of Tragicomic Misunderstanding

Having distinguished between barriers to love that are internal rather than external as the basis of romantic tension in need of resolution, Taciturnus highlights misunderstanding as the "Tragic and Comic-Tragic Principle" he employs in his upending tale. Of course, misunderstanding can be just as external as internal, and is frequently mixed. If as a result of some stroke of fate a crucial letter from a certain Franciscan Friar Laurence gets interrupted, that is straightforwardly external. In contrast, if two are looking each other straight in the eye and cannot manage to make their anxious meaning clear, then we may have some internal ghost haunting the story with no third-party status. Writing around these possibilities Taciturnus states that

> as soon as misunderstanding between two people is posited, then as long as they misunderstand each other no other reason can be given for it than misunderstanding. If the reason…can be given, then the *discrimen* [distinguishing element] of the misunderstanding is removed. Thus the two could go on misunderstanding each other but nevertheless also basically understand each other. (416)

At the extreme limit of tragicomic explanations a misunderstanding between two parties becomes tautological because it seems due to a misunderstanding so fundamental there simply is no common point of contact. In that case the underlying existential orientations of the two parties do not even share the same language, a solipsistic nightmare from which the diarist regularly startles himself awake. But it is hardly ever as neatly circumscribed as these alternatives indicate. The way Taciturnus articulates this quagmire is that misunderstanding occurs

> whenever the heterogeneous are brought together, a heterogeneity, please note, of such a kind that there is a possibility of a relation, for otherwise the misunderstanding *is* not—therefore it can be said that as the basis of the misunderstanding there lies an understanding, that is, the possibility of understanding. If the impossibility is present, then misunderstanding is not present. With the possibility, however, there is misunderstanding, and looked at dialectically it is both tragic and comic. (416–17)

Once again, the dialectical element forms the crucial undercurrent, wrenching our feet back and forth beneath the surface. Normally the poet can find a way to comically expose malicious information in time or tragically air good intent moments too late, but combining them in a setting where the lovers' passion is itself the conflicted element in such a way that neither of them can quite account for their separate but equally ballistic fear and longing lies beyond aesthetic type-setting, though it could issue in a mere "negative unity of a life-view not given in poetry but rising out of it, so to speak, as a presentiment" (417–18). As a tactile example of such negative unity Taciturnus cites Socrates' left-handed, incarcerated rumination about how rubbing his leg after removing his chains provides an uncanny pleasure. The reason Taciturnus favors this example is because he thinks of Socrates as someone so cavalier about death, so self-assured of his own integrity, and furthermore one who looks upon the prospect of Athenian exile as much worse than hemlock, that he can simultaneously tip his hat at life's small pleasures. This combination is truly baffling. Should we expect—and this is a genuine question—one sentenced with capital punishment to actually delight in a final choice of sirloin and caramelized onions, side of steamed asparagus, and baguette with real butter? Even as a negative unity Taciturnus claims "Socrates specifically posits a duplexity that poetry cannot express" (419). If poetry could express it—and who knows, perhaps a writer can try—then grace would mock cruelty in "a rare combination of joy and sorrow" with very few believing it, with very few knowing whether to laugh or cry. The death sentence of a hero is simple enough, but if one "simultaneously gets a hint that the man himself assumes that the situation could also be comic, then poetry must declare bankruptcy" (419).

It seems doubtful from this Socratic example that Taciturnus is simply deploring the limitations of poetic composition *per se* by genre and standard protocol, but rather diagnosing the limits of our own imaginations, even as these typically go hand in glove. In either case, the limitation emerges when our art and subsequent imagination, or our imagination and subsequent art, lack the point of contact between the comic and tragic "that places the misunderstanding together in a unity or by which they situate themselves together in such a way that they simultaneously are kept together and yet apart in misunderstanding, and yet cannot be separated because the point of contact is there, and its existence is a relationship that is simultaneously comic and tragic" (419). One result of this limitation is merely tragic when a "generation of dunderpates" cannot digest the message of an "enthusiast" because there is no underlying point of common understanding. Taciturnus does not provide a literary example in this case, perhaps because he is unwittingly thinking of his own construction, without saying as much. (After all, the paradoxical insinuation is that only Plato himself uniquely understood even his teacher's merely negative passion.) However, Taciturnus does cite *Gulliver's Travels* as a potential candidate for tragicomic unity, but then dismisses it as mere comedy due to its "fantastic" element (419). As an example, what is interesting about Gulliver's faux travelogue is that readers encounter a race of miniatures who engage in a bitter civic and then military dispute over whether to cut eggs from the large or slender end, a corresponding race of prodigious simpletons so apparently underdeveloped they mock the distinction between Whigs and Torys, and then a race including a horrified king who flat-out refuses to hear further about the recipe for gunpowder, replete with a set of scholars utterly amazed to find that so diminutive a creature as Gulliver appears comparatively endowed with reason. Later in the book Gulliver has occasion to meet a highly developed scientific culture whose academic department of language has adopted the task of clarifying speech by eliminating all verbs and reducing all communication to the silent perception of direct objects. Gulliver is then once again cast upon a land where the most elegantly endowed creature is a genteel breed of horse (Houyhnhnms) that finds Gulliver's description of English character so below itself that it cannot appreciate the difference between Gulliver and the Neanderthals (Yahoos) that otherwise occupy the region. In the end poor Gulliver is literally at sea in a morass of conflicted self-knowledge, all of which could be as tragic as it is comic, depending on how you read it. As satire, Swift's construction lies below the dignity of Taciturnus' desire to raise our conscious apprehension of where we really stand as personally affectionate and politically astute, rational animals, which apparently requires a nectar-laden study of falling in love. Pinching his own earlobe, the scenario Taciturnus offers that might come closer in actual life is when a deaf man enters a meeting hall, and not wanting to disturb the proceedings, opens a creaking door with increasing patience as those inside increasingly lose it (420). The unintentionally annoying disturbance here might seem insignificant on a literal level, but imagine if the rudely interrupted meeting in question was about whether introducing casinos into the economy would help fund primary education, or in an adjacent scenario, if a beloved got smacked on a spiritual funny bone and then stumbled about trying to recover. Apology becomes increasingly uneven as the hurt deepens. And the more salient the passion, the more slippery such roughshod apology becomes, as "the dialectically infinitized spirit simultaneously sees [the tragicomic] elements in the same situation" (420). In *that* case, *both* are left hanging, including the audience members, were an artist audacious enough to wish it upon them.

One might interpose a Freudian gloss on Taciturnus' imaginary project by noting possible links between childish play (as serious as it is opposed to reality), the way such play goes underground in adult life as a strictly private, shameful fantasy, and the role creative writers take in transforming our consciousness, not into something as directly "productive" as their own but into an actively receptive and forgiving audience, all due to a common proclivity for living imaginatively. According to Freud's conjecture, the aesthetic pleasure we receive from literature proceeds "from a liberation of tensions in our minds" and "that not a little of this effect is due to the writer's enabling us thenceforward to enjoy our own day-dreams without self-reproach or shame."[20] The stories Freud has in mind are not only ones in which love conquers and heroes go free but also those in which villainy wins out. However dark or romantic, some unrealistic expectation gets imaginatively fulfilled, and Freud does his best to remain characteristically amoral in his analysis. What this account does not explain, however, is the interest an artist may have in imaginatively heightening tensions within our minds in order to bring us closer to reality, and the paradoxical pleasure this may afford a mature audience prepared for the kind of resolution that results from honest discomfort. While any given audience member might remain puerile enough to only enjoy either schmaltzy or vile outcomes given their own private fantasies, neither counts as an accurate assessment of the range of aesthetic production nor of what constitutes its genius. Nor can one appeal to a particular medium in support of Freud's one-sided account, since a comic book can be as childish as a graphic novel is mature, and vice versa. No doubt the same would apply to musical scores and whatever libretto may accompany them, in both classical and popular instances.

---

[20] "Creative Writers and Day-Dreaming," *The Complete Psychological Works of Sigmund Freud,* Volume lX (London: The Hogarth Press, 1959) 153, translated by James Strachey.

What Taciturnus announces is that the characters he has conjured—a certain Quidam and Quaedam—are opposing foils. "Him I have kept in the power of spirit in the direction of the religious; her I have kept in esthetic categories" (420). Two hermeneutical confusions we should avoid in this regard are taking this admitted artifice too literally, as if by authorial intent we are supposed to encounter one dimensional silhouettes; and second, importing full human subjectivity to either of them. The first approach would erase the evident realism in play while the second would give rise to overwrought judgments concerning unflattering caricatures. Both of these readings are tempting because it is always easier to avoid the sticky mess of our concrete inner lives by reverting to either distorted animation or some deconstructive theory about gender, both of which amount to the same thing. More fruitful than such cartoons is to understand the electric clash between two individuals we ecstatically wish joined at the hip and mouth, provocatively turned toward one another as if life itself depended upon it, lovers truly. This reading is both more difficult and more rewarding, if we can stomach the contrast within our own selves. "The point of unity," we are told, "is that they are united in loving each other. The misunderstanding, then, is not due to some third factor, as if they understood each other and were separated by some alien power—no, ironically enough, everything favors their misunderstanding" (420). Furthermore, although the "conjunction in this misunderstanding" is their mutual affection, in their "heterogeneity this passion must express itself in essentially different ways, and thus the misunderstanding must not come from outside but develops in the relationship itself that exists between them" (421). The tragic element is they do not understand each other; the comic part is they nevertheless love one another. Even more fundamentally, love itself "has an ethical and an esthetic element" (421). These two elements are by apparent design ponderously split between the lovers in question, and it is only when we join the two characters that we get a fully human sensibility.

What particularly engages Taciturnus is that the diarist "sees the comic and with this fortifies himself for the tragic" but does not see it "as a seasoned observer" (422). The status of such seasoned observation, however, remains ambiguous. On the one hand the diarist apparently picks out the comic side of things, which "serves to illuminate the religious," when as a matter of analytical opinion a more elevated passion "chooses the tragic part of this unity," the true point where "religiousness begins—that is, the religiousness for which immediacy is over" (422). As part of this mixture, according to Taciturnus, "Paganism culminates in the mental fortitude to see the comic and the tragic simultaneously in the same thing" (422). Such historiographical typology aside, the comic and tragic are both "necessary extremities of movement for the person who wishes to exist by virtue of spirit and after having abandoned immediacy," just as one needs two legs to walk. Reminiscent of such evocative coordination is a journal entry Kierkegaard once wrote:

> If I did not know that I am a genuine Dane, I could almost be tempted to explain my self-contradictions by supposing that I am an Irishman. For the Irish do not have the heart to immerse their children totally when they have them baptized; they want to keep a little paganism in reserve; generally the child is totally immersed under water but with the right arm free, so that he will be able to wield a sword with it, embrace the girls.[21]

Adding this amusing quip about ethnological-religious heritage to our recipe, the truly ideal stance still eludes us and seems to unfold just above the author's head, since anyone "who has one leg and yet wants to be spirit by virtue of spirit is ludicrous, be he ever so great a genius" while only in a "balance between the comic and tragic lies the condition for proper walking" (422). The trouble with the "knight" Taciturnus has composed is that "when he is on the point of becoming integrated in the religious, he becomes extremely dialectical" (422). This could suggest he limps, is bowlegged, has a clubbed foot, or that he jaunts more uncharacteristically and is simply faster than most. However, in claiming that his hero picks the comic element out of the synthetic ideal, Taciturnus insists he displays "a demonic qualification of approximation to the religious" (422). Nevertheless it is hard to believe this fellow is simply lame or not serious enough. Not hard to believe is that he has a

---

[21] *Søren Kierkegaard's Journals and Papers, Volume 5, Autobiographical, 1829–1848,* 5556. Underneath this entry one could add 5247: "I have also united the tragic and comic; I crack jokes and people laugh—I cry."

peculiar, fascinating, and finally attractive gait, all things considered. Together with this, we would do well to recall that the Gospels record the possessed are some of the few who recognize Jesus for who he really is along the way. "Demonic" qualifications are not simply pejorative but also positive in this context. On this reading demonic possession is a kind of madness over thwarted ideals one hopes to recover with a tragic optimism that truly is an "approximation" of divine resolution. I think it hard to imagine something more romantic than a guilty penitent in actual love. This would apply to both God and a girl, considered as the beloved. The diarist is fully and blessedly *caught*. On this reading the divine comedy is as light and dark as either Dante or Milton paints it. Sharing elements of infernal twisting or a long day's dying, the diary has the realistic feel of pleading downcast eyes desperately trying to figure something out.[22]

Imaginary Contrasts

At this point Taciturnus goes over the structural elements of his "imaginary construction," his creative venture in outlining the contrasts we must all somehow come to perceive and stitch together. Warming up to the details, the formal structure of the diary is an exploration of the disjunction between two kinds of idealization, one esthetic and the other religious, each containing their own potential for self-absorption. As concrete illustrations of their difference and final similarity, Taciturnus states that just as a lover can endow a beloved with beauties that are not there due to an initial distance between them both physically and psychically "prior" to actual encounters, so can one imagine horrifying and unfair traits after the fact (426). We could just as well turn these around and suggest how arrestingly drawn we are to merely perceptible features and how wonderfully we might cherish the particularity of another's faults up close and personal. Putting it positively, gazing at the angelic figure in red or then bathing and dressing her due to a broken limb are two sides of the same dialectical coin. The movement of love turns and flips in exactly this fashion, but is difficult to describe without

[22] Dante Alighieri, *Inferno*, Canto V, and *Purgatorio*, Cantos XXV–XXVIII; and John Milton, *Paradise Lost*, Book X, line 964.

imaginative embellishment, an existential art that may be the test of one's mettle either way. Interlacing the various values at play in and against reality, Taciturnus purports: "So the story begins twice."

> In the morning he recollects actuality; at night he deals with the same story but is permeated with his own ideality. This ideality, therefore, is not an illusory anticipation that still has not seen the actuality but is an act of freedom after the actuality. This is the difference between esthetic and religious ideality. The esthetic is higher than the actuality prior to the actuality, that is, in illusion; the religious is higher than the actuality after the actuality, that is, by virtue of a relationship with God. The duplexity is expressed. A poet or a lover can certainly have an ideal conception of the beloved but cannot simultaneously have an actual consciousness of the extent to which it is not true. Only the new ideality that comes after the actuality can endure this contradiction. (422–23)

In addition to passing the stringent requirements Judge William levels at his own imaginary exception, part of what this implies for the diarist during the extended interim is that his beloved both vanishes and becomes a "gigantic figure" (423). Appropriately enough, all this double-edged idealization "requires that he see her again," both in church and on the street, encounters that "prove nothing to him"—as if there were something to "prove"—as pale or vigorous as she may seem either on Hauser Square or in a pew (424–25). For her part, she pleads a hopeful case against his arguably morbid, presumptively protective but explicitly deceptive care. In an artistically romantic, philosophically puzzling but psychologically astute mood, Taciturnus surmises "[f]rom his point of view, this is just as energetic an expression of his love as her violent outburst was of hers," concluding that this "of course, was mutually the worst thing they could do to each other" (425). Revisiting the connection between the sublime and demonic, Taciturnus reminds us the diarist remains *in suspenso*, simultaneously imbuing his passion with a mixture of comic anticipation and tragic resolve (426). It could have gone differently for him; he could have found rest and let his decision stand without becoming "dialectical because of her," but in this precise, aberrant state the diarist "illuminates many a religious issue" (426). Interpretively reconstructing at least one of these religious issues,

Taciturnus states that the darker, "demonic" side of Quidam's ordeal lies in this: "that with a presentiment of a possibility he is unwilling to relate himself to himself in his religious idea but understands her in esthetic categories and cheats the ethical a little, as if he were—if he is guilty—less guilty because she came out of it all right, less guilty even if she had dealt wrongly with him" (427). Predictably, these comments evoke an equivocal judgment and intimate that a particularly illuminated place to reside is one where a person cannot get on top of themselves, cannot preside over their guilt or innocence, but must remain at the anxiety-riddled call of someone else altogether, not unlike the young prophet Nathan, or a Romeo. With hope leading on, faith and love put us in such a position, whether the one who calls out is Quaedam or YHWY. What makes either name unspeakable is the privileged seat they hold in broken and contrite hearts alike, a holy of holies fearsome to approach given the melancholy dispute between our angelic and beastly natures, and only entered by means of an unveiled, repentant divine madness just as Socrates sat before the young Phaedrus.[23]

Sorting through the heterogeneous characteristics that animate his two protagonists, Taciturnus invites us into this baffling citadel. First, Quidam remains enclosed with a depressed reserve that "is the condensed possibility that must be experienced through a crisis in order that he can become clear to himself in the religious" (427). What this reserve contains and implies our author has "deliberately" dropped at "the frontier of understanding that posits the misunderstanding," thereby hollowing out the mere "intimation of a higher life" (428). While the diarist "can say a lot, and with a lightness, about what *has* made him reserved, he does not and cannot say what *is making* him reserved. Therefore, inclosing reserve can scarcely be taken from the reserved person and there is no real healing for him except religiously within himself" (428). In contrast, his beloved is immediately open, pronouncing her devotion with a range of vowels an abstractly enclosed person lacks. Correspondingly, he is crushed beneath a specific depression that in "the pain of sympathy for her wins out," but on the whole is animated by a "sheer enthusiasm" that is "in itself ludicrous, tragic because of his suffering, comic because he does the most foolish

[23] Plato, *Phaedrus*, 237a –238e.

things" without even suspecting that it "signifies something else" and "is bound to help him" (429). In further contrast, according to the construction she offsets his confusion with a vivid joy in the face of an intermittent, half-lit distress such that her lover "must be esthetically developed in his imagination, must be able to grasp the ethical with primitive passion in order to take offense properly so that the original possibility of the religious can break through at this turning point" (430). The upshot of this comparative contrast is that one can no more walk with one leg than speak with a string of consonants. What we are looking at is not simply the prospect of mobility and speech, but poetry and dance, the existential elegance of movement and expression that lies just above our heads and just beneath the surface of the text as a whole. There is no path around this conundrum but to move forward. That movement implies a balance, a balance between our immediate affections, our grave doubts, our higher selves, and fickle desires, all spread in a perplexing field of crimson and clover, violets and various irises, and peppered with a handful of schwarzkopfs strewn amidst the lilies, liturgically speaking. Taciturnus is not entirely clear or reliable in this regard, since he claims he has constructed the scenario in such a way that the diarist "leaves her, but not in order to give her up, but in order to persevere, just in case it might help" (430). What Taciturnus means is that he helps her, but he could just as well mean that he helps himself, because in the string of consonants the diarist delivers it is "uncertain and unsure whether it is insulting to her to put her off with such a hope" (430). Either way, the diarist is "altogether consistent, it is this that is to help, but how he does not know. One word between them and his development would surely have been disturbed" (430). In the meantime, she "cannot carry on by herself" and has little option but to change her mind about the whole affair (430). This reticence on her part is predictable since that is how Taciturnus has "designed the imaginary construction—simultaneously comic and tragic" (430). Oddly enough, the "declining fund" of her "lightheartedness" which could have helped resolve his turmoil contributes to "what he was supposed to be," a literary fact about which the conjured diarist "does not dream" but "merely feels his misery so deeply that he is incapable of being what everyone is capable of—being a married man" (430–31).

This comparative portion of Taciturnus' letter includes an interpretive gloss that may not have occurred to us if all we had was the diary itself. Specifically, when he says that Quidam is essentially a "thinker," unacquainted with the world and the opposite sex in particular, and that she is about as interested in his existential brooding as she would be if he were preoccupied with the Syro-Chaldaic or Elamitic languages, we might wonder about the author's evidence (431–32). Of course Taciturnus nuances these bald pronouncements with the fact that "on the other hand his unsophisticated veneration of the opposite sex has something touching about it, plus a certain epigrammatic force superior to knowledge of the world" and that she "pooh-poohs learned and curious subjects, which is a lovable trait and not devoid of charm" (431–32). One gets the sense that Taciturnus is not just the author but himself a reader. And in this instance he is hashing out how two such limited personalities could possibly understand one another. But these limitations are also *our* limitations. The diarist would not be the only one to overthink his affection and endow it with difficulties that an assistant professor might easily explain away, if that is what Quidam is doing. Nor would she be the first with "life and days before her" to endearingly bat her eyelashes at such notions, if that is what Quaedam is doing. Coordinating these differences is the task. "If he has her honor on his conscience, then she has had his thought-existence on hers" (432). Put otherwise, the internal dynamics of romantic ideals set us apart from ourselves as much as they do from one another. On the other hand, they also might keep us together. Taciturnus completes his comparison and contrast of the two by suggesting how their divergent existential comportments cause incomparable suffering on each of their parts, further breaking up whatever corresponding sympathy they might have for and accentuating the misunderstanding between them. He assesses this by saying the diarist cannot abide her possessive attachment and she cannot comprehend his guilt-ridden agony (432). The tragicomic result is that Quidam's strategy to restore her liberty and gain back his own shipwrecks on her healthy desire for felicity and fledgling confidence that she could hold up her own end of the existential bargain. The whole scenario, as the author has constructed it, prompts Taciturnus to claim the following:

> [I]f he is guilty of having begun, then she is guilty of making use of the ethical side of the relationship to bind him to herself and of risking the steps the results of which she neither dreams nor is able to estimate. He sees the comic, but with passion, so that out of that he chooses the tragic (this is the religious and something that I, who see there both elements in equilibrium, cannot understand); she sees the tragic, and so clearly that she makes it the comic. (434)

Ending these critical rounds of his literary experiment in which both parties make fools of themselves, Taciturnus summarizes the "stages" his dubiously armored, pigeon-toed knight illustrates: "an esthetic-ethical life-view under illusion, with the dawning possibility of the religious; an ethical life-view that judges him; he relapses into himself, and he is just where I want him to be" (435). Clearly this is not a neat and shining description of an exemplary figure "great systematic thinkers, who have so much to traverse," are likely to entertain (436). Rather, what we witness is a cloudy individual paired with an equally opaque beloved, each of whom "has a share of the elements of erotic love" but together do not deliver the soporific resolution of cheaply won third acts (436). This is not to say the diary simply unfolds a painfully ridiculous stalemate between two ill-fated partners, but rather allows an "individuality…to come into being in all its possibility" (436). The fabric of this stage of life is basted at all the seams, making up an outfit stitched together from swatches of impulse and resignation, impetuous flairs of sheer demand and utter heartbreak, all trimmed by moral sensitivity and religious longing. The thread Taciturnus uses is a barely visible underlying agreement that romantic ideals are a patchwork of competing values that threaten to expose us at our best and strengthen us at our worst, an "affair" which "is always a usable theme in relation to what it means to exist, even though *philosophice*, in relation to rote reciting, it is folly," with "marriage as the dialectically most composite disclosure of actuality" standing as a representative backdrop.[24] In this

[24] Here I quote Johannes Climacus since both he and Taciturnus cite Constantin Constantius' little book, *Repetition*. See *Concluding Unscientific Postscript*, 265, 294. In support of Climacus' own set of theses that subjective inwardness contains a regrettably neglected truth, that suffering is a distinctive mark of authentic piety, and humor a precursor to a genuinely Christian feeling

regard the ineffective fig leaves we may provisionally don along the way are matched by the divinely granted animal skins one wears at the advantageous cost of a first taste of death, a fact that no doubt despairingly preoccupies the Fashion Designer 370 pages earlier.[25]

As elsewhere in *Stages*, the gendered language here can be distracting. One might even go as far as to say the construction under question is especially, though underhandedly patriarchal by perniciously casting the male in the form of an emasculated penitent who nevertheless continues to treat the female as a ruse of his own corrupt imagination. However, by another estimation, some actual female readers will honestly identify with Quidam rather than Quaedam, and vice versa, four ways. Both experiential and literary evidence suggests that whatever gender constructions we might detect are anything but airtight. Moreover, in the life of a person with usual emotional depth, conflicts between religious aspiration and ordinary comfort, solitary intellectual proclivity and interpersonal sensitivity, moral reserve and bodily desire, depressive tendencies and delightful expectations—along with all the available discordant models of love and marriage with their attendant politics inside and outside the bedroom—tend to go hand in hand, notwithstanding the pressure of cultural normalization. In or even out of historical context, the overall tone of *Stages* is an attempt to place the universal and particular dimensions of both actual and possible human experience in mutual relief against the backdrop of one another.

Unresolved History

The third section of Taciturnus' letter is a further attempt to delineate the genre of his imaginary construction, taking his initial cue from Aristotle's claim that poetry is more philosophical than history, that the

---

for life, Taciturnus also relevantly lauds the fact that the imaginary construction under examination here "does not take as its starting point a later moment in time and relate a remarkable conflict as something past, nor does it slacken the tension of conflict in a reassuring conclusion, but by means of its teasing form makes the reader even more contemporary than he is able to become by way of a contemporary actuality and leaves him stuck in it by not giving a conclusion" (289).

[25] Genesis 3:7, 21.

literary arts have a greater power to express ideal human capacities and possibilities where actual records only dwell upon some historically located, contingent case. What Taciturnus adds to this is that if such historical results are comic, we do not really care whether what happens actually occurred because the cheerful resolution of any incongruity—whether real *or* fictional—poses no existential threat to what we want to believe. In contrast, if the results are tragic, we suddenly become interested in whether the proposed conflict is somehow inevitable, and in that case the reader casts about for an answer in the form of material precedent. The difference is not that comic relief and tragic failure are not equally possible but that we want to evade the gravity of the latter by pointing to contingent examples. The sheer possibility of a tragic outcome is so disquieting that we would prefer a final judgment that places blame at a comfortable distance from ourselves. In short, we *want* a comic ending and flee from a tragic one. As a rather odd result, we tend to feel offensively duped by what we know is a theatrical venture if the outcome is not a happy one. Thus in a paradoxical attempt to render heroism ubiquitous, audiences regularly get hermeneutically twisted by either reducing idealized representation by the diminutive factor of actual history or demanding of it a preferable outcome. Needless to say, in the light of such a pretzel, the whole matrix of esthetically suspended disbelief and spiritual doubt renders us, as either spectators or scriptwriters, creatures over which one could just as well laugh as cry. Thus Taciturnus wants to dispel our fascination with the historical so that we can face reality proper.

> In order to grasp the ideality, I must be able to dissolve the historical in the ideality or do (to use a pious expression) what God is said to do for one who is dying: shine upon it. Conversely, I do not enter into the ideality by repeating the historical jingle. Therefore, anyone who, with regard to the same thing, does not reach the conclusion just as well *ab posse* [from possibility to actuality] as *ab esse ad posse* [from actuality to possibility] does not grasp the ideality in this same thing. He is nurtured only on fancies. Ideality as the animating principle does not automatically become historical. That which can be transmitted to me is a multiplicity of data, which is not ideality, and thus the historical is always raw material, which the person who appropriates it knows how to resolve in a *posse* [possibility] and

> assimilate as an *esse* [actuality]. There is nothing, therefore, more foolish in the religious sphere than to hear the commonsensical question that asks when something is being taught: Now, did it actually happen this way, for if it did one would believe it. Whether it actually happened this way, whether it is as ideal as it is represented, can only be tested by ideality, but one cannot have it historically bottled. (439)

As a contribution to a state of affairs in which audience members are both invited and tempted to ask not whether what transpires is possible and whether they are willing and able to follow in the designated footsteps, but whether it actually occurred and if "my neighbor Christophersen [has] done it," Taciturnus resolves *this* conflict by making his own creative endeavor lack a result altogether (440). Refusing to foist upon the reader the darkest outcome and simultaneously avoiding the safeguard of some Hollywood ending, Taciturnus forges his own "negative unity" of winter and spring in a gospel that figures Holy Week all at once, without respite and prior to closure, eluding poet and historian alike. Suspended above both hilarity and depression readers enter a never-never-land of interiority in which they are barred from either sneaking "past the ethical toward metaphysic's freedom from care" or remaining "stuck in an ethical difficulty" (438). In one of the more unforgettable images within the text as a whole, that place is where

> the believer continually lies out on the deep, has 70,000 fathoms of water beneath him. However long he lies out there, this still does not mean that he will gradually end up lying and relaxing onshore. He can become more calm, more experienced, find a confidence that loves jest and a cheerful temperament—but until the very last he lies out on 70,000 fathoms of water. (444)

One of the reasons this literary construction and analysis is a vast ironic stretch is because very few would be tempted to emulate "the story of suffering" Taciturnus offers. Comic and sad at the same time, readers are left wondering where *they* truly stand. If we are ethically concerned about an esthetic "misalliance" in matters of personal love—or in political, artistic, or any other civic matters—and look forward to a more "glorious alliance" with the religious, then we are in a true, representative pickle (444). Distancing himself from an actual religious stance, but without arrogating a "desire to take it by force," Taciturnus states the following:

> The religious seeks no foothold in the historical, does not seek it, even less and for a higher reason than the comic does. It presupposes the unity of the tragic and comic in passion, and with a new passion or with the same one it chooses the tragic, and this relation in turn makes every historical foothold meaningless. It is never finished, at least not in time, and therefore can be represented as such only by a deception. If, then, a man who had been regularly listening to a speaker discoursing on religious matters were to go to him and say, "Now that I have listened to you so regularly, do you think that I now have faith?" the speaker, in a fit of what one calls good nature, concerned sympathy (for which one inserts a card of thanks in the newspapers), answers, "Why, of course, that is my opinion, set your mind at ease; just don't miss my discourses, and feel free to come to me if you ever have any doubts again etc." My constructing scrutiny, devoid of all good nature and concerned sympathy, is of the opinion that he would have done better to answer, "My dear fellow, are you making fun of me? I do not even dare vouch for my wife—indeed, not even for myself, for I am lying out on 70,000 fathoms of water." (445)

Thus, without the tempting promise of "moon and stars, the favor of young maidens, and applause of the reviewers," Taciturnus flat out refuses any demand to answer whether his imaginary construction "is a real-life story" (445). As a matter of fact, however, it nevertheless is "based on something actual, namely, on the categories" (445). The pulled punch here is that tragedy "has the interest of actuality" and comedy contains "metaphysical disinterestedness," while the production under scrutiny is absorbed with "the invisible unity of jest and earnestness" that "evades the formidable handshake of earnestness and jest's fellowship with jolly companions" (446). In so doing Taciturnus is not attempting to improve upon the story of Genesis 22, or even Johannes De Silentio's *Midrash*, but retelling it once again by subtractive addition. One of the more judicious things we can say about Taciturnus at this point, along with the diarist, is that for all his indirect, deceptive circumlocution he is desperately trying to be clear about how, when it comes to a life suffused by ideals of faith, hope, or love, the one road is as equally enticing as the other, which often makes all the difference.[26] The authentic trick of great art, a truly good story, is that it allows us to come to terms with our own *possible* selves, for better or worse, without illusions about our *actual* lives, also for better or worse.[27]

Along with its form, the content of this positive lack of narrative resolution within the diary suggests a distinctly dialectical form of guilt and responsibility in which repentance is "prevented from constituting itself" (446). By way of comparative illustration Taciturnus reimagines King David's plot to have Uriah sent to the front lines in order to have Bathsheba for himself:

> I am assuming that he has sent a messenger with secret orders to the commander; I am assuming that it takes the messenger three days' journey to reach the camp. The historic actuality makes no difference here. What happens? The very same night the messenger departed, David, trying to find the rest of sleep, does not find it but finds terror wide awake; it grips him, and he collapses in repentance—in the next paragraph, to be sure, comes the atonement. No, wait a minute. That same moment David realizes that it might still be possible to prevent the murder. An express messenger is sent, and David stays behind. I am assuming that this takes five days more. Five days—how much is that? After all, it is not a phrase in a paragraph; at most it is a particle, a "meanwhile" that merely begins a sentence, but five days could very well make a man gray-haired. (450–51)

So composed, what is telling about this narration is the gaping suspense David must endure before a definitive result is announced by reality. He has indeed repented of a murderous intent, but the question is whether he must repent of actually committing the crime. As old as David might age in the span of these five days, "all this is a far easier

[26] Some readers mistake the title of Robert Frost's famous poem as a road "less traveled," which implies the cheerful independence of a frontier character. But that outcome is a future revision of history, and its implication is as comic as it is tragic, which the author *shall* be telling, "somewhere ages and ages hence" and "with a sigh." The actual title refers to a road "not taken."

[27] A good guage of this is to measure reactions to Tim O'Brien's *The Things They Carried*. In that case one will witness fully adult veterans back into a corner and those born twenty years after the Vietnaam war throw the book across the room, and still others leak tears sweeter than either obedience or sacrifice.

case" than that of the diarist (451). For one thing, the murder at issue for Quidam is not literal but is nevertheless equally grave on another level as a possibility. Dying of a broken heart is no joke, especially if one goes on living. And that is what the diarist rightly suspects he has perpetrated. Yet we often witness cases where people recover from such a wound, all limbs intact. But the question *here* is whether the relevant organ will be somehow permanently damaged. That will take time to discover, and usually more than five days. In David's case, the result can perhaps be clearly determined one way or the other. But while finding Uriah alive and well would be a tremendous relief, such a happy outcome would not really be particularly comic for any of the three parties involved. For his part, David is fully prepared to accept responsibility for the worst given the thoroughgoing nature of his original intent, a fact he would nevertheless have to live with. In Quidam's case, his intentions are not directly criminal, and his repentance perhaps unnecessary, but his strategy to rectify it remains entirely dubious. The real guilt, if there is any to attribute, is to have loved at all and risked drawing another into a troubling web of ludicrous and depressing ideals. To summarize, "He could have a murder on his conscience; the whole thing can be a gust of wind" (447). The diarist will just have to wait and find out, an interim entirely lost on those who would rush, as on a systematic "roller coaster," toward a paragraph designated "Atonement" (447). Perhaps in eternity we will be able to laugh at all this, where our hair does not turn gray with longing, suspense, or some other "dialectical agony" (451). The way Taciturnus looks upon it, *in medias res* and not *sub specie aeternitatis*, ironically and without passion as a mere observer, is to "sit elated with my reckonings and look simultaneously at the comic and the tragic. The tragic girl who dies and the comic sinner who becomes a murderer, the tragic sinner who suffers and the comic girl who goes on living" (448–50). As readers the question becomes how representative the case of the diarist might be, whether "such things are found only rarely in actual life or not found at all" or "found most frequently but amounts to nothing at all" since "the perfectly normal perhaps is found simply and solely in handbooks and in lectures by men who do not exist in themselves or know how to spy on life and on others" (447). To pick out a different example from that of

David, we could cite Aristotle's claim that regret is a measure of character when the result of our action specifically does not match our intent, as when, for instance, we slam a friend's finger in a car door by accident.[28] Only a morally insensitive person would not immediately and profusely apologize but instead impassively declare, "Well, it's not *my* fault; I didn't *mean* to." Compound this example with the more tender spiritual feelings involved in matters of personal affection and then we have a drama of inner life on a greater scale, a drama rather difficult to chart because we may lack a proper vocabulary for so alternately stormy and calm and fathomless a sea, which turns out to be 140,000 deep (471). That is enough to drive one mad, if we don't drown first.

While Taciturnus rewrites the story of David, Bathsheba, and Uriah as an internal drama, what possibly inspires him to offer an appendix to this section on *Hamlet* is because it includes one of the more famous versions of the prophet Nathan's literary strategy to call out David's guilt in the form of a play within a play.[29] Hamlet employs such a tactic to confirm the fratricidal guilt of his mother and uncle. What interests Taciturnus is how the simultaneously obvious but ghostly premonition about the right or wrong of Claudius and Gertrude might be a signpost of Hamlet's own inner strife. The standard witness to this drama supposes Hamlet has justice on his side and that, for inexplicable and decidedly undramatic reasons, he vacillates over his grandiose and vengeful plan to expose the truth. According to Taciturnus this reading makes Hamlet an essentially comic figure, one so clearly in the right and yet so pathetically reticent: "If the plan remains fixed, then Hamlet is a kind of loiterer who does not know how to act; if the plan does not remain fixed, he is a kind of self-torturer who torments himself for and with wanting to be something great. Neither of these involves the tragic" (453). According to another reading, Hamlet harbors "religious presuppositions that conspire against him in religious doubt" under which he sinks (453).

> If Hamlet is to be interpreted religiously, one must either allow him to have conceived the plan, and then the religious doubt divest him of it,

[28] Aristotle, *Nicomachean Ethics*, line 1110b 20.

[29] 2 Samuel 12.

> or do what to my mind better illustrates the religious…—give him the demonic power resolutely and masterfully to carry out the plan and then let him collapse into himself and into the religious until he finds peace there. (454)

Unfortunately, such an explanation makes for very little drama in external terms, which is exactly why Taciturnus finds it so appealing, for reasons not the least of which is that to imply *Hamlet* is a comedy would leave critics and bookbinders alike at a considerable loss. What resonates here is the way in which an "unrivaled" poet like Shakespeare—and lovers like the rest of us—can barely manage to hold our own with anything like innocence and therefore cast about for answers that not even a prophet could provide without calling upon an internally conflicted script. In a rather garbled message, as sobering as it is hilarious, Taciturnus seems to write: welcome to the human condition.

Real Suffering

As Taciturnus further tries to distinguish his literary hero from other sorts, along with the specific sort of sympathy we are supposed to feel and catharsis we might undergo, he makes some rather confusing observations about suffering. Merely "esthetic" heroes apparently experience difficulties from outside whereas a "religious" individual like Quidam exhibits a "qualitative qualification" that renders him useless for a standard poetic portrayal (455). Indeed, the uniquely contrived scenario even puts the author himself under an interpretive strain. To cite the two relevant options, the whole story would make a lot more narrative sense if the diarist were merely a demonic figure who essentially says, "I see my idea of existence being stranded on this girl, *ergo*, she must go; my road to a great goal runs over her downfall," or in contrasting conjunction with this reading, to "bow before" an unnecessarily tortured heroine who in faithful resignation gets stuck on a corresponding ideal (455–56). But this is not the story Taciturnus wants to tell, which strangely and predictably enough tells us something about *him*. Rejecting these readings of his own work, being both unwilling to think of Quidam as purely demonic and unable to bow before Quaedam, Taciturnus reveals:

> Because of the relationship this could not be done, and it is the relationship that gives me my dialectical satisfaction. I am not interested in how they happened to begin, in their individual fates. If I were, I would instantly be influenced essentially by his passion, and that would be the end of my equilibrium. As soon as I add passion and consider each one individually and his fate, then I must say of *him* that he is the one who eventually suffers more. He began, and by doing so he insulted her since he did not understand the distinctive characteristic of female existence; he began, and therefore he deserved more suffering. Of *her*, I must say that she is the one to whom life does the greater wrong in the imaginary construction, that by having become involved with him she always appears in a wrong light from the moment he by his deception prevents her from expressing the sympathy she certainly could have felt. Because he exists in the deception, a comic light falls upon her whatever she may do, even if she chose to remain faithful to him. He is very sensible of this wrong against her, and yet from his viewpoint he is acting in sympathetic passion, and this is one of the coiled springs in his suffering—that from his viewpoint he is doing the utmost and yet the most lunatic thing he can do; because they do not have a common viewpoint, he does not form a contiguous angle with her. Neither from his viewpoint nor from hers is it like for like: feminine attractiveness, loveliness—and a spiritual existence by virtue of the dialectical. His most desperate efforts are of no help, do not make up for the disparity, for feminine attractiveness has a claim that demands precisely what he lacks. Here is the source of his suffering. On the other hand, the opposite holds, that a spiritual existence by virtue of the dialectical must ask with regard to feminine attractiveness as the mathematician asks: What does that demonstrate? This he does not do, for he is not in spiritual equilibrium but in passion and therefore is concerned about the former and here chooses his suffering. (456–57)

The relevant passions and ideals this lengthy passage illuminates tend to derail our imagination, mainly because the track is so bent. The sheer collision that results leaves both "feminine" loveliness and "masculine" deceit fully intact, with an upending lack of resolution that is just as hopeful as it is unnerving. We are simply not allowed to know whether to laugh or cry, or on either of whom to pin these emotional responses with their curiously gendered presuppositions. Like love itself, it is both scary and exhilarating, a train-ride one may not want to venture at all. Taciturnus himself does not even know quite what to make of it, so thrown off is he by his own construction. Presumably this is part of the narrative trajectory, in which demons regularly betray the truth of the matter. So delivered, what we can know is that between any two lovers, and indeed within ourselves, the conflict between a fully embodied open receptivity, along with all its attraction, and a more or less disembodied spiritual reserve, marks our hands and sides. Such a conflict is not allegorically but literally, androgynously projected onto the screen of the text.

In terms of the heroic suffering that may be involved two literary references are embedded in this portion of the text. The first reference is to Sophocles' *Philoctetes,* which Taciturnus cites in passing as a better example than *Oedipus* in some local German controversy over whether Greek esthetics makes proper use of physical malady—blindness in particular—as a tragic motif. The tale of Philoctetes itself is about a resentful hero rendered invalid by a divine snakebite odious to his human companions but graced with a bow that always aims true, a bow which keeps him alive while marooned by Odysseus on a deserted island by shooting fowl that might otherwise consume him before being called upon once again to join Neoptolemus to bring down Paris, in part, according to one version of the story, because Philoctetes himself was at one time smitten with Helen. Not only is this the sort of complicated story that would interest Taciturnus but it also affords the opportunity to simultaneously evoke and renege the distinction between physical, external pain and the existential reality of hurt feelings due to ruinous ideals, whether personal or political. In light of the diarist and his tale, the lesson may be that all of us are both wounded by mysterious snakebites and armed with arrows that fly straight, largely in terms of the demise and retrieval of personal love. Nevertheless, patriotism plays a secondary but corresponding role, since Philoctetes is after all a Greek, just as anyone is presumably both a citizen as well as a lover. In any case, the rather elliptical way Taciturnus weighs in on this obscure debate about dramatic poetry is to say that *Philoctetes* "in a way is an exception to the universal esthetic concept but yet such that the exception by no means can invalidate it but rather itself relapses" (458). Without being able to tell exactly what the dispute is over, we can reasonably say the use of physical malady as a narrative device in moving readers toward true sympathy can be either cheap or apropos. This may well depend on how well that malady fits and contrasts with corresponding aspects of spiritual agency and pathos. The balance is a delicate one to realistically strike. Any half-wit can toss off a script in which a paraplegic transparently walks all over everybody and is thereby even more crippled than he thinks, although one can also imagine someone doing it well minus two-dimensional cliché.

Two paragraphs later Taciturnus chides Friedrich Schlegel for cowardly standing behind beauty and health against physical malady as the only qualities worthy of dramatic interest and any ensuing conflict or resolution that might result. The literary reference here is to *Lucinde*, a "novel" that charts the thoughts and sensibilities of a lover which has often been read as an autobiographical veil of Schlegel's own enduring affair with Mendelssohn's daughter Dorothea Veit, who left her banker husband Simon. Scandalous in its time, Hegel thought the book an adulterous attack on the stabilizing institution of marriage while Schleiermacher defended it as an arresting testimony to our potential religious aspirations. In casting Quidam in the odd role he plays, Taciturnus distances himself from both the official romantic tradition stemming from a book like *Lucinde* as well as the disparaging Hegelian attack on it. What Hegel found so irritating and one-sided about the romantics of his generation is how they seemed to elevate purely individual, subjective thoughts, feelings, and inclinations to a divine status, which he implies is the polar opposite of an exceptional form of virtue that could only appear in a relatively uncivilized context. His counter-veiling example to such sniveling, reclusive, melancholy lovers is Hercules. Of course he says this in the same breath as he writes that liberal sexual relations are the natural prerogative of men rather than women because men have a higher ethical substance outside the more fundamentally natural, monogamous home. He cites *Antigone* in support of such a civilized way of thinking because Antigone as a female representatively chooses family obligations over the state. Adding to this perplexing mix, Hegel then levels a characteristically mediated criticism against both unbridled sensuous delight and monastic asceticism, casting suspicion on each, especially if they are surreptitiously soldered together under the heading of "platonic" love.[30] It is as if Hegel had never sat alone simultaneously laughing and crying while reading the *Phaedrus,* in which the beautiful youth lures Socrates outside the city limits with a little essay on love tucked beneath his cloak and his *daemon* forces Socrates to repent of his own "Platonism."[31] Schleiermacher was more cheerful and measured in his estimation of romantic sensibilities even as he had problematically fallen in love with a married woman. In his famous speeches to cultured despisers of religion he writes:

> Let me disclose to you a secret that lies concealed in one of the most ancient sources of poetry and religion. As long as the first man was alone with himself and nature, the deity did indeed rule over him; it addressed the man in various ways, but he did not understand it, for he did not answer it; his paradise was beautiful and the stars shone down on him from a beautiful heaven, but the sense for the world did not open up within him; he did not even develop within his soul; but his heart was moved by a longing for a world, and so he gathered before him the animal creation to see if one might perhaps be formed from it. Since the deity recognized that his world would be nothing so long as man was alone, it created for him a partner, and now, for the first time, living and spiritual tones stirred within him; now, for the first time, the world rose before his eyes. In the flesh and bone of his bone he discovered humanity, and in humanity the world; from this moment on he became capable of hearing the voice of the deity and of answering it, and the most sacrilegious transgression of its laws now no longer precluded him from association with the eternal being.[32]

---

[30] G.W.F. Hegel, *Philosophy of Right* (Oxford: Oxford University Press, 1967) 105–16, 263, translated with notes by T. M. Knox. Just beneath the surface here is the example of Hamann already cited in the 5 June morning entry of the diary. Hegel himself seems to have cowered behind the issue by snubbing any suggestion that one might cancel a church-state sanctioned wedding ceremony as a purely external betrayal of the inner sanctity of love. Such a suggestion clearly does not satisfy the requirements of a genuine *Aufhebung.*

[31] Plato, *Phaedrus,* 238d.

[32] Friedrich Schleiermacher, *On Religion, Speeches to Its Cultured Despisers* (Cambridge: Cambridge University Press, 1988) 119, translation and notes by Richard Crouter. Genesis 2.

The conclusion of this story, as it were, is that "in order to intuit the world and to have religion, man must first have found humanity, and he finds it only in love and through love" since each one of us "embraces most ardently the one in whom the world is reflected most clearly and purely; each one loves most tenderly the one in whom he believes he finds everything brought together that he himself lacks for the completion of humanity."[33] The "confusion" that *Lucinde* perpetrated, echoed by both its critics and supporters, haunts the present text from the inside. It turns out that a so-called happy but plastic Greek conception of worth and beauty *and* the humanistic lyricism of early German romanticism, with their outright celebration of corporeal existence, deserve one another by each remaining internally conflicted. Taciturnus weighs in amidst these voices to say that our sympathies might waver, and that in matters of love it is just as denigrating to dismiss a poor, sickly soul desperately trying to put it all together and repeatedly failing along the way as it is potentially pornographic to reserve sole worship for perky, well-forged citizens and intimates. The author here is simply trying to assemble something out of the universal mess with his own tale of tortured eroticism that usually turns human lovers toward God in the bifocal image of an endearingly childish Cupid and an alarmingly authoritative YHWY. Appropriately enough, the centerpiece of *Lucinde* contains a yarn about how the narrator stumbled upon a fortuitous emotional and spiritual healing in the embrace of someone who helped him sort through his "alternation and mixture of passion, friendship, and sensuality" and thereby restored him to a new social world with her refreshing "air of grotesque universality and cultivated vulgarity."[34]

Under his own name, Kierkegaard himself wavered as well. In his dissertation on irony he both defends and criticizes the romantic liaison articulated by *Lucinde*. Against Hegel—or Judge William—he insists Schlegel is right to alert us to "the many degradations that have crept into a multitude of life's relationships and have been especially

---

[33] Ibid., 120.

[34] Frederich Schlege, *Friedrich Schlege's* Lucinde *and the Fragments* (Minneapolis: University of Minnesota Press, 1971) 101–103, translated with introduction by Peter Firchow.

indefatigable in making love as tame, as housebroken, as sluggish, as dull, as useful and usable as any other domestic animal—in short, as unerotic as possible."[35] In even stronger terms he claims there is "a moral prudery, a straitjacket, in which no reasonable person can move. In God's name, let it break to pieces."[36] On the other hand—and inexplicitly against the endorsement of someone like Schleiermacher—he fails to applaud "the moonlit theater marriages of an exaggerated romanticism for which nature at least can have no purpose and whose unproductive labor pains and weak embraces are of no more service to Christian than to pagan countries."[37] The days are over when our sheer humanity could serve as a reliable image of our creator, "when everything lived for love alone and for the happy lovers everything in turn was a myth about love."[38] In contrast the young Kierkegaard evokes a postlapsarian "Christian view of marriage that in the very hour of the wedding has had the boldness to pronounce the curse before giving the benediction."[39] Somehow, while this view "places everything under sin" without exception, including children, it contains an earnest thought "too high to be grasped by the bustling laborers in prosaic, everyday life, too rigorous to let itself be mocked by marital improvisers."[40] Kierkegaard implies that *Lucinde* portrays a purely negative affirmation of sensuality by resisting "the spirituality in which sensuousness is an assimilated element."[41] In doing so the book not only appropriately suspends an established social ethic but cancels it altogether and thereby

---

[35] Søren Kierkegaard, *The Concept of Irony* (Princeton: Princeton University Press, 1989) 286, translated by Howard V. and Edna H. Hong. In passing, George Pattison evocatively likens the scandal *Lucinde* caused to the one following D.H. Lawrence's *Lady Chatterly's Lover*, a work correspondingly replete with irresolute compromise, difficult longing, and tender confusion, and scandalous only to the degree it heartbreakingly pits *both* the exigencies of industrial wage-earning and proper social standing against all genuinely human feeling. See *Kierkegaard, Religion and the Ninteenth-Century Crisis of Culture* (Cambridge: Cambridge University Press, 2002) chapter 6.

[36] Kierkegaard, *The Concept of Irony*, 288.

[37] Ibid.

[38] Ibid.

[39] Ibid.

[40] Ibid.

[41] Ibid., 291.

inadvertently substitutes for it "an actuality that is no actuality," throwing us into a dreamy "ideal climate" not more southern "compared with ours in the north," but in reality "nowhere to be found."[42] Continuing with his wavering estimation Kierkegaard states at length that

> If we ask what poetry is, we may say in general that it is victory over the world; it is through a negation of the imperfect actuality that poetry opens up a higher actuality, expands and transfigures the imperfect into the perfect and thereby assuages the deep pain that wants to make everything dark. To that extent, poetry is a kind of reconciliation, but it is not the true reconciliation, for it does not reconcile me with the actuality in which I am living; no transubstantiation of the given actuality takes place by virtue of this reconciliation, but it reconciles me with the given actuality by giving me another, and higher and more perfect actuality. The greater the contrast, the less perfect the actual reconciliation, so that when all is said and done there is often no reconciliation but an enmity. Therefore, only the religious is able to bring about the true reconciliation, because it infinitizes actuality for me. Therefore, the poetic is a kind of victory over actuality, but the infinitizing is more of an emigration from actuality than a continuance in it. To live poetically, then, is to live infinitely. But infinity can be either an external infinity, because in my enjoying, I am continually outside myself in that other something. But an infinity such as that must cancel itself. Only when I in my enjoying am not outside myself but am inside myself, only then is my enjoyment infinite, because it is inwardly infinite. Even if he enjoys the whole world, the person who enjoys poetically nevertheless lacks one enjoyment, for he does not enjoy himself. But to enjoy oneself (of course, not in the Stoic or egotistical sense, for there is no true infinity in that, either, but in the religious sense) is the only true infinity.[43]

Such authentic religiously poetic existence "comes only through resignation," which contains a pleasure unknown to those who would—to cite his example—in complete self-absorption egotistically seek and gain revenge when the sweet smell of it belongs only to divine

---

[42] Ibid., 286, 290.

[43] Ibid., 297.

personages already equipped with the reliable self-confidence and knowledge that renders such external means of satisfaction unnecessary.[44] Given this example, one might wonder how this confluence of poetic and presumably passive theological justice bears on the dynamics of personal love. Our clue in the extended parenthesis of the longer quote is that we should be neither stoic nor egotistical, but engaged in the true romance of the religious that amounts to neither bourgeois compromise nor libertarian decadence. To take an example closer to that of the diarist, it would require considerable courage and "inward infinity" to stomach *not* treating a beloved suffering from childish depression *as* a depressed child *by* embedding a bitter dose of deceit in one's care. Equally difficult would be receiving such a dose. But this kind cruelty is the larger, more truly expansive romanticism that creates a moral context for a more local, tender, and immediately pleasurable affection.

In his own way Taciturnus too suggests esthetics is ill equipped to handle the kind of unity one might seek in romantically joining our most spiritual and sensual ideals. The point on which he and Kierkegaard certainly agree is the degree to which a literary production can or should reconcile one with life and may or may not cause one to despairingly revolt in a given situation. The way in which Taciturnus approaches the power and limitation of popular esthetics is by pointing out that it only makes use of the "preferred" sufferings of healthy and wealthy characters in reconciling a viewer with life, since the "unpreferred" suffering of the poor and hunchbacked would simply reduce poetry to the kind of "blubbering" one might witness in a hospital or unemployment line. For those who have experienced such tears in their actual lives, esthetics demands more of them in order to identify with and "lose" themselves in the pain of more privileged characters. This is precisely the artistic scenario Taciturnus cites: the power it takes for an under-classed citizen to identify with the suffering of a well-placed nobleman. As a matter of fact, poetry could just as well make use of sickly and disenfranchised characters, but this would place particular demands on a corresponding audience member. If the spectator is healthy and wealthy, he or she might indignantly object to the suggested

[44] Ibid., 289, 298.

premise that only the leprous or economically destitute truly suffer. Implying no small amount of responsibility for a writer, all this is to say that poetry could just as well give rise to laughter at trouble in paradise as it could incite disgust in a cancer ward, without provoking any genuine feeling or any real catharsis either way. Spiritual tuberculosis is a hard shot to frame for any cinematographer. "In this exigency," Taciturnus writes,

> when that which one has learned from poetry does not reconcile one with actuality, the religious appears and says: Every suffering is commensurate with the idea, and as soon as the relation to the idea is there, it has interest—otherwise it is culpable and it is the sufferer's own fault. It makes no difference in the matter whether the suffering is not to be able to carry out his big plans or to be hunchbacked; it makes no difference at all in the matter whether it is to be deceived by a faithless lover or to be so unfortunately misshapen that even a kindly person cannot help laughing when he sees such a one, with whom it would never enter anyone's head to fall in love. (459)

"This," he concludes, "is how I have understood the religious in composing the imaginary construction" (459).

We should be clear that the way Taciturnus has understood this "exigency" is that the religious does not become "so high-spirited that it goes to the opposite extreme and says: 'The lame, the crippled, the poor are my heroes—not the privileged'—which would be unmerciful of the religious, which is mercifulness itself" (460). Pausing to point out that Feuerbach's unapologetically humanist distillation of Christianity corroborates Pascal's dying dictum that suffering is the natural condition of the regenerate, he turns back to Aristotle's classic description of the catharsis dramatic arts accomplish in purifying our emotions by awakening fear and compassion and then stripping audience members of egotism as they lose themselves in the hero's agony (460).[45] Of course,

[45] Feuerbach's healthy-minded desire that theology become reborn a third time as anthropology that so attracted and repelled someone like Karl Barth and inspired the iconoclasm of figures like Marx and Freud, seems to have impressed Taciturnus with its remarkable, even orthodox faithfulness. A relevant passage in this context is the crucial expansion of Freuerbach's claim that Christianity is a religion of suffering: "The Passion of Christ, however, represents not only moral,

whether any given literary production has this effect in large measure depends on the existential status of the spectator who, if they are a "purely sensuous person has no fear whatsoever of that which preoccupies the poet." Such a spectator "feels neither fear nor sympathy" and is rather the sort of person for whom all real danger amounts to walking tightropes or facing the prospect of execution (460–61). Taciturnus here weighs in on the prognostic debate over whether the arts are beneficial for the citizens of a just republic. Plato was skeptical, and is often read as a draconian censor, although Socrates' whole point is that the poets regularly teach us to laugh or cry about the wrong things, or the right things to the wrong degree, and generally instill in us a fear and sympathy for images a third remove from reality. Such entertainment by

---

voluntary suffering, the suffering of love, the power of sacrificing self for the good of others; it represents also suffering as such, suffering in so far as it is an expression of possibility in general. The Christian religion is so little superhuman that it even sanctions human weakness. The heathen philosopher, on hearing tidings of the death of his child exclaims: 'I knew that he was mortal.' Christ, on the contrary—at least in the Bible—sheds tears over the death of Lazarus, a death which he nevertheless knew to be only an apparent one. While Socrates empties the cup of poison with unshaken soul, Christ exclaims, 'If it be possible, let this cup pass from me.' Christ is in this respect the self-confession of human sensibility. In opposition to the heathen, and in particular the stoical principle, with its rigorous energy of will and self-sustainedness, the Christian involves the consciousness of his own sensitiveness and susceptibility in the consciousness of God; he finds it, if only it be no sinful weakness, not denied, not condemned in God." *The Essence of Christianity* (New York: Harper Torchbooks, 1957) 60–61, translated by George Eliot. Similarly apropos, Pascal's terminal declaration is tempered by one of his prayers recorded in *Prières pour les Maladies* that so struck William James with its apparently resigned but debatable pessimism: "Deliver me, Lord, from the sadness at my proper suffering which self-love might give, but put into me a sadness like your own. Let my sufferings appease your choler. Make them an occasion for my conversion and salvation. I ask you neither for health nor for sickness, for life nor for death; but that you may dispose of my health and my sickness, my life and my death, for your glory, my salvation, and for the use of the Church and of your saints, of whom I would by your grace be one...I know not which is more profitable to me, heath or sickness, wealth or poverty, nor anything else in the world. That discernment is beyond the power of men or angels, and is hidden among the secrets of your Providence, which I adore, but do not seek to fathom." William James, *Writings* 1902–1910 (New York: The Library of America, 1987) 262.

falsehood would amount to a pernicious, even though highly popular education. Thus Plato seemingly bans the poets with what amounts to an NC-35 rating. As for the celebrated status of the poet himself, Plato has Socrates provocatively assert anyone should be more eager to be the subject of a eulogy than merely the author of one, a rather upending bit of self-irony on Plato's part.[46] Of course none of this is an indictment against poetry *per se*. Plato's own student Aristotle is more direct and diplomatic in both his estimation of the dramatic arts and his relative trust in the reliability of common opinion by picking up on his teacher's invitation to welcome back the poets from exile if they can but put their own charm to better use.[47] Taciturnus saunters into this perennial courtroom dispute between philosophers and poets with a copy of *The Republic* hidden in his left hand and "A Story of Suffering" in his right, declaring

> it is a mistake for the religious to be angry at poetry, because poetry is and remains lovable. For the spectator it is another matter if he is unaware that such things exist. It is, of course, stupidity or cowardly callousness to want to be ignorant of the existence of poverty and sickness because a person is himself healthy; for even if the poet does not make it manifest, nevertheless anyone who has thought two healthy thoughts about life knows that in the next moment he can be in the same situation. It is not wrong of the spectator to want to lose himself in poetry; this is a joy that has its reward, but the spectator must not confuse theater and actuality, or himself with a spectator who is nothing more than a spectator at a comedy. (461)

Virtually in the same breath Taciturnus displaces the significance of external goods and the blows of fate that threaten us—however stoically or weepily one would or should respond to such blows—and points out how the *religious* poet "begins in another quarter" with: "What you must fear is guilt, and your compassion must be for the person who falls in this way, for the danger is first here. Yet your compassion must not go astray so that you forget yourself over some other person'" (462). Whether or not critics or the general public in a Greek, German, Danish,

---

[46] Plato, *The Republic*, line 599b.

[47] Aristotle, *Politics*, line 1341b 20ff; and *Poetics*, lines 1449b 21, 1452b 30, 1453b 1.

or American republic would welcome Taciturnus as a writer, his literary aim is clear. In contrast to a merely poetic healing in which the individual, "staring himself into the esthetic dizziness, disappears from himself, like an atom, like a speck of dust, something thrown into the bargain along with what is the common lot of all human beings, of all humanity, disappears like an infinitely brief fractional consonance in the harmony of the spheres of life," Taciturnus advocates a distinctively religious catharsis that

> consists in transforming the world and centuries and generations and millions of contemporaries to something vanishing, transforming jubilation and acclamation and esthetic hero worship into a disturbing diversion, the idea of being finished into a phantasmagoric hallucination—so that all that remains is only the individual himself—this particular individual placed in his relationship with God under the qualification: guilty / not guilty. (462–63)

Needless to say, from the pen of the dairy's actual author such bold artistic clarity is internally complicated. In the overall rabbit hole of *Stages on Life's Way,* Taciturn identifies himself with "the parish clerk, that lowly servant" who "by virtue of his office, a humble-proud high priest of inner emotion, tells us 'that we should sorrow over our sins,' something, of course, that the perish clerk does not dare say to the reverend superiors, the assistant professors in the pulpit," and then explicitly confesses even he cannot quite imagine, for himself, what it would be like "to get into the predicament where it would be doubtful whether I was guilty, and I therefore remain outside" (462–63). Neither offended nor truly pious Taciturnus remains thoroughly fascinated by this paradoxical point of view. His *own* point of view emerges from a simultaneously feigned and earnest, coy observatory position that does in fact leave the reader quite alone, since what *he* sees in the contrast between the esthetic and religious is a unity of the comic and tragic such that "in poverty I see the tragedy in the fact that an immortal spirit is suffering and the comedy in the fact that it all revolves around two shillings" (463). What is so lonely about this invitational perspective is how difficult it is to tell whether physical distress is more or less important than spiritual malaise—or in the case of romance, whether duty is more important than desire, along with the heavenly and earthly host of competing thoughts and feelings that invariably ensue. A genuinely religious person, a genuinely poetic person, recognizes and honors each, but few of us manage to put them together, a failure for which one should feel both terribly guilty and oddly unapologetic. As a sermon this is a hard one to write, even with every muse, every flower and ash, and every *trompe l'oeil* on one's side since "world-historical surveys, systematic conclusions, gesticulations, wiping sweat from the brow, a stentorian voice, and pulpit pounding, along with the premeditated use of all this in order to accomplish something are esthetic reminiscences that do not even know how to accentuate fear and pity properly in the Aristotelian sense" (463).

To his credit—if this is what he actually accomplishes—Taciturnus does not "do the astounding thing of ripping the clouds asunder to show heaven open, the judgment day at hand, hell in the background, himself and the elect triumphantly celebrating," but rather "lets heaven remain closed, in fear and trembling does not feel that he himself is finished, bows his head while the judgment of the discourse falls upon thought and mind." He does not "thunder so that the congregation might be kept awake and be saved" but

> lets God keep the thunder and the power and the honor and speaks in such a way that even if everything miscarried he nevertheless is certain that there was one listener who was moved in earnest, the speaker himself, that even if everything miscarried there was one listener who went home strengthened, the speaker himself, that even if everything miscarried and everyone stayed away there was still one person who in life's difficult complications longed for the upbuilding moment of the discourse, the speaker himself. (464)

As sly and open as this will no doubt seem, Taciturnus is as little assured of his own affect until he has an actual reader as he is confident of his explicit authorial intent. Shall we add *intentionally* so?

A Torturous Appendectomy

In the appendix to this section Taciturnus once again parses the comic and tragic in an attempt to negatively unify them under the heading of the religious, swallowing laughter and halting tears in a kind of awful wonder in the face of which angels regularly enjoin us to fear not. The topic is self-inflicted wounds and how we should react to and evaluate them. From the perspective of mundane esthetics such wounds are merely comic because unnecessarily needless. If someone is stabbed or starved from without, then we presumably witness a kind of tragedy; if they stab or starve themselves it just seems laughable in the sense that paranoia or hypochondria cannot be taken seriously as real threats. A sensitive reader of this section might become reasonably distracted by the fact that anorexia nervosa and other forms of self-mutilation are far from comic and indeed tragic as they graphically articulate various inner compulsions prompted from without. But in that same spirit we must keep in mind that the case under interpretation here is of a social misfit who brings harm upon himself due to agonizing over a potentially unfounded responsibility in light of a purportedly mediocre passion on the part of his beloved. Bracketing the purely somatic dimensions of self-torment, we must note how quickly Taciturnus switches the matter to how it might be presented, diagnosed, and addressed by an author who presumably knows better in conjunction with an audience (or patient) who should know better but may not. "Precisely because," he writes,

> it is esthetically correct that all self-torment is comic, one is psychologically wise in an actual situation to use the comic explorer before dealing with self-torment another way. One of course does not bring the patient to laugh immediately at his own fixed idea but by means of analogies comes closer and closer to him. If he laughs excitedly at the analogies, then it is possible that one can take him by surprise by means of a *coup de main* [surprise stroke]. However, this can only be developed specifically in practice, but in practice there is nothing so ridiculous than to see religious categories used in deep and dumb seriousness where one should use esthetic categories with humor and jest. (466)

From a purely esthetic perspective the reader is prompted to conclude that Quidam is laughable and Quaedam is silly, since his passion is so prodigious and hers too small for either of them to be taken seriously, which in its own way is quite sad, even tragic. And echoing his equivocation over purely physical suffering versus spiritual trial, the final assessment from an esthetic point of view is that "it considers any inward direction a desertion, and since it cannot have the deserter shot it makes him ludicrous," which Taciturnus takes as his cue to turn back to a religious perspective, since that perspective "does not consist in an immediate relation between strength and suffering, but in the internal, when this relates itself to itself" (467–68). On the surface, this final esthetic, dismissively pejorative judgment is that the lovers bring their pain upon themselves. However, according to an adjacent reading, self-torment is not laughable but reprehensible, not an occasion to brush something off but to repent of a fresh and original sin. The line here between poetry and piety is extremely thin, since an ubiquitously "sly religiousness" would say, "One must not evoke the dangers oneself; our Lord will surely send them if necessary," whereas an authentically religious person precisely fears for himself and a truly "religious healing consists first and foremost in arousing this fear," a dangerous insight one only properly discovers *"by himself"* (468). In contrast, inauthentic religious talk is "half-esthetic" in placing us in a purely external relation to God that amounts to this:

> Our Lord can certainly bring danger and misery to your house; indeed he can take your property, your beloved, your children, and he will surely do it if it is beneficial for you—*ergo*, since he has not done it, then there is no danger. This is esthetics with imitation religious gilding. From the religious point of view, the greatest danger is that one does not discover, that one is not always discovering, that one is in danger, even if otherwise one had money and the most lovable girl and adorable children and was king of the country or one of the quiet ones in the land, free from all cares. (468–69)

What Taciturnus does here is raise the existential ante by leveling the field and suggesting sickness of heart and loss of limb are both similar and incomparable. Anyone faced with the choice between being a drunk driver or the paralytic victim should know the horrifying moral hiatus that threatens all of us. We are simply unprotected either way, and no amount of good will, anger, or self-pity can help. It takes a singularly curious imagination to simultaneously stand up straight and bow down low and have the "knightly blood" to recognize "it could indeed happen to you also" and honestly ask "why should I be exempt in preference to others?" (469). Once again, this is a difficult sermon to write and deliver with the appropriate tone, imagery, and mood. Rather than "deceive" his audience (or patient) and "by way of religious fancy" merely help him "to play hooky from life," Taciturnus' tenor of choice is the thought of being "joyful out on 70,000 fathoms of water, many, many miles from all human help" and with virtually neck-breaking speed adds: rather than swimming "in the shallows in the company of waders" (470). These expressed thoughts are his way of composing how "he who truthfully and simultaneously can say he is always in danger and always joyful is saying simultaneously the most disheartening and the most high-minded words spoken" (470). It turns out that authoring such words poses an additional threat to and responsibility of the speaker himself, since

> here there are not hard-hearted fathers as with the unhappy lovers in the tragedy; here there is not the superiority of the enemy, before which the hero in the tragic drama falls; here there is not the betrayal by the person one trusted most so that the outstanding person is caught in the trap—here there is only one person who can be the betrayer, oneself, and next to him, but infinitely far removed, the speaker who would advise one to leave it alone instead of doing the only thing he can do—helping one out into the depths where there are 70,000 fathoms. And when this has happened and he now perceives that he can do no more, cannot do more to help the person he loved more than his own life (as is possible in the story of the play) but only in this anxiety discovers that he has 140,000 fathoms beneath him, there is still one thing left to do; he can shout to the beloved, "If you do not become happy now, then know this, know that it is your own fault." (471)

All the Hebrew prophets put together would tremble and immediately fall on their faces at the prospect of delivering such a message. The self-torment under examination here is thus a "halfway point" of helpless self-discovery, with the addition that if an informant happens to be called upon to send such a letter he would likely be considered a "national scourge" delivering an unaccountable invoice. Of course, tongue in cheek, Taciturnus would "imperturbably receive money for it" even as he would have gladly compensated rather than condemned Socrates (471). The thinly embedded, dual irony here is that Taciturnus no more claims to be religious than Socrates claimed to have knowledge. Apparently it is thus how we learn from self-undermined masters to laugh at ourselves amidst the perils of treading our own personal and political waters.

Returning to the particulars of the diary, Taciturnus states Quidam "is something of a self-tormentor" (472). (According to the author's interpretation) the diarist recognizes the danger of the "sortie" with his beloved but remains stuck there and "does not retrieve himself in joy quickly enough to repeat the movement again" (472). With almost tangible indirect self-irony, Taciturnus claims for his hero that it "is possible that things will go better for him if he is sufficiently sensible to regard a whole life as compatible with such a course of instruction and to reconcile himself to remaining a dawdler among those who are quickly finished, a retarded pupil among those who go infinitely further" (472). As for Quaedam, Taciturnus remains obviously guilty (or not?) of restricting the scope of her character to a girl who is helpful enough in getting the diarist "out upon the deep" and "lovely enough to stir him, but also weak enough to misuse her power" rather than painting her as "more spiritually qualified and less femininely lovable" and "magnanimous" enough for her to say to Quidam (in lines he nevertheless grants her):

> My dear, you distress me with your deceit. I do not understand you, and do not know whether you are irresponsible enough to want to leave me because you want to be out in the world or whether you are hiding something from me and are perhaps better than you seem. But whichever it is, I do realize you must have your freedom; I fear for myself if I were not to give it to you, and I love you too much to deny you it. So take it, without any recriminations, without any anger between us, without any thanks on your part but with the awareness on my part that I have done the best I could. (473)

If this was her expressed character, Taciturnus informs us, then the diarist "would have been crushed; he would have been sunk into the ground for shame," not before God but before a perfectly human being (473–74). No doubt more than one reader has actually *wanted* her to deliver these or some such lines if only just to be finally through with the whole affair, an "esthetic" life preserver Taciturnus dangles out above the 70,000 fathoms but holds onto within the imaginary construction as such. Given this unresolved narrative tension, what stands out here as transcendently revealing is how we are in point of fact supposed to be crushed, and apparently lift ourselves—romantically, politically, artistically, even somatically, and including, above all, religiously. Quaedam, according to *my* reading, plays that humanly divine role, both within and outside the text of actual life. Peeling back the various layers we notice that it *is* Quidam who is humbled, and not entirely by himself. Whether he found joy amidst the struggle is definitely not an answer one can find in this or perhaps any script. So it goes.

In a parting interpretive shot concerning his own literary invention, Taciturnus productively teases us with the observation that anyone

> will see how many new constructions could be made from this point by changing him or her a little and seeing what would result for him and for her, how he might have been in order to crush her (if, for example, he had cruelly made her responsible for his life and perhaps terrified her so that she never recovered from it), which he simply cannot do, or how both of them must have been constituted for both of them to be crushed (if, for example, he had not had religious presuppositions and perhaps in desperate pride ended by celebrating their union with suicide) instead of both being helped as they are now. (474)

So presented, for the reader, such "help" amounts to an entirely uncomfortable passing of the baton. Demand more or expect less of either or both of the characters as we might in an effort to achieve resolution, we apparently must run faster or swim harder, if possible, although the average "reader of novels" can only "make other and greater demands and feel that when everything revolves around only two characters it must be boring, which it is indeed if it does not also revolve around the categories" (474). Arguably the "categories" in question are the conflicting set of ideals and emotional habits our words and actions imperfectly display as we work out what really matters to us while we care for and draw from others around us presumably doing the same. Actual people, including ourselves, often prove unreliable in this regard, which despite noble intentions no amount of television can make up for. And so we turn to literature. As for the diarist and his story of suffering, it may be as useless as an actual appendix in need of extraction or one of the more indispensable organs in the social body. It is left for the reader to decide, which will doubtlessly tell them something about themselves.

The Moral of the Story

In the penultimate section to his "Letter to the Reader," Taciturnus presses upon us a moral to his story, but that moral is by no means straightforward and light years away from being moralistic. Perhaps the most helpful way to unpack the initially bizarre adage "to repent of nothing is the highest wisdom" is to begin with his central example and then work through the more abstract claims.

> A gambler comes to a standstill, repentance seizes him, he renounces all gambling. Although he has been standing on the brink of the abyss, repentance nevertheless hangs on to him, and it seems to be successful. Living withdrawn as he does now, possibly saved, he one day sees the body of a man drawn out of the Seine: a suicide, and this was a gambler just as he himself had been, and he knew this gambler had struggled, had fought a desperate battle to resist his craving. My gambler had loved this man, not because he was a gambler, but because he was better than he was. (477)

As an example this one operates on several levels at once. First, as a particular instance of sinful proclivity gambling is itself ambiguous, in fact "dialectical." It can incapacitate one by becoming an obsession that occludes all other capacities by pure loss. But taking risks has a positive side and is an actual virtue. Like lust, risky proclivities are not pointlessly destructive and without direction in the way that—to take the classic examples detailed by Dante—pride, envy, and anger usually are, although these more basic vices are often not fearfully appreciated as such by puritan imaginations that give so much press to gluttony or lust. The midpoint in Dante's account of purgatorial ascent of course is sloth, the lethargic sorrow over good things that immediately precedes the open-ended sin of greed that happens to be joined with prodigality as its apparent opposite. In the black light of this schema gambling hangs up there with other unpruned vices that have virtues in their roots. To take risks, or harbor lusty desires, are thus as positive as they are pejorative.[48]

On another level, the deeper sin that shines through in Taciturnus' example is a despair culminating in suicide, the ultimate rejection of all difficulty. At this level it is once again important not to draw moralistic conclusions, and also where Dante's set of divisions and narrative distinctions is correspondingly helpful and illuminatingly dissonant. While an icy, treacherous thanklessness is Satan's thoroughgoing crime that binds him in the sheer center of nothingness, and prefigures pride as the chief vice, one can nevertheless overcome arrogance in an ascent to earthly paradise. And while lust figures as a stormy self-torment just below limbo and is the least of the barriers to heavenly bliss, the suicidal are relegated to the seventh infernal circle, locked in a thorny, incorporeal punishment for making an irrevocably self-destructive decision. Infamously, we are told that those who resign their earthly life in this fashion are indeed rejoined with their bodies, but in the form of lifeless corpses stuck on the tree in which they have been randomly imprisoned, which presumably only entrenches and extends their original despair. Attending the dark wood of self-inflicted harm are the simultaneously beautiful and horrible harpies who both feed on one's soul and give it voice. The particular suicidal instance Dante provides is that of Pier della Vigna, who experienced a strategically agonizing, steadily rising, but faithful political career in the court of Frederick II before falling among envious comrades and being imprisoned with his

---

[48] Dante, *Purgatorio,* Cantos X–XXVl. It is relevant here to emphasize that vices less teleologically oriented and which arrest spiritual development have a much more tenuous link to corresponding virtues. Seneca, for example, was entirely reticent to admit anger had any salutary aspects in either war or peacetime. "Virtue needs no vice to assist it," he writes, although as a Stoic he may falsely generalize that strong emotions play no positive role in the life of a rational animal. While anger is linked to a cognitive perception of injustice, reasonable assessments of it are often residual and the effects of its emotional impetus largely negative. Thus anger is perhaps not so much pointless as useless. Seneca, *Moral and Political Essays* (Cambridge: Cambridge University Press, 1995) 27, 42, edited and translated by John M. Cooper and J. F. Procopé. Dante's typology suggests this is less true of other passionate perceptions and their corresponding emotional excesses.

eyes gorged out, a fate as politically frequent as it is personally regular, if we have the stomach and courage to recognize and honor it.[49]

On yet another level the example Taciturnus offers contains the additionally arresting element that the gambler had loved his fellow, "not because he was a gambler, but because he was better than he was." Ambiguously, this could mean he loved him not because he was simply a gambler, but a better gambler. That would fit with the initial dialectical nature of vice. But it may be more helpful at this level to comparatively consider the existential fates of Peter and Judas. The Gospels leave the complex impetus of the two disciples' actions for us to wonder about and interpret, but the canonical agreement is that Peter did not end his own life after his threefold denial of association with Jesus while Judas, after selling out his iterant leader for thirty pieces of silver, hanged himself. However that story is variously told, then and now, it prompts us to ask which guilt-ridden response takes more courage: to humbly repent and suffer the shame of accepting a corresponding threefold form of forgiveness and then carrying on and feeding sheep, or simply throwing in the towel and ending it all? One of the more glorious ambiguities of the New Testament telling is whether, before hanging himself, Judas simply threw back the silver he received on the temple floor, which the chief priests then used to purchase a potter's field in which to bury strangers since blood money could not properly be put in the official treasury, or whether Judas himself kept the money and used it for such himself after formerly repenting and being told by his employers: "What is that to us? See to it yourself."[50] In any case, how *would* we go about judging the variously embedded alternatives and sympathizing either way? As a purportedly mere observer and writer the manner in which Taciturnus weighs in on this matter is to say we need to accept and forgive his troubled hero and in this way fear for ourselves in the face of his story as "*de te narratur fibula* [the tale is told of you]" (478). Through indirect correspondence he admonishes us not to be a "modern fool who believes that everyone should court the colossal objective task of being able to rattle off something that applies to the whole human race but not to himself" (478). Along the way he claims it

[49] Dante, *Inferno*, Canto XIII.

[50] Luke 22:1–62; Matthew 27:3–10; John 18:15–27, 21:15–23; Acts 2:15–26.

"unnecessary to consult romances and novels" and then castigates pious readers who would "very likely break off my story a little earlier and have it end with my gambler, shocked by the sight, going home and thanking God for his rescue"; or worse, to callously condemn the other gambler for not wanting to be saved. And even worse than this, to falsely and contemptuously assure a fortunate audience with a "doctrine of predestination" and thereby only help imprison them in the guise and consciousness of a person "who does not have sympathy but has a fear of water" and "finds it unreasonable to take another person's fate so hard" (477–78). In the actual case of his spared but anxiously stunned gambler, the way *Taciturnus* tells it "is not that it is a proclivity to condemn that makes him so keen" but the sense that "he himself cannot be saved by chance" and that "if he says that the other gambler went down despite his good intentions, then he himself goes down; and if he says that consequently the other was unwilling, then he shudders, because he still saw the good in him and because it seems as if he is making himself better" (478).

The roundabout message here is about the mercy and terrible forgiveness we all at some point may have to offer and accept, and even more deeply, about how if we have managed to either thoughtlessly or sagaciously avoid such a prodigious fate, we should not count ourselves lucky but simply broken in a different way. A central preoccupation of his letter is once again with how the existential trials of life are in some sense universal and that no one makes it through by simply avoiding certain trials or anxiously succumbing to the cowardice or defiance that plagues us in familiar forms of hereditary sin. Abel was no more innocent than Cain, or either of their parents, though Cain's particular crime gets a lot of press, and those of his parents remain ambiguously baffling, just as most crimes of previous generations and a full half of our own typically do. What we *all* must acknowledge is our equal fragility and general fault in this common history by "repenting of nothing"—that is, by simultaneously confessing and somehow celebrating we are finally *human* as creatures. Anyone affectionately entangled with another, as a parent, child, friend, or lover should know this. According to some reports even certain sea-born animals—the first within creation—know something about the mourning and delight this entails (although presumably the least of their fears is an allergy to water).[51] Our education in these facts does often begin and continue with a consideration of creatures both higher and lower than ourselves, which at least sheds some light on Taciturnus' confession that although "I am not a gambler, that phenomenon is sufficient, unless, of course, I am an angel," in addition to the follow-up statement that anyone "who goes undauntedly through life on the category that he is not a criminal but not faultless, either, is of course comic" and off-hand assertion that such a person should be "extradited" as such in the name of authentic religiosity and thereby properly serve poetic wherewithal (479).

We do well to read both these understatements and the hallmark generalizations about "the three existence spheres" often quoted in scholarly excerpts against the backdrop of this thicker narrative description of a discombobulated ex-gambler. According to Taciturnus' abstract characterization of the stages,

> The esthetic sphere is the sphere of immediacy, the ethical sphere the sphere of requirement, (and this requirement is so infinite that the individual always goes bankrupt), the religious sphere the sphere of fulfillment, but, please note, not a fulfillment such as when fills an alms box or a sack with gold, for repentance has specifically created a boundless space, and as a consequence the religious contradiction: simultaneously to be out on 70,000 fathoms of water and yet be joyful. (476–77)

What makes the ethical sphere a "passageway—which one nevertheless does not pass through once and for all" is that once the innocent immediacy of youth is over and we gain a sense of sin more "radical" than some particular one-time offense, repentance becomes "dialectical" such that "if one gives it a finger it takes the whole hand" and forgiveness then looms above one's head as an unbelievable necessity for restoring an original sense of integrity. It then appears that the task of being moral becomes impossible and only gives rise to the further, even more difficult task of resisting unmitigated despair. Indeed, to "become so transparent to oneself that one knows that one does not exist at any

[51] See Alasdair MacIntyre's *Dependent Rational Animals* (Chicago: Open Court, 2001).

point by virtue of immediacy" is positively alarming (477, 481–83). Hence we must relax enough to tread water without sinking, whatever one's particular sinful proclivity may be. The most difficult question is about the "second" immediacy of religious faith that has lost its naiveté in a furnace of doubt but finds tragicomic relief in the midst of helplessness. The way Taciturnus formulates this issue, which we must simply live with *as a question* rather than a problem to be solved, is the following:

> But since immediacy is indeed something simple but also something highly compounded, with this one difficulty (of being annulled), together with the other, which is just like it (that immediacy is even canceled as sin), the signal is given for the *difficileste* [most difficult] questions, all of which are included in the one: how an immediacy comes again (or whether the cancellation of immediacy for the existing person means that he does not exist [*er till*] at all), how such an immediacy is different from an earlier one, what is lost and what is gained, what the first immediacy can do that the second one does not dare, what the first immediacy loves that the second does not dare, what certainty the first immediacy has that the second does not have, what is its joy that the second does not have, etc., for it is a very prolix matter. (483–84)

Such abstract claims and questions would be difficult to make sense of if not for the various layers of stories, characters, and points of view each of them represent and coordinate among and often despite themselves. In the current illustration, the fortunate gambler who happened to have been saved from despair might have looked upon the fate of his fellow as an occasion to nurse a sense of self-assured superiority, a crime at least as self-destructive and even more thoroughgoing than literal suicide. Or prompted by an equally destructive, morose anxiety, he might have simply drowned himself. Rather, Taciturnus thinks of his gambler as one fortuitously purged by sympathy and fear, which may contain an embedded argument for why contemplating suicide is so instructive and even spiritually healthy. Gambling aside, the virtue at the core of suicide is its profound sense of helplessness. Far more scary would be the arrogant sensibility that we can simply help ourselves, which is the main reason why to repent of nothing may indeed be the highest wisdom. In that sense Judas ought to be a patron saint, even if Dante wouldn't know exactly where to place him. Affairs of the heart naturally illuminate this lesson, like carefully etched images profligated throughout a kerygmatic text and planted like so many parabolic seeds giving rise to a left-handed union between the esthetic and religious.

In a final jarring comment Taciturnus claims the recent ink spent on this issue of repentance and forgiveness "is extraneous to the task the imaginary construction has assigned itself, for Quidam is only a demonic figure oriented to the religious" (484). We are prepared for this comment since he introduced his central character as such at the beginning of his analysis. But it may remain baffling because the diarist seems so agonizingly conscious of his situation, feelings, obligations, and religious proclivities, tearing him asunder short of the suicidal sorrow of a young Werther, who for his own part had problematically fallen in love with someone already betrothed.[52] Consonant with interim comments on the topic, perhaps we should say here that the terminology and phrasing of "a demonic figure oriented to the religious" is more representative than pejorative. That is, we may all of us be more like self-tormented figures longing for healing than one-dimensional ghouls any self-respecting audience member would rightly dismiss out of hand. Such a reading is indirectly confirmed in a roundabout manner when Taciturnus immediately adds "the issue is beyond both my understanding and my capacities. I shall not shirk it by saying that this is not the place, as if it were the place and perhaps the time and the space on paper that I lacked, since on the contrary I rather much believe that once I had understood it myself I would surely find the place and time and the space for exposition" (484–85). Such circumlocution may just be a literary tease or it may be an honest confession. For one thing the theme of repentance and forgiveness cannot be entirely extraneous given the title "Guilty/Not Guilty?" What we can say is that, just above the author's head, to repent of nothing suggests at least two things at once. First it implies being unapologetic about our mishaps. Second, it unfolds an ethic of taking responsibility for our complexities that often do harm to

[52] Goethe, *The Sorrows of Young Werther*. This work is also contrastingly cited in *Concluding Unscientific Postscript*, 288.

both ourselves and our neighbor. Love stories, lived and well-written, are no doubt the most tangible examples of what this duality might feel like and require. A similar dynamic would apply to broader social aims such as being the Secretary of Defense, or Education for that matter. Our common frailty is something for which we all must ambiguously but thoroughly repent, without either a neat explanation or an excuse. That Taciturnus would make this point in an offhand way and then seemingly take it back by saying it is beyond his capacity to understand may be as good a transition as any to his truly final "concluding word."[53]

Concluding Words

In his "concluding word" Taciturnus attempts to wrap himself up as an author and leave his reader—if there are any left—singularly alone. On an equestrian model Taciturnus figures he has, far from outrunning anyone, not only fallen behind but stayed in one place, "captured by one idea" while "the favorably disposed reader reined in his swift steed and thought I was riding a pacer, but when I did not move from the spot, the horse (that is, the reader) or, if you please, the rider, became impatient, and I was left behind alone: a nonequestrian or a Sunday rider whom everybody outrides" (485). Unhorsing himself he then admits being a sophist in regard to the religious perspective that preoccupies him and pauses on the spot to make the following distinctions: First, the person

---

[53] John J. Davenport helpfully illuminates Taciturnus' letter by supporting the following four claims: (a) The critique of "sagacity" over against infinite passion, whether personal or political, can be understood by way of a critique of utilitarian consequentialism as inadequate for explaining the fundamental, value-laden passions and commitments that constitute the narrative identities of our lives; (b) Quidam's existential conflict is between two equally fundamental, salient passions/commitments that is decidedly unlike an addict who more fundamentally wants to be free of her addiction; (c) Such conflict is representative of the human condition generally and drives one to either preside over and manage the conflicted and anxiously guilty feelings that typically ensue or receptively accept a mysteriously grounded religious grace; and (d) The whole scenario invokes a rough-hewn theodicy of self-formation through suffering. See "The Ethical and Religious Significance of Taciturnus's Letter in Kierkegaard's *Stages on Life's Way*," *International Kierkegaard Commentary*, Volume 11, Stages on Life's Way.

who fancies they are religious without actually being so is simply a fool while the person who only "sees one side of the religious" is obviously a sophist. For his part, Taciturnus sees multiple sides, although his voracious agility renders him no more fat than the skinny Egyptian cows consuming the fatter ones.[54] And so he makes further distinctions between various kinds of sophists: (a) those who "reach an immediate relation to the religious" by means of poetic enthusiasm, (b) those who reach it through an untested immediate ethical sensibility as "a positive doctrine of obligation" rather than recognizing "repentance" as "the supreme task of the ethical and expressly negative," and (c) those who confuse purely abstract "metaphysical" speculation with actual, lived achievement, as if all existential issues were a mere history for cool contemplation (486). In contrast to all such options, Taciturnus is at least cognizant that

> the religious consists precisely in being religiously, infinitely concerned about oneself and not about visions, in being infinitely concerned about oneself and not about a positive goal, which is negative and finite because the infinitely negative is the only adequate form for the infinite, in being infinitely concerned about oneself and consequently not deeming oneself finished, which is negative and perdition. (486)

But merely knowing this "with a balance of spirit," Taciturnus is nevertheless "a sophist like the others, for this balance is an offense against the holy passion of the religious" (486). Apparently his familiarity with infinitely negative regulative ideals and having a truly balanced view of them falls short of the actual elegant double-movements required for the dance floor. And so he admits to standing on the sidelines merely looking on. Even so, he has a contribution to make, since his tragicomic "balance," "which in the Greek sense (not in the infinite religious concern about oneself), is not devoid of significance in illuminating the religious" (486–87). What this series of caveats implies is that he is both closer and further away from actually *being* religious. As a mere writer he at least knows he can claim no real authority on the matter. Thus his concluding self-estimation is that

[54] Genesis 41.

"[s]atisfied with the lesser—hoping that the greater may some day be granted me, engaged in the pursuits of the spirit in which it seems to me every human being is bound to have abundance enough for the longest life, even if this were composed of nothing but the longest days—I am happy in life, happy in the little world that is my environment" (487). Should we pity the actual author here, truly feel for him, or dismiss him, and get him out of our head, as it were?

Mid-paragraph Taciturnus then addresses a series of popular sensibilities about the cultural literacy of Danish urbanites. For starters, he reports that some think Copenhagen is a small and boring town. From this he dissents and asserts Copenhagen is large enough to be "fair-sized" but small enough such that the "statistical consolation they have in Paris over so and so many suicides, the statistical joy they have in Paris over so and so many superlative people, cannot intrude disturbingly and churn the individual into a froth so that life has no meaning, his Sabbath no comfort, his festival day no joy, because everything slips away into emptiness or surfeit" (487).[55]

[55] For readers coming later one could place Taciturnus' comments on the burgeoning field of statistical analysis in conversation with Emile Durkheim's landmark treatment in his study *Suicide* (Tampa FL: The Free Press, 1951), translated by John A. Spaulding and George Simpson. Durkheim's thesis is that the collective, social dimension of human life is more fundamental than individual temperament and proclivity and applies a more uniform and lasting pressure on it than we might otherwise assume, and is therefore uniquely equipped to explain what turns out to be merely relative statistical variations in behavior. For though he offers a pluralistic account of suicidal tendencies under different and even opposed rubrics, an irreducibly collective background informs and modifies individual desire, conscience, and expectation like a moral carbon base. We cannot even begin to speak intelligibly about particular cases without a sociological analysis such that extraordinary hybrids and anomalies, if they exist at all outside our imagination, offer surprisingly little useful information. In his own way Taciturnus might agree that any given society—with its domestic codes, political ideals, and economic structures—is formidably greater than the sum of its parts. But he would clearly add the dramatic caveat that even so there are still individuals who can, do, and perhaps ought to be informed by other individuals not under the heat lamp of statistics, but rather in the white lightning of a *de te narratur fabula*. The real difference may be that while Durkheim initially emphasizes the social cohesion of traditional religious identity as part of the overall social mixture, Taciturnus highlights its individuating effect. As the

Underneath this, in a deliberate parody of and indirect agreement with Judge William's pastoral defense of settled married life over against traveling far and wide, not to mention being well-read, Taciturnus gushes about how the comparative lack of Danish urbanity affords one the chance to discover something "on which one has in vain sought enlightenment in books." Such enlightenment "suddenly dawns on one upon hearing a servant girl talking with another servant girl" given how "a phrase that one has tried in vain to torture out of one's own brain, sought in vain in dictionaries, even the dictionary of the Academy of Sciences and Letters, is heard in passing—a soldier says it and does not dream what a rich man he is" (488). Part of what is oddly amusing about this rushing prosaic stream of thoughts is that it is not clear who holds such a low view of Copenhagen and whether they are even Danish in the first place, or perhaps from Minnesota, Tokyo, or wherever.

It gets worse and funnier still. Even as "some" find Copenhagen small and boring, still others suppose the Danish language "is not adequate to express difficult thoughts" (489). On this point Taciturnus

---

diarist evokes: alone before God, out there amidst the howling of wolves where households are spaced much farther apart than in large and dense urban settings. Durkheim would respond that this view and role of religious sentiment are largely the result of the Reformation and quickly point out that egoistic suicide rates turn out higher in Protestant countries. Here the debate might become a wash, with each modifying the other's fundamental case in such a way that a sufficiently nuanced statistical analysis could form a *de te narratur fabula* of its own kind. If Taciturnus reintroduces the Socratic element into traditional piety, perhaps Durkheim introduces it for the first time into sociology. To this degree the fact that Durkheim is focused on why religiously disillusioned bachelors prey to an industrial culture in the throws of chronic economic upheaval might be more prone to suicide in spite of themselves may not be that far from Taciturnus' imaginary example of an anxiety-riddled gambler gazing upon his cohort being drawn out of the Seine. Or as Graham Greene's character in *A Burnt-Out Case* rehetorically demands with unwitting prescience: "Who remembers what happened to Lucien de Rubempé in the end?" (New York/London: Penguin Books, 1961) 45. As a matter of literary fact Balzac's own character did end his own life after a protracted, dissillusioned travail, the account of which can be found in *A Harlot High and Low* (New York/London: Penguin Books, 1970) 402–406, translated by Rayner Heppenstall. The back-story can be found in *Lost Illusions* (NewYork/London: Penguin Books, 1971), translated by Herbert J. Hunt.

also disagrees and feels happily bound to his mother tongue, "bound as Adam was to Eve because there was no other woman," but more positively because, among having other qualities, his native language "does not puff and sound strained when it stands before the unutterable but works at it in jest and earnestness until it is enunciated" and which "in relation to the object it goes in and out like an elf" (489). When reading this long and lugubrious defense of Danish, one gets the palpable sense our author is celebrating the qualities of a beloved that "others" do not recognize, and may even find ridiculous, particularly if they themselves are not in love. It is as if Taciturnus had encountered other languages like so many different animals and finally declares of his own tongue: "this one at last, bone of my bone, flesh of my flesh," which is as contagiously amusing as it is seriously evocative.[56] The message of this effusive glossolalia is about the local ties and personal preferences that exercise a hold on all of us, a fact which may or may not get lost in translation depending on whether this feature of human life is taken as a crippling limitation or a fortunate point of departure.

Having sophistically but unapologetically vindicated the Danish tongue, in a swing-vote of anti-provincialism Taciturnus further distances himself from the opinions of his fellow countrymen by simultaneously rebuffing the opposing sentiments that Denmark is either living on old memories or faces a matchless future. On the contrary, his cultural perception is that there is no "great difference between one generation and the next" since in gaining any critical distance a living participant "is in the situation of extolling what a former generation of contemporaries misjudged" (490). This stance is a real mindbender if one considers the implications of critically embracing what is at hand without recourse to either stodgy nostalgia or childish optimism. For example, one could say we haven't moved beyond Socratic wisdom and this constitutes our greatest hope for the future. If true, this would make ancient Athens a contemporary scene and many a contemporary entirely backwards. Presumably the same would apply to Abraham or Jesus. Or shrinking generational gaps, one could say Millennials are not so different than Baby Boomers, presumably depending on the books they read, or not, or whom any given individual

[56] Genesis 2:23.

emulates as a hero. More pointedly, a third-wave feminist might only detect a hair's worth of difference between Virginia Woolf and D. H. Lawrence where her predecessors would recognize an entire world of distinction. Rounding out all this critical distance and receptive appropriation, Taciturnus fully accepts the view that to be a Danish author is a poor way to make a living. But he is quick to add that, if true, this could just as well be a tribute as a slur since in that case his homeland would at least not have to recognize "authors by the dozens" (491). This is the tail-side of the Socratic coin where the notorious teacher, having refused money for his maieutic services, claimed at his trial that far from being condemned he should receive free meals in the Prytaneum at state expense ordinarily awarded to Olympian athletes.[57] One could slice the irony here with a knife, one of the earliest instances of geeks in competition with the jocks, who regularly condemn the former to death.

Only a few pages from the end of his letter, where Taciturnus has not assumed he will even have any readers left, he nevertheless envisions at least one reader who might turn and ask his fellows what to make of this strange literature, to which the imaginary response of "some" is: "Pay no attention to such an author, do not listen to him—he is a seducer" (491). Along the way, at least "one" of this fanciful "some" might go on to make the distinction between a purely erotic, demonic seducer like Don Juan and an "enthusiast" who

> does not go to dances with girls (in this respect he is far behind), but he seeks a place in a small sideroom off the ballroom and in a corner of the parlor. Then when the girls are somewhat tired from dancing, or when twilight falls and work stops and thoughts want to flap their wings, then he sits down; now it is his time. Then they listen to his talk, and with his imagination he lures them on into seductive ideals, and as he talks he stretches the expectancy of the aspiring soul and the claim of presentiment. He craves nothing for himself. And once again they seek the pleasure of the dance and the daily pursuits begin again, but secretly they ponder the lofty things he had talked about and they long to imbibe once again the spellbinding illusion. He himself remains unchanged, for his delight is only in the longing for

[57] Plato, *Apology*, 36d.

> the ideal in his words and thoughts. And when he is silent, it seems to him as if there were a deep sorrow in his soul; in his depression he feels like a blind old man whom talking, like a child, leads through life. So the little misses listen to him, and little by little they are seduced; they seek in vain for what he described, seek it in vain in him, seek it in vain in themselves, and yet they long for his conversation and grow old by hearing it. (491–92)

Among the items we should attend to in this passage is the meticulously crafted link between the power of language, audience reception, erotic passions, the loneliness never entirely absent from the heart of romantic love itself and that is the source of a greater part of its craving and close-quartered activity, and the aging sensibility that we are all in some salient sense both physically and spiritually helpless. Significantly, such an "enthusiast," such an author, a mere poet—according to this singular imaginary report—remains in one sense "far behind" a Don Juan and yet leagues ahead and is therefore far more dangerous. Why might this be the case? Because Taciturnus wants to join the dance? Because he disdains the dance? Because he wants to join his own body *in order to* join the dance? Because he thinks too much, or because others do not think enough? Because hell hath no fury as when enervating jealousies intervene and tender intimacies become bloody? Because there is a Minervan owl overlooking the terraced garden outside both the dancehall and the parlor, tucked in a tree, remaining presciently mute? There is something true in all these affirmative rhetorical answers, which can be summed up in how his whole manner of being disturbs the life of the party by enticing the listener with a problematic platonic ascent. As it turns out, the "girls," such as they are, do not listen to the warning of the "old aunt" but simply smile and say, "He! He is the nicest man, and in his association with us he is so careful, so reserved, as if he did not see us or as if he were afraid of us, and what he says is so beautiful, oh, so beautiful!" (492). Perhaps what it most arresting about this imaginary self-characterization by a pseudonymous author of how others might perceive him is how utterly true to life it comes by articulating the both guilty and innocent, fragile and wonderful erotic bond we are able to forge through mere conversation. This characterization really is both sad and delightful, a negative unity of the comic and tragic. At our best we all know, if we have experienced it, how like a kiss reading a book can be, certainly startling and perchance welcome.

At this final juncture Taciturnus continues to split into a third person by perorating on how "some" "one" might go on to insist how this given author surely does not have such poetic powers of seduction, "nor does he chase after women, but nevertheless in a different sphere he is a seducer" (492). The narrator here is starting to evaporate, just as William Afham did earlier in the text: "Anyone who looks at him with a genuinely speculative eye sees with half a glance that he, himself defrauded by life by being merely an observer, has become not the deceiver but the deception, the objective deception, the pure negation" (492). Nevertheless there is something positively intoxicating about Taciturnus and his production in that "he wants to induce everyone to believe that the single individual has infinite significance and that this is the validity of life" and "seduce you in a period of ferment to sit still in the undivided estate of quietism in the futile thought that everyone is supposed to attend to himself" (492–93). Which is precisely why he must be warned against as a potential threat, though "without having any evil intention" (493). Thus our first-person third party to himself concludes: "do not incite him, for then he could possibly become dangerous; let him go for what he is, a mocker and an enthusiast *in uno* [in one], a bourgeois-philistine *in toto* [throughout], a deceiver, pure negation" (493–94). At this point it sounds like *he* is the confessional demoniac with a religious orientation, seduced by the very character he has conjured. Disappearing in this way into a crowd of voices and alternate orientations, Taciturnus then leaves us finally alone, a punishment whose only harm is "being allowed to shift for oneself when it is the only thing he wishes," not unlike the punitive damages awarded by tossing a wriggling eel back in the water (494).

An Inconclusive Word from the Present Reader

Amidst *Stages on Life's Way* there is as much agreement as contention between the various voices and perspectives we encounter. Readers are often enjoined to consider the esthetic, ethical, and religious orientations as rivals, each competing for precedence, and that the task is to somehow fit ourselves into one or another of the so-called spheres of existential orientation through primary identification and defense. In contrast, I think we witness a prospective ideal of smoldering beauty, ethical warmth, and ascetic heat all coalescing in an arresting development of heartbreakingly faithful ecstatic repose. Put otherwise, *Stages* forms a whole and does not outline three entirely distinct stages of programmatic development that often appear on dust jackets. Anyone more closely familiar with the details of the book, and even more attentive to his or her own life, should be skeptical of such a caricature. The insights about love that *Stages* unfolds and explores and leaves the reader to simply face without solution must be called forth from the tensions within each prospective "stage" as well as between them. One could, as it were, start anywhere, with any given claim, because any perspective points to or raises a contrary. If we had to divide up and organize the stages, it would be: (a) a smattering of ironically detached revelers full of meaningful longing despite themselves, (b) an anxiously defensive middle-aged, married Judge vocationally divided, and (c) a wide-angled snapshot of conflicted passion taken at a distance by a self-confessed literary observer, altogether which could just as well amount to a single, internally complicated stage. Whatever progression occurs will be circular and cumulative, not linear and disjunctive. For example, even if one were tempted to neatly identify the moral center of the book with Judge William against the tipsy bachelors and solitary diarist on either side, one could just as well point to his arguably deluded and faithless idolatry of a staid bourgeois marriage as the truly demonic "exception."[1] Thus, one could say the book stages in three acts a *sui*

[1] Reading Kierkegaard, even Denis de Rougemont concludes by emphasizing the series of dissatisfying disjuncts between the philistine sagacity of practical

generis universal that resists disambiguation. The sheer disorientation of this striking hermeneutical possibility evokes a poetic, moral, and otherworldly simultaneity, an internally differentiated simultaneity that over time *is* the stage, whether in the theater or actual life.[2]

---

association, the "interim" romantic reaction to this, and the religious sublimation that falls short of full humanity as he keeps careful, defensive watch over the affectionate duties of faithful marriages. See *Love in the Western World* (Princeton: Princeton University Press, 1983) 299–323.

[2] Interpreting the formally disparate portions of *Stages* as a literary whole, and how the esthetic, ethical, and religious moments of existential orientation are internally related and flow back and forth to become mutually modified over the course of a lifetime, may shed some light on how tempting but finally unnecessary it would be to make it structurally correspond to *Three Discourses on Imagined Occasions* from the parallel authorship Kierkegaard intentionally signed and published alongside his pseudonymous writings. "On the Occasion of a Confession" takes as its theme the ambivalent mixture of wonder, guilt, and joy, born of solitary stillness before an eternal beloved we properly seek, only to find it is we who have been sought. If this discourse directly corresponds to anything it might as well be C.S. Lewis's *Till We Have Faces*, in which the terrifying and wonderful dimensions of human and divine love remain inextricably intertwined. "On the Occasion of a Wedding" emphasizes the internal threats and good fights that occompany the otherwise immediate joy of romance, threats, and fights that are worse than death and call for a corresponding fragile peace born of dutiful resolve. The third discourse, "At a Graveside," focuses on the inexplicably sure sense of mortality that silently attends the variable range of experiential fortune and bad luck with uncertain intimations of possibility, and paradoxically encourages us, of all things, to face *life*. Sythe in hand, in this portrayal death is neither a grim reaper nor a comfort to be suicidally embrassed. Various scholars have drawn parallels between these discourses and the so-called stages along the way. That scholars agree the second discourse corresponds to the manuscript stolen from Judge William is naturally justified insofar as both the manuscript and the discourse suffer from internal bleeding. My own take is that we best imagine—on any of the three occasions—Quidam, Judge William, and the banqueteers all reading these discourses, all listening, each of them separately disturbed or comforted, but certainly moved. No doubt it is likely the banqueteers as subjective personalities might prefer to sit in the balcony or stand in the narthex, perhaps joined by Quidam in the back somewhere. Naturally Quaedam is there among them, probably in a pew down front next to William, and no doubt occupied with her own thoughts and torn assunder by nameless feelings of love lost and regained. In any case, the troubles of erotic passion, marriage, and otherworldly ascetic longing are all soldered

If we did cast about for theoretical scaffolding with which to peer more closely at the structural details of the existential edifice *Stages* erects, our best available option would be the dramatic and dialogical model of Plato's *Symposium*, clearly signaled by the very form and content of "In Vino Veritas." But this reference does not end there and helps illuminate *Stages* as a whole, partially to the degree that the model itself is thoroughly literary, partially to the degree that actual life itself is inherently dramatic, and partially because such drama is periodically didactic, often pedantic, but finally—hopefully—edifyingly, even intuitively discursive. In the penultimate speech by Socrates, itself a report of a conversation he had had with Diotima, he describes an ascending teleology of thought and desire that begins with loving particular embodied individuals. The next rung of this ladder includes a view of all instances of embodied attraction. Climbing higher we catch a glimpse of the beauty of another's mind and moral character. Further up we become enamored with beautiful thoughts and institutional practices more generally. Ascending higher and higher one finally and longingly gazes upon Beauty Itself, in the light of which all lower forms are both recognizable and appear imperfect by comparison.[3] Most readers find the upper reaches of this ascent at least disorienting if not frankly nonsensical. What could it possibly mean, for example, to find the Athenian Constitution more beautiful than Bathsheba, not to mention what it means that the Form of Beauty Itself makes even the Athenian

---

together to form a three-way electrical switch. To say the least, love and death continually haunt and inspire a complete, integrated life and simultaneously call for confession. If we must conclude anything definite about Kierkegaard's overall authorship, his writings are thouroughly dialectical throughout, in both their whole and parts, and cannot be neatly compartmentalized into distinct picture-perfect moments of esthetic, ethical, or pious self-comportment. Each of them have integrity only in relation to the others. See Walter Lowrie's introduction to his translation of *Stages on Life's Way* (Oxford: Oxford University Press, 1940); the historical introduction by Howard and Edna Hong in their translation of *Three Discourses on Imagined Occasions* (Princeton NJ: Princeton University Press, 1993); and Andrew J. Burgess's "*The Relation of Kierkegaard's* Stages on Life's Way *to* Three Discourses on Imagined Occasions," from *International Kierkegaard Commentary,* Volume 11, Stages On Life's Way (Macon GA: Mercer University Press, 2000), edited by Robert L. Perkins.

[3] Plato, *Symposium*, lines 210a–211d.

Constitution look like a ragdoll to which I might otherwise be tenderly attached as an infantile self? Or to take another part of his dialogical report about the generative qualities of love, how can we compare the competing progeny of a newborn babe with a Pulitzer-prize-winning novel? Would or should we trade the significance of an actual child for a copy of Homer's *Odyssey*?[4] But as with *Stages*, we must pay close attention to the internal irony. Following Diotima's lead Socrates reports that Love—conceived at an exalted celebration of Aphrodite's own birth—is the hybrid child of Poros and Penia, a mixture of poverty and plenty, homeless but resourceful, always in need but full of ingenuity, a genius with enchantments, potions, and clever pleadings, an entirely ardent but mere lover of wisdom altogether.[5] Of course this is merely a *story* about the defects and nobility of love, meant to cast light on the prose of real life. Along the way, it suggests that the very height of philosophical ascent is poetically replete with proper names and particular individuals, beginning right here with our greatest philosopher-ironist.

In terms of *Stages* I have suggested we could begin on a middle rung, with Judge William, there on a crisp morning, having tea with his spouse, having in all likelihood slept a solid eight hours while the demolition crew hired by Constantin was breaking up a nefarious gathering down the road. Although he is himself middle-aged, he is far from jaded, and in fact remains an idealist. This sounds good, and often inspires readers with the thought of how sweet and secure and happy such a life can be such that as he and his wife can travel from country inn to country inn on holiday while amusing themselves at the prospect of having corns on one's feet being grounds for divorce ahead of time. Judge William's passion is steady, comfortable, and relatively noiseless. Other readers find his very idealism off-putting. Married love, we are informed, is a synthesis of all titular excitement consistent with moral respect and devotion. Cupid with his quiver of arrows sits obediently in the presence of YHWY and all is right with the world. It seems there is no danger, for example, of being shot twice, or from different directions, or even worse, not at all. As for the diarist, he is shot only once, but in

[4] Ibid., lines 208e–209e.

[5] Ibid., lines 203b–204c.

respect to the wrong person, or on a more unsettling interpretation, in respect to any person. Apparently the synthesis is not so easily or even ever achieved. This drives Quidam further in YHWY's direction, which leaves his beloved standing there, by the end, reticently heartbroken, with one last request: think of me sometimes, which the diarist promises to do in a cavalier way without revealing how seriously he will in fact do so (395). As in the midst of Socrates' paradoxical report on the wondrously glorious pitfalls of love's passion, we are left disoriented, straddling an additional rung, glancing down, and more than a bit shaky.

The way Plato tells the story after Socrates recounts the mystical ascent towards Beauty in Itself, the already inebriated Alcibiades interrupts the otherwise sober proceedings in celebration of the Dionysian festival and delivers the final speech. It is an encomium just as divided as the others, but far more personal, as delighted and alarmed as he is to find Socrates in company and on whom he impetuously decides to base his rhetoric. Vain and jealous, Alcibiades simultaneously praises and criticizes the notorious maieutic teacher by comparing him to a figure of Silenus, snub-nosed with double flute in hand, hollow and split down the middle with statues of the gods inside, looking much like the beastly and erotically charged satyr Marsyas, punished for impudently competing with Apollo but whose music was later played on Olympus because the melodies were so divine. The difference is that in Socrates' case his only instrument is verbal, though his mere words instill a corresponding bacchanalian frenzy within the soul of the one with ears to hear. Alcibiades clearly intends to confuse his audience with a mad, overlapping mixture of worship and complaint as he recounts his lover's ascetic acts of temperance and fortitude. At the apex of this elegy he confesses how jilted he felt at Socrates' refusal to embrace him beneath his mantle in exchange for the wisdom the reluctant teacher brought to a private dinner arrangement.[6] This tragicomic scene is fraught with the kind of enticing and embarrassing tension familiar to all those who have ever been truly and problematically in love, a scene in which inner beauty and external attraction, fine words and flirtatious antics, noble

---

[6] Ibid., lines 215a–222c.

deeds and repressed desires all feverishly vie for equal attention in an ambivalent blend of shame and reverence.[7]

Kierkegaard himself manages to add his own "stages" to this ancient and treacherous but nevertheless buoyant body of water as a correspondingly complicated, but fresh tributary. If he does so in spite of himself as either a lover or a writer, this would be par for the course and neither a reason for embarrassment nor an invitation to dismiss him out of hand. It rests with us to feel, to know, and resolve, no doubt from a place located outside *Stages* and within the text of our own lives. Perhaps along the way we should in fact read the book backwards, starting with the diarist's religiously distended melancholia, followed by Judge William's sober good cheer, and ending with the Seducer's tipsy categorical imperative: "Enjoy!" Let us all raise a toast to the intoxicating, tragicomic difficulty, and ultimate delight of romantic ideals before smashing our goblets against the wall; and with Alcibiades, let us crash this party with an agonized internal respect for his feeling vulnerably jilted by Socrates, recalling above all Quaedam—petulant, reserved,

---

[7] This Platonic interpretive framework is itself a subject of interpretion. There is a long, popular, and scholarly tradition of reading the final entry of Alcibiades as a kind of offhand, ridiculous confirmation of the presumably superior delivery of Socrates' description of a purified ascent above the material, emotionally mixed, and romantically charged dimensions of particular loves as experienced on the ground. On this view the highest earthly legacy of Platonic love is an outward and upward friendship in which we no longer primarily value and desire the inward-looking embrace of a bodily other. One of the more compelling and least facile versions of this view is expressed by Andrew Sulivan, writing in light of Montaigne's relationship to La Boétie in the aftermath of a promiscuous HIV scare that witnessed partners senselessly die. Sulivan heartfully lauds a kind of friendship that "existed rather as a platontic longing so intense that we have almost forgotten it today. It is a form of union which is truer than love, stabler than sex, deeper than politics, and more moral than family." *Love Undetectable* (New York: Alfred A. Knopf, 1998) 228. Compare this with Martha C. Nussbaum's *The Fragility of Goodness* (Cambridge: Cambridge University Press, 1986) chapters 6 and 7. In "Does Love Cure the Tragic? Kierkegaardian Variations on a Platonic Theme," Adriaan van Heerden adds another piece to the puzzle by asserting the "religious imperative commands the pursuit of the 'erotic ascent' and the 'erotic descent' simultaneously towards the limit." *International Kierkegaard Commentary*, Volume 11, Stages On Life's Way, 89.

amorous, resigned, piqued, amused, anxious, hopeful, angry, and humanly pious—along with her penultimately situated, corybantic lover.

Bibliography

Augustine. *Confessions.* Translated with notes by Henry Chadwick. Oxford: Oxford University Press, 1991.

The Autobiography of Goethe. Illustrated Sterling Edition. Translated by John Oxenford, Esq. Boston: Dana Esthes & Company, n.d.

Baldwin, James. *Collected Essays.* New York: The Library of America, 1998.

———. *Just Above My Head.* New York: The Dial Press, 1978.

Balzac, Honeoré de. *A Harlot High and Low.* Translated with introduction by Rayner Heppenstall. New York/London: Penguin Books, 1970.

———. *Lost Illusions.* Translated with introduction by Herbert J. Hunt. New York/London: Penguin Books, 1971.

Capallanus, Andreas. *The Art of Courtly Love.* Introduction, translation, and notes by John Jay Parry. New York: Colombia University Press, 1960.

Chopin, Kate. *The Awakening.* New York: W. W. Norton & Company, 1994.

The Complete Works of Aristotle. Two volumes. The revised Oxford Translation, edited by Jonathan Barnes. Princeton: Princeton University Press, 1984.

Dante. *The Divine Comedy.* Translated by Allen Mandelbaum with introduction by Eugenio Montale and notes by Peter Armour. New York/Toronto: Alfred A. Knopf, 1995.

Day, Dorothy. *The Long Loneliness.* New York: Harper & Row Publishers, Inc., 1997.

Diogenes Laertius. *Lives of Eminent Philosophers,* Volume I. Translated by R. D. Hicks. Loeb Classical Library, LCL 184. Cambridge MA/London: Harvard University Press, 1925.

Dostoevsky, Fyodor. *The Brothers Karamozov.* Translated by Richard Pevear and Larissa Volokhonsky. San Francisco: North Point Press, 1990.

Durkheim, Emile. *Suicide.* Translated by John A. Spaulding and George Simpson. Tampa FL: The Free Press, 1951.

Encounters with Kierkegaard, A Life Seen by His Contemporaries. Collected, edited, and annotated by Bruce H. Kirmmse and translated by Bruce H. Kirmmse and Virginia R. Laursen. Princeton: Princeton University Press, 1996.

Feminist Interpretations of Søren Kierkegaaard. Edited by Céline Léon and Sylvia Walsh. State College: Pennsylvania State University Press, 1997.

Fenger, Henning. *Kierkegaard, The Myths and Their Origins.* Translated by George C. Schoolfield. New Haven: Yale University Press, 1980.

Feuerbach. *The Essence of Christianity.* Translated by George Eliot. Introductory essay by Karl Barth and foreword by H. Richard Niebuhr. New York: Harper & Row, Publishers, 1957.

Freud, Sigmund. "Creative Writers and Day-Dreaming." In *The Complete Psychological Works of Sigmund Freud,* Volume IX. Translated by James Strachey. London: The Hogarth Press, 1959.

Furtak, Rick Anthony. *Wisdom in Love, Kierkegaard, and the Ancient Quest for Emotional Integrity.* South Bend: University of Notre Dame Press, 2005.

Gadamer, Hans-Georg. *Truth and Method.* Second revised edition, translated by Joel Weinsheimer and Donald G. Marshall. New York: Crossroad Publishing Corporation, 1989.

Garff, Joakim. *Søren Kierkegaard, A Biography.* Translated by Bruce H. Kirmmse. Princeton: Princeton University Press, 2007.

Goethe, Johann Wolfgang von. *Elective Affinities.* Translated by R. J. Hollingdale. New York/London: Penguin Books, 1971.

———. *The Sorrows of Young Werther.* Translated by Michael Hulse. New York/London: Penguin Books, 1989.

———. *Wilhelm Meister's Apprenticeship.* Translated by Thomas Carlyle. New York: The Heritage Press, 1959.

Greene, Graham. *A Burnt-Out Case.* New York/London: Penguin Books, 1961.

Hall, Amy Laura. *Kierkegaard and the Treachery of Love.* Cambridge: Cambridge University Press, 2002.

Hannay, Alstair. *Kierkegaard, A Biography.* Cambridge: Cambridge University Press, 2001.

Hegel, G.W.F. *Aesthetics, Lectures on Fine Art.* Two volumes. Translated by T.M. Knox. Oxford: Clarendon Press, 1975.

———. *Lectures on the Philosophy of Religion, One-Volume Edition, The Lectures of 1827.* Translated by R. F. Brown, P. C. Hodgson, and J. M. Stewart with the assistance of H. S. Harris and edited by Peter C. Hodgson. Berkeley, Los Angeles, London: University of California Press, 1988.

———. *Philosophy of Right.* Translated with notes by T. M. Knox. Oxford: Oxford University Press, 1967.

Heidegger, Martin. *Being and Time.* Translated by John Macquirrie and Edward Robinson. New York: Harper and Row Publishers, 1962.

Herodotus. *The Histories.* Translated by Aubrey De Sélincourt and revised with notes by John Marincola. New York/London: Penguin Books, 1972.

Hesiod. *Works and Days.* Edited and translated by Glenn W. Most. Loeb Classical Library, LCL 57. Cambridge MA/London: Harvard University Press, 2006.

Hoffman, Kevin. "Kierkegaard, Compassion, and the Descent of Love." *International Philosophical Quarterly* (July 2007).

Ibsen, Henrik. *Brand.* A version for the stage by Geoffrey Hill. New York / London: Penguin Books, 1996.

*International Kierkegaard Commentary,*Volume 11, Stages on Life's Way. Edited by Robert L. Perkins. Macon GA: Mercer University Press, 2000.

James, William. *Writings* 1902–1910. New York: The Library of America, 1987.

Kierkegaard, Søren. *Christian Discourses/The Crisis and a Crisis in the Life of an Actress.* Edited and translated by Howard V. Hong and Edna H. Hong with introduction and notes. Princeton: Princeton University Press, 1997.

———. *The Concept of Irony.* Edited and translated by Howard V. and Edna H. Hong. Princeton: Princeton University Press, 1989.

———. *Concluding Unscientific Postscript to* Philosophical Fragments. Edited and translated by Howard V. and Edna H. Hong. Princeton: Princeton University Press, 1992.

———. *The* Corsair *Affair, And Articles Related to the Writings.* Edited and translated by Howard V. and Edna H. Hong. Princeton: Princeton University Press, 1982.

———. *Either/Or, I.* Edited and translated by Howard V. and Edna H. Hong. Princeton: Princeton University Press, 1987.

———. *Fear and Trembling/Repetition.* Edited and translated by Howard V. and Edna H. Hong. Princeton: Princeton University Press, 1983.

———. *Philosophical Fragments/Johannes Climacus.* Edited and translated by Howard V. and Edna H. Hong. Princeton: Princeton University Press, 1985.

———. *The Point of View.* Edited and translated by Howard V. Hong and Edna H. Hong with introduction and notes. Princeton: Princeton University Press, 1998.

———. *The Sickness Unto Death.* Edited and translated by Howard V. and Edna H. Hong. Princeton: Princeton University Press, 1980.

———. *Stages on Life's Way.* Translated by Howard V. and Edna H. Hong. Princeton: Princeton University Press, 1988.

———. *Stages on Life's Way.* Translated with introduction by Walter Lowrie. Oxford: Oxford University Press, 1940.

———. *Three Discourses on Imagined Occasions.* Edited and translated by Howard V. and Edna H. Hong. Princeton: Princeton University Press, 1993.

———. *Without Authority.* Edited and translated by Howard V. and Edna H. Hong. Princeton: Princeton University Press, 1997.

———. *Works of Love.* Edited and translated by Howard V. and Edna H. Hong. Princeton: Princeton University Press, 1995.

Kjaeldgaard, Lasse Horne. "'The Peak on which Abraham Stands': The Pregnant Moment of Soren Kierkegaard's *Fear and Trembling*." *Journal of the History of Ideas* 63/2 (April 2002).

Krishek, Sharon. *Kierkegaard on Faith and Love*. Cambridge: Cambridge University Press, 2009.

Lawrence, D.H. *Lady Chatterley's Lover*. Edited with an introduction and notes by Michael Squires. New York/London: Penguin Books, 1994.

Lebowitz, Naomi. *Kierkegaard, A Life of Allegory*. Baton Rouge: Louisiana State University Press, 1985.

Léon, Céline. *The Neither/Nor of the Second Sex, Kierkegaard on Women, Sexual Difference, and Sexual Relations*. Macon GA: Mercer University Press, 2008.

Lewis, C.S. *The Allegory of Love*. Oxford: Oxford University Press, 1936.

———. *Till We Have Faces*. New York: Harcourt, Brace and Company, 1957.

Lowrie, Walter. *Kierkegaard*. Gloucester MA: Peter Smith, 1970.

MacIntyre, Alasdair. *Dependent Rational Animals*. Chicago: Open Court, 2001.

Mann, Thomas. *Lotte in Weimar: The Beloved Returns*. Translated by H.T. Lowe-Porten. New York: Vintage Books, 1983.

Maugham, W. Somerset. *The Moon and Sixpence*. New York/London: Penguin Books, 1944.

Milton, John. *The Annotated Milton, Complete English Poems*. Edited by Burton Raffel. New York: Bantam Books, 1999.

Moore, George. *Heloise and Abelard*. Two volumes. New York: Boni & Liveright, 1925.

Nussbaum, Martha C. *The Fragility of Goodness*. Cambridge: Cambridge University Press, 1986.

Nygren, Anders. *Agape and Eros*. Philadelphia: Westminster Press, 1953.

O'Brien, Tim. *The Things They Carried*. New York: Broadway Books, 1998.

O'Neill, Caroline Coleman. *Loving Søren*. Nashville: Brodman & Holman Publishers, 2005.

Pattison, George. *Kierkegaard, Religion, and the Ninteenth-Century Crisis of Culture*. Cambridge: Cambridge University Press, 2002.

Plato Complete Works. Edited by John M. Cooper, associate editor D. S. Hutchinson. Indianapolis/Cambridge: Hackett Publishing Company, Inc., 1997.

Plutarch. *The Lives of the Noble Grecians and Romans*. Translated by John Dryden and revised by Arthur Hugh Clough. New York: Modern Library, 1975.

Ricoeur, Paul. *The Conflict of Interpretations*. Edited by Don Ide. Evanston: Northwestern University Press, 1974.

Rougemont, Denis de. *Love Declared, Essays on the Myths of Love.* Translated by Richard Howard. New York: Pantheon Books, 1963.

———. *Love in the Western World.* Translated by Montgomery Belgion as a revised and augmented edition with a new postscript. Princeton: Princeton University Press, 1983.

Rousseau, Jean-Jacques. *The First and Second Discourses.* Translated by Roger D. and Judith R. Masters. New York: St. Martin's Press, 1964.

Schlege, Frederich. *Friedrich Schlege's* Lucinde *and the Fragments.* Translated with introduction by Peter Firchow. Minneapolis: University of Minnesota Press, 1971.

Schleiermacher, Friedrich. *On Religion, Speeches to Its Cultured Despisers.* Translation and notes by Richard Crouter. Cambridge: Cambridge University Press, 1988.

Seneca. *Moral and Political Essays.* Edited and translated by John M. Cooper and J. F. Procopé. Cambridge: Cambridge University Press, 1995.

Shakespeare, William. *The Tragedies of Shakespeare,* Volume 2. New York: The Modern Library, n.d.

Singer, Irving. *The Nature of Love,* Volume 1, *Plato to Luther*, second edition. Chicago: The University of Chicago Press, 1984.

———. *The Nature of Love*, Volume 2, *Courtly and Romantic.* Chicago: Chicago University Press, 1984.

———. *The Nature of Love*, Volume 3, *The Modern World.* Chicago: Chicago University Press, 1987.

Søren Kierkegaard's Journals and Papers, Volume 5, *Autobiographical, 1829–1848.* Edited and translated by Howard V. and Edna H. Hong assisted by Gregor Malanstschuk. Bloomington: Indiana University Press, 1978.

Søren Kierkegaard's Journals and Papers, Volume 6, *Autobiographical, 1848–1855.* Edited and translated by Howard V. and Edna H. Hong assisted by Gregor Malanstschuk. Bloomington: Indiana University Press, 1978.

Stendal. *Love.* New York/London: Penguin Books, 1975.

Sullivan, Andrew. *Love Undetectable.* New York: Alfred A. Knopf, 1998.

Swift, Jonathan. *The Portable Swift.* Edited with introduction by Carl Van Doren. New York: The Viking Press, 1948.

Unamuno, Miguel de. *Tragic Sense of Life.* Translated by J. E. Crawford Filtch. New York: Dover Publications Inc., 1954.

Wittgenstein, Ludwig. *Philosophical Investigations.* Translated by G.E.M. Anscombe. Oxford: Basil Blackwell, 1968.

Index